No Oil in t

CW00968103

Faith and the Lamp

No Oil in the Lamp

Fuel, Faith and the Energy Crisis

Andy Mellen and Neil Hollow

DARTON·LONGMAN+TODD

First published in 2012 by
Darton, Longman and Todd Ltd
1 Spencer Court
140 – 142 Wandsworth High Street
London SW18 4JJ

ISBN: 978-0-232-52944-9

A catalogue record for this book is available from the British
Library.

Thanks are due to the following: Green Books for permission to
use material from *The Transition Handbook* and *The Transition
Companion* by Rob Hopkins; SPCK for permission to use material
from *Surprised by Hope* by Tom Wright; Carlin Music for
'Iris of the World' – Written by Bruce Cockburn –
© Rotten Kiddies Music LLC (BMI). All Rights Reserved.
Lyric reproduced by kind permission of Carlin Music Corp.
London, NW1 8BD.

Phototypeset by Kerrypress Ltd, Luton, Bedfordshire

Printed and bound by Bell & Bain, Glasgow

Contents

Foreword

I have been involved in the energy industry for nearly 25 years now, but was still surprised and honoured when Neil and Andy asked me to write a foreword to their book. It made me reflect on the changes I've seen over the years. When I first started out people weren't that interested in the industry I had chosen and frequently sought to change the subject if I talked about work. More recently however, I find that more and more people want to debate energy issues. What do I think about shale gas and the risks from its drilling technology? Why are gas and electricity prices going up? Should I install solar panels? Does it matter that an increasing proportion of our energy will have to be imported? Should we build new nuclear power stations? How reliable or economic is renewable energy? I could go on. These debates, and many others, are being conducted in board rooms, government and parliamentary circles, academic institutions and Green groups. All this shows how important energy is. Barely a week goes by without another contribution coming from someone; usually pushing his or her particular agenda and it is sometimes difficult to sort out the truth.

Even within the energy community, however, the discussion tends to focus on climate change and carbon emissions and largely ignores the issue of resource availability. I fully acknowledge the importance of decarbonisation but have felt for many years now that this misses part, and a big part, of the energy debate. Let me illustrate what I mean by looking at two issues. First, the demand for energy just keeps on growing. Global energy consumption increased by 2.5 per cent in 2011 and in the last 10 years is up 30 per cent largely driven by growth in China and other emerging countries. Even when we in the UK are seeing year on year reductions in energy consumption, mainly from much needed improvements in the efficiency with which we heat and power our homes, demand from around the world continues to put strains on the energy industry's ability to meet expectations. To give one specific example, China accounted for 11% of global primary energy demand back in 2001. A mere ten years later it is already at 21%. The modern world is addicted to energy and the number of countries with the addiction is growing.

Secondly, we still remain dependent on fossil fuels for our energy. For all the momentum behind renewable energy and a potential nuclear renaissance, at least in the UK, fossil fuels account for 87% of global energy use. While oil's share has been reducing recently, that has been because growth in oil production has not been keeping pace with the overall increase in energy demand. Oil still accounts for one third of all the energy we use. The other two fossil fuels of natural gas and coal make up the balance. By their nature, fossil fuels are a finite resource. They represent the accumulated energy from the sun captured, processed, cooked and stored over millions of years. They can literally be described as God's gift to modern man and once we've used them they are gone, unless we've got a couple of millennia to wait.

These two factors combine to mean that our modern way of life and the prospects for future economic prosperity both in the UK and in the developing world remain dependent on oil and its cousins. We, therefore, have to consider the availability of future supplies of fossil fuels. When this does get an airing in the energy debate it gets called 'peak oil'. This is probably not a helpful title because it artificially focuses on just oil and implies a looming and rapid descent. Whilst this may be possible it ignores the fact that simply failing to meet the world's insatiable appetite for more energy each and every year is enough of a problem without adding the double whammy of falling output. And that constraint applies equally to gas and coal as well as oil. However, peak oil is the term we have and I suppose it will have to do.

There are signs that we are starting to see the onset of 'peak oil' or at least the problems of constrained resource availability. Over the last decade or so, geopolitics has become increasingly determined by energy issues. The current political stand-off with Iran is partly about nuclear energy. We are concerned about Middle Eastern politics mainly because that region still accounts for 48% of the world's proven oil reserves and 38% of its gas. We are increasingly reliant on drilling and mining in more technologically and environ- mentally challenging areas such as the Brazilian pre-salt offshore fields and the whole Arctic region. Finally, prices have become increasingly volatile and seem to be on a long-term one-way path. If you adjust for inflation then average oil prices in 2011 were the second highest on record behind 1864 when the oil industry was in its infancy. We have all seen this trend played out at the petrol pump.

If, as I suspect, resources are going to get scarcer and scarcer in the years ahead these problems will only get worse. Wars and rumours of wars about oil will become everyday news, we will see more threats to habitats and ecosystems and price rises will force radical change in our lifestyles. We tend to think that higher energy prices just mean we might have to buy a smaller car but this misses the point. Energy and its price and availability affect far more than just the cost of the school run. Almost everything we buy and use has either a direct link to oil or has a significant embedded energy component. Food is the obvious example with its use of petro- chemical based fertilizers and transport requirements. The threat of 'peak oil' or even just a more constrained and hence expensive supply of energy will have fundamental consequences for how we live our lives and, as is often the case, the affect will be most acutely felt by those least able to cope.

To a large measure discussion of these issues and the risks to our way of life are confined to the fringes of the energy world. A few renegade geologists and some environmental campaigners do try and keep the issue of 'peak oil' on the table. Some businesses have tried to get government to look at the resource issue from a risk management perspective. The odd research analyst looks at long- term trends in company reserves and energy prices. It would be easy to use the cliché to say that we are burying our heads in the sand. However, despite the well-known saying, ostriches don't, in fact, do this. They actually lower their heads and put their ears to the sand to listen for impending danger. We would do well to take a leaf out of their book.

Against the background of some debate about peak oil in energy circles, there is a distinct and deafening silence from the wider

Christian community and therefore a lack of a Biblical perspective on this vital issue. In 'No oil in the Lamp' Neil and Andy have tackled this gap head on. They have set out the background to the issue of 'peak oil' and exposed some of the consequences of an energy-constrained future. They have also developed the outlines of a theology of peak oil. These issues need and deserve proper consideration in both Christian and wider circles and Neil and Andy's book is a timely contribution to the debate. If it stimulates more people to take a long, hard look at energy issues and to get involved in the debate they will have done a worthwhile and valued job.

Ian Marchant

Chief Executive, SSE (formerly Scottish and Southern Energy)

Introduction

The fool doth think he is wise, but the wise man knows himself to be a fool.

William Shakespeare, *As You Like It*, Act 5 scene 1

In 1994 the photographer Peter Menzel published *Material World: A Global Family Portrait*, a book containing photographs he had taken of people standing outside their homes with all their belongings. One picture shows an American family outside their attractive suburban house. The street is adorned with furniture, kitchen equipment, beds, clothes and of course two cars. The point here is not to knock the American lifestyle (would anyone in the developed world be very different?) but to show the average household's oil dependence. Almost everything shown in that picture can be linked to oil in some way – either it uses oil, is made from oil, or has been manufactured and transported using energy from oil. Our way of life is built on what many analysts contend is the teetering edifice of cheap fossil fuels. In developed countries, and increasingly in the rest of the world, we are oil addicts and sooner or later we are going to have to go 'cold turkey'.

This book is not primarily another Christian book about the environment, climate change and the effects of fossil fuels (although the authors fully accept the fact of human-made climate change and the need to urgently address it). This book is about the other half of the fossil fuel equation, not the 'cannot live with it', but the 'cannot live without it'. The environment in general and climate change in particular have received belated attention in Christian circles over the last few years. The issue of shrinking oil supplies, and the forced and very dramatic changes this will mean to western lifestyles has not. We recognise that is also true of wider society (although there is a great deal of concern and interest in oil depletion in academic circles).

As we explain in the first few chapters, we believe that changes in energy supplies will constitute a paradigm shift that will fundamentally change our society. This is an issue the Church cannot ignore. The problem is commonly summed up by the phrase 'peak oil', which you may hear in the news or read in your newspaper. This is a useful shorthand for describing the predicament. However the situation is a complicated one which resists simplistic analysis. We look first at oil, the most important fossil fuel, then at the other conventional energy sources, and then examine the range of renewable technologies and their scope for meeting future energy needs. For each area we attempt to provide not just a scientific analysis of the challenges and potential, but also try to examine the moral questions linked to specific energy sources. We also consider some overarching questions: Can and should we try to maintain our current lifestyles? Will the alternatives allow us to fly and drive as much as we do at the moment? How can we feed ourselves when fossil fuels are largely used up?

August 2008 saw oil prices spike upward to a record peak before falling back. The rollercoaster ride since then, with energy costs on a continuing upward trend, has caused enormous disruption to the global economy. Yet if some analysts are correct, we are only in the foothills of the crisis, with unknown obstacles and peaks lying ahead. However, the view is not completely negative: there could be many benefits in retreating from our oil dependence, and in fact there are communities that have already taken the initiative and started thinking about a better future, de-coupling themselves from globalisation and building up local resilience. We examine this movement, Transition, and what the church can learn from it.

The western world's addiction to oil has led to corrupt governments, economic havoc, environmental destruction and human-made climate change. Christians have been complicit in this misuse and exploitation of the earth's resources. However, at its best, Christianity has been a faith centred on simplicity, sacrifice and a passion for social justice. We have therefore much to contribute to shaping a post-oil society. The realisation that the world's resources are finite is going to come as a profound shock to most of our society who find their meaning in life from ownership of things or through travel. There will be huge potential for reaching out to people in an age when happiness will have to be decoupled from possessions.

The Church as an institution is in no way ready for a post-oil world. Many of the churches we attend are gathered congregations with people travelling many miles by car to every meeting. In addition, the energy use of the buildings we meet in can be huge. Chapters 11 and 12 look at the practical lifestyle and institutional changes individual Christians and the Church will face in a post-peak oil world. In a future where material goods are much more expensive we will need to discover the kind of fellowship of believers outlined at the end of Acts 2. Churches will need to cut their energy use dramatically and we look at some exemplar congregations that have done this. However, arguably even these churches will face the challenge of how to 'do church' in a changed social and economic context.

Parts of this book are not going to be an easy read. The age of cheap fossil fuels is coming to an end. That is not in doubt. What is in contention is how humanity copes with this change. It is no exaggeration to say the answer to this question will decide the shape of the twenty-first century. As Christians we should be able to lead the way following a saviour who owned little and told us not to store up treasures on earth. The overall aims of the book are twofold: first, to raise awareness of peak oil among Christians, and, second, to prepare the Church in practical ways for life post oil. After all, if the rest of society is going to have to be transformed, then so will the Church. As Christians we believe God has a way through this for us, and peak oil is not all bad news. Read on, and see if you agree.

1

What's the problem?

Crossed the border laughing, never know what to expect
they wanted to know what church I'm in and what things I
  collect
they're trying to plug holes in the hull while flames eat up the
  deck
the captain and his crew don't seem to get the disconnect.

Me and peak oil and love; from the song
'Iris of the World' by Bruce Cockburn

The modern world is not perfect, but if you were born in a developed country sometime in the last sixty years, it is likely that you have experienced a rising standard of living, with increasing comfort and convenience. Yet we only need to look back a few generations to see how much has changed, and how much we take for granted. We flick a switch, assuming that electricity will be there to light up the bulb. We expect to be able to travel long distances quickly, in comfort and at reasonable cost. We think nothing of sitting down to a meal whose ingredients have been transported across the globe to our table. These things and many more besides have become basic expectations for most in the developed world – and as Christians living within a modern, developed country we share them. While we may bow our heads and give thanks for God's provision at the start of a meal, in most other ways we take the conveniences of modern life for granted.

Progress, however, comes at a cost. It takes energy, in fact an enormous amount of energy, to make the modern world work.

Despite continued technological progress (in fact partly because our houses now contain more technology), the average household is using more energy today than at any time in the past. Globally, use of oil, coal and gas has at least almost doubled since 1970 and shows little sign of slowing down (Figure 1).

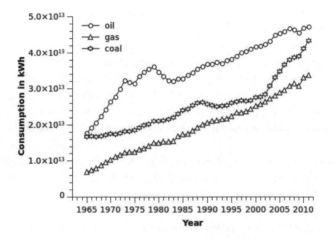

Figure 1: Global oil, gas and coal consumption trends (source: BP Statistical Review of World Energy 2012).[1]

We use energy to heat and light our houses, work places and churches; to transport us around; to make electricity; to produce and cook the food we eat; and to provide us with all the accoutrements of modern life. Despite all the talk and enthusiasm about renewable energy, our lives are mostly powered by four energy sources we get out of the ground, namely oil, gas, coal and uranium. Each of these provides energy in a different way. Uranium is used to produce electricity in nuclear power stations. Coal is used mostly for heating and electricity. Gas, too, is burnt to produce electricity and for domestic heating and cooking; it is also used to make the fertiliser which underpins modern food production. Oil, though, is arguably the most important energy source for the world today, because, among many other uses, oil fuels transport. Ninety-five per cent of all travel today – both people and goods – is powered by oil.

Oil is a mixture of different hydrocarbons, which, through a process called fractional distillation, can be separated into the familiar products that keep our world moving: petrol to run our cars; diesel for cars, trucks, tractors and trains; kerosene, which is blended into fuel for planes; and heavy fuel oil for ships. We are so used to life with oil that we can easily overlook just how incredibly energy dense oil is (in fact only nuclear fuels like uranium produce more energy per gram). Just think how much energy it takes to push a car along: run out of fuel and it takes two or three strong adults just to move the car on to the side of the road – let alone push it up a slight slope! Yet pour just one gallon of petrol into the tank and it will speed a modern car along effortlessly for up to 70 miles. However, oil is used for much more than transport. Some is still used to produce electricity. Some is used for heating homes and workspaces, but more importantly oil can be processed in a multitude of ways to provide useful products: plastics, fibres, paints, agrochemicals, glues and cosmetics are all oil derived. In fact, when you start to look around, oil is everywhere. The clothes and shoes we are wearing, the computers on which we wrote this, the radio playing in the background and the plastic bottles from which we drink water from are all largely made from oil. Almost everything we use today has either been made directly using oil or has employed the energy from oil somewhere in its production and transportation to us. Oil is so useful, it's little wonder that we have become totally dependent on it. It has become the lifeblood of the global economy and any interruption to its supply would have a catastrophic effect.

Well, here's the problem: oil, together with the other three sources of energy mentioned above, is finite – there is a limited amount available and one day it will be used up. Coal, oil and gas are the 'fossil fuels' – made by geological action of the earth on deposits of organic matter over millions of years. Uranium is different in that it is an element which occurs widely across the planet at low concentrations. However, there are only a few locations where deposits of uranium ore are found in sufficient concentrations to be worth mining and extracting, so it too should be classed as finite.

Given that we are so dependent on these four key sources of energy, and that in each case we are gradually depleting them, the important question is this: how soon could we start running short?

We have written this book because we believe that the availability of energy will quickly become a critical issue in the years ahead, in particular because oil production, on which the modern world is totally dependent, is starting to run down. The other energy sources will also decline, but oil depletion will hit us first. That stark statement is what undermines old expectations, and provides a new and challenging foundation on which we have to try and build a different future.

The facts of oil depletion are not widely known or understood, so we hope that in reading this book you will gain a better understanding of what we face. We also hope to provide some pointers towards what a Christian response might be, as we try to understand the context in which we will live and minister in the future. As Christians we have ultimate hope through Jesus, yet for now we live in this world and experience the problems and limitations that humanity suffers. Our lives may point towards the Kingdom of God which will one day be fully revealed, but unless we start to live differently we are likely to be dependent, for now, on the resources of Saudi Arabia – the world's largest oil exporter.

You may already be asking yourself, 'Is this for real? Can reports of an imminent oil crisis possibly be true? How could humankind have painted itself into such a tight corner?' The rest of this chapter aims to detail how we have arrived at this situation and give some analysis of the consequences, but first we need to go way, way back.

A brief history of oil

Oil formed when the remains of ancient organic matter were pressure-cooked thousands of feet underground.[2] The source material for the oil we use today is thought to have been vast areas of algae which bloomed in warm lakes and shallow seas during periods of warmer temperatures millions of years ago. Over many years, the remains of these algae built up in thick layers of sediment which were eventually covered by other deposition, or thrust down by tectonic activity. Eventually, in some areas of the world, these rich sediments found themselves between 7,500 and 15,000 feet below the earth's surface, where the temperature and pressure were just right to cook them into hydrocarbon-saturated rock.[3] In some places, due to forces thrusting the rock up from below, or erosion of the rock above over many millions of years, this oil-bearing rock ended up at the earth's surface and pressure caused oil to ooze out. These places were where humankind first came into contact with oil, and there are many historical reports of oil being laboriously harvested from these 'seeps', and used in various ways: in Genesis 6, Noah waterproofs the ark by sealing it with pitch (most likely the tar residue left when the lighter portions of oil evaporate). There are reports of ancient civilisations in China and the Middle East burning oil for heating or light, and oil tar was reportedly used to pave the streets of Baghdad as early as the eighth century AD. However, the use of oil in quantity began only 150 or so years ago when the technology of the industrial revolution was applied to oil extraction, probably first in the area around Baku, now in Azerbaijan but then part of the Imperial Russian Empire. Better known but slightly later was the emergence of a nascent oil industry in the US.

The first man to successfully drill for oil in the US was Edwin Drake, who adapted a salt well drilling rig. On 27 August 1859 he struck oil 69 feet below farmland in Pennsylvania. A lack of business sense meant that Drake never made his fortune from oil, and the early pioneer drillers struggled to find a market for this new product! However, the properties that have made oil so useful to us today soon became clear: refined into kerosene, oil could be used for both lighting and heating, and began to displace the increasingly scarce whale oil. Even shallow wells like Drake's provided plenty of oil, which could be transported easily and relatively safely. Once the technology to refine it in quantity caught up with its production, the modern oil industry was born.

In the last years of the nineteenth century the internal combustion engine was developed and in the early twentieth century the diesel engine. Initially used as stationary engines for pumps and industry, the mounting of engines on four wheels ushered in the era of the 'horseless carriage', which became a major user of petrol or diesel, and caused a boom in oil exploration and extraction. The twentieth century could arguably be called the century of oil, such was its impact. The early years saw the first experiments in powered flight, and in 1908 the first mass-produced car, the Model-T Ford, began to roll off the production lines. Oil production and use rose steadily throughout the early decades of the twentieth century, but the cataclysm of the Second World War changed all that – the need to provide fuel for many thousands of planes, tanks, trucks and ships took oil production to new heights. While it took many years for oil to displace coal as the fuel of choice in some areas, by the end of the 1960s the steam ships and steam trains were almost all gone, as oil became the predominant source of energy for transport. The amazing technological progress throughout the century was underpinned by energy from oil.

Today, in the second decade of the twenty-first century, humankind is dependent on oil as never before. Modern transportation and international trade would be impossible without oil. But it is at this point, with the oil price increasingly volatile and on a generally upward trend, that we need to be asking ourselves a very important question: 'Just how much oil is left?'

The first predictions about future oil supply were made back in the 1950s by a remarkable character called Dr Marion King Hubbert. He was an American oil geologist and already a scientist of considerable achievement when he started making some calculations about oil reserves and future production. He quickly discovered that the principle 'what goes up must come down' applied to oil production. Although his methodology is a little technical it is worth looking at, because it forms the crux of the issue. Hubbert noted that the production from a typical oil field, plotted on a graph over time, tended to form a bell-shaped curve. In the initial stages production increases rapidly, but then slows and eventually peaks, followed by a decreasing flow of oil as the field depletes. This was well understood, but what Hubbert did was to show that it could also apply to oil production from a region such as the United States. The production from hundreds of individual oil fields in a country or even the world, combined into one big graph, also showed the same bell-shaped curve (see Figure 2). From production data on oil that had already been produced and information about oil field discoveries (which had peaked in the 1930s) Hubbert was able to calculate that production in the lower 48 States in the USA would reach an all-time peak in the early 1970s. His forecast was presented in a paper entitled 'Nuclear Energy and the Fossil Fuels' at the American Petroleum Institute conference in San Antonio, Texas in 1956.[4] The prediction drew immediate derision – he was pretty much laughed out of the conference. At that time, production in the United States was on the upward part of the bell curve, increasing rapidly, more oil was being found, and it seemed unbelievable that oil production could one day slow and drop. But Hubbert was proved right when US oil production peaked in 1970, exactly in the middle of the dates he had predicted. Despite massive efforts in exploration and new extraction techniques since, it has continued to decline. Why is this important? Well unfortunately, the US situation provides us with a template for the global situation: worldwide oil production will also reach a peak and then go into terminal decline. Hubbert realised this, and his 1956 lecture even included a ballpark prediction that this global peak would happen 'in around 50 years'. After continuing to refine his calculations over the years, Hubbert died in 1989 before this prediction could be verified, but it seems he was not far out. His legacy is summed up in a phrase you may well have heard: 'peak oil'. These two words have a technical meaning – the point in time when global oil production will reach its maximum and start to fall. However, they have also become a kind of shorthand for describing the fundamental problem of finite oil supply and the consequences which will result once production starts to fall.

Hubbert was a prophetic pioneer in terms of forecasting, and in his wake a whole industry of oil production analysis and comment has grown up – nowadays there are excellent books, websites and other sources of information on the subject. In the 1970s US production peaking and two oil crises kept the idea of peak oil in the news, but in the 1980s the oil price fell, and concern over long-term oil supplies was forgotten. Then in the 1990s a group of industry insiders retired and started whistle-blowing. Two of these, Professor Colin Campbell (ex BP and Texaco) and Jean Laherrere (ex Total), together initiated the Association for the Study of Peak Oil (ASPO).[5] Their concerns were first brought to public attention in 1998, in an article they co-authored for *Scientific American*, entitled 'The End of Cheap Oil',[6] in which they argued that there may be less oil around than everyone thinks. They highlighted the problem that, during the 1980s, the oil producers in OPEC (the Organisation of the Petroleum Exporting Countries) were negotiating about production quotas (how much oil each member could pump).

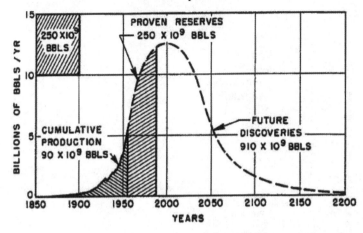

Figure 2: Hubbert's original global production estimate peak. Combining the production graphs for individual oilfields and regions produces a global bell-shaped production curve, allowing an estimate to be made of the date of maximum production (peak oil). The actual production curve is much more ragged but follows a similar trajectory.

These were drawn up based on the declared reserves (the amount of oil estimated to be in the ground) in each country. The problem is that everybody suddenly inflated their declared reserves (allowing them to pump more oil) – basically they cheated and as a result oil reserve figures have been questionable ever since (see Figure 3). The reported reserves of Kuwait, Iraq, Iran and Saudi Arabia all increased dramatically during the 1980s – and have stayed high ever since, despite billions of barrels being extracted. This alarming discrepancy leads to wide differences in the estimated size of the remaining global oil reserves, depending on who you believe.

While it is accepted in the oil industry and among analysts that oil production will one day peak and decline, analysts differ over the timescale. If you are optimistic and believe the OPEC data, you will have a high estimate for the ultimate reserves, and will expect a production peak in the 2020s or beyond, by which time the world will be prepared. Adherents of this view are termed 'late-toppers' in peak oil terminology, and most oil companies and governments fall into this category. If, like Campbell and other analysts, you believe a much lower figure for ultimate reserves, you are likely to be an

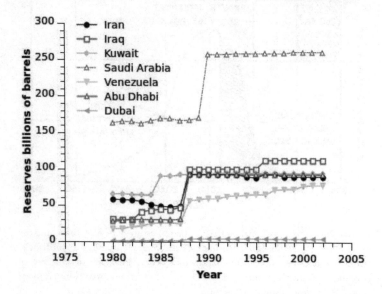

Figure 3: OPEC reserve revisions (data from Dr C. Campbell in presentation to Scottish and Southern Energy).

'early-topper' with peaking sooner. (In his most recent analysis, Campbell suggests that we may have passed the peak sometime between 2008 and 2010.) It is fair to say that there are a wide range of views on this subject, with many analysts predicting a later peak than Professor Campbell. In their 2009 report on Global Oil Depletion, the UK Energy Research Centre listed the problems that analysts face when grappling with the data: 'Reserve estimates are uncertain, reporting is restricted, auditing is insufficient, harmonisation is limited, field data is unavailable, distortions are likely.' Despite this, after reviewing 500 studies on future oil production they concluded that a peak beyond 2030 was 'at best optimistic and at worst implausible. There is a significant risk of a peak before 2020 – and a possibility that it has already passed.'[7] What experts do agree on is that we will only be able to see the peak in the rear-view mirror, maybe some years after it has occurred. That said, the exact date of 'peak oil' production is not as important as the consequences of what follows. As Professor Campbell states:

The peak itself has no great significance; it is the perception and the vision of the long decline that comes into sight on the other side of the peak, that's what really matters. We do not face the abrupt end of oil, but merely the onset of a gentle decline in the rate of extraction. That said, the change from growth to decline of this critical energy supply on which the modern world depends is a discontinuity of epic proportions.[8]

Campbell's language here is circumspect and measured, but the meaning is clear: when the world starts to run out of oil, the consequences could be devastating.

Robert Hirsch, an energy expert who was commissioned by the US government to write a report on the effects of peak oil, wrote:

the peaking of world oil production presents the U.S. and the world with an unprecedented risk management problem. As the peak is approached, liquid fuel prices and price volatility will increase dramatically, and, without timely mitigation, the economic, social, and political costs will be unprecedented. Viable mitigation options exist on both the supply and demand sides, but to have substantial impact, they must be initiated more than a decade in advance of peaking.[9]

At peak oil, although half the oil is still there in the ground, we will have used all the easy-to-extract and best quality oil. What we will be increasingly left with is the lower quality oil, in unstable parts of the world, in inhospitable environments, or in places where it is difficult to extract. James Howard Kunstler, a writer on these issues, puts it apocalyptically: 'We have been using oil like there is no tomorrow. Now there may not be.'[10] That view may be pessimistic, but since nobody can say for certain how much is left, or accurately predict when supplies might run short, who can say how concerned we should be? We might look to our governments for certainty, and for evidence that this problem is being planned for. However, at least in the UK this evidence is hard to find – only very recently a UK

Energy Minister, Malcolm Wicks, stated that ' ... none of us know when the oil is going to run out, but it's not in the foreseeable future'.[11]

As well as the geological question of how much oil is left in the ground, other factors also play a part in the unfolding story of future oil production. Many commentators have expressed concern that, however much oil is there, the industry may not have the ability to extract it fast enough to match demand. The low oil price of the 1980s and 90s led to a lack of investment in production capacity, from drilling rigs through to refineries, which may cause a supply bottleneck in the future. Another concern is the ageing workforce in the oil industry. A task force of major companies in the UK has highlighted these two factors as real concerns over the next decade, predicting a supply crunch around 2015.[12]

Given the recent high price of oil, it is no surprise that the search for new oil fields is continuing apace. Until recently, you had to look back to the late 1960s and early 1970s for really major discoveries (North Alaska and the North Sea respectively). However, the last decade has seen an increase in discoveries, including some fields off the coast of Brazil. Unfortunately these barely offset the reduced production from older fields which are past their peak and declining. To maintain the current oil production we would have to keep on discovering and exploiting new finds at a rate far higher than we have historically achieved, even with recent finds. High oil prices encourage companies to look for oil in places where it would have previously been uneconomic – difficult environments like the Arctic and Antarctic and in deep water. Not only does this make the exploration and extraction much more expensive, it is also inherently riskier. The largest ever marine oil spill was caused by a catastrophic accident on the BP Deepwater Horizon exploration rig, which blew up while drilling in the Gulf of Mexico in April 2010. Eleven workers died in the initial explosion, huge volumes of oil were released. These continue to pollute the environment and may have long-term detrimental effects. Increased oil exploration and production in these difficult and testing environments could well produce more accidents like this – a worrying prospect.

Overarching all these concerns, geological, environmental, technological and human resources, is the question of politics – and in particular the situation across the main oil producing region of the Middle East. Early 2011 saw the so-called 'Arab Spring' – an abrupt and unexpected change in the political landscape across the Arab world. Starting in Tunisia, widespread street protests took place as ordinary citizens demanded human rights and political change. The leaders of Tunisia and Egypt were deposed, while protests in Syria and Bahrain have been brutally repressed. In Libya, intervention by NATO to prevent the repression of a grass-roots uprising led to the overthrow and murder of Colonel Gadaffi and in other countries there have been rumours of discontent. How things will develop is anyone's guess at present, but the wind of change is blowing right across the Arab world. This is welcome and long overdue in terms of political and human rights, but raises concerns in terms of oil supply. (This was reflected in the price of oil spiking upwards with every uncertain step in the unfolding drama.) Were the key oil-producing states, such as Saudi Arabia, Iran, Kuwait and others around the Persian Gulf to become politically unstable, it would have very serious implications.

The expectations of governments, industry and consumers around the world are based on the premise that oil and gas will continue to flow out of the Middle East for the foreseeable future. The ruling elites in oil exporting countries also want this to continue – their lavish lifestyles and economies are dependent on the inflow of petro-dollars. (Saudi Arabia has thousands of minor members of its extended Royal family supported by generous hand-outs, the so-called 'oil dole'.) But what would happen if a revolution affected one of the major oil-exporting countries, and it ended up with a government that was antagonistic to the West? A new regime could simply turn off the taps, with devastating effect. Or it could decide that, rather than pumping oil flat-out to satisfy oil-consuming nations, it would prefer to reduce exports and conserve the resource for production over a longer period. This might be quite a wise thing to do for such a country, if it could cope with the reduced income, but again it would play havoc with global supply in the short term. Another worrying scenario would be a civil war where oil infrastructure gets damaged, production stalls and the price sky-rockets.

The Middle East holds a critical position in terms of future oil supply simply because such a large proportion of the remaining global reserves of oil (and gas) are there. On a list of the world's largest oil fields, 28 out of the top 40 are located in the region. (The world's largest, the Ghawar field in Saudi Arabia, was discovered in 1948, started producing in 1951, and is still pumping out around 5 million barrels per day 60 years later.) The Middle East is also, crucially, a place of unresolved conflict over the existence of the state of Israel, the position of the Palestinians and their competing demands for land and sovereignty. These seemingly insurmountable problems remain as a point of tension with the Arab world, and are likely to continue to do so whatever political changes take place.

This is where we are in the unfolding story of oil: dangerously dependent, with a finite supply, and a host of uncertainties to boot. In the next chapter we look at why all this should matter to Christians.

Notes

1 Since the units of production and consumption are different for each fuel source, they have been converted to kWh which the reader is familiar with. It is not so much the large numbers that are of interest, as the trend.

2 For some Christians this is a contentious statement, particularly if you believe in a literal six-day creation and a world that is only about six thousand years old. This book is not the place to rehearse these arguments; suffice it to say that there are many Christians who see no conflict between the texts in Genesis and geological evidence which tells us that the world is many millions of years old.

3 J. Leggett, *Half Gone: Oil, Gas, Hot Air and the Global Energy Crisis* (Portobello Books, 2006) gives a geologist's comprehensive guide to the formation and extraction of oil.

4 M. K. Hubbert, *Nuclear Energy and the Fossil Fuels*, American Petroleum Institute, 1956.

5 ASPO details can be found at www.peakoil.net.

6 C. J. Campbell and J. H. Laherrere, 'The End of Cheap Oil', *Scientific American*, 1998.

7 Global Oil Depletion Report, UKERC, 2009.

8 C. Campbell. Quotes are taken from several of his monthly newsletters for ASPO Ireland – found at www.aspoireland.org.

9 R. Hirsch *et al.*, *Peaking of World Oil Production: Impacts, Mitigation, and Risk*

Management, Report for the US Government Department of Energy, 2005. We disagree with his solutions, which take no account of climate change, but his analysis of the problem was spot on.

10   J. H. Kunstler, *The Long Emergency: Surviving the Converging Catastrophes of the Twenty-first Century*, Atlantic Books, 2006.

11   Malcolm Wicks, speaking to the UK Parliament's Sustainable Energy Group, 12 July 2005. Things may have changed, however. When Neil made an FOI request for government policy documents relating to peak oil, he was refused on the basis there were too many!

12   UK Industry Task Force on Peak Oil and Energy Security, Report 2010.

2

What about Christians?

Some trust in chariots and some in horses,
but we trust in the name of the LORD our God.
They are brought to their knees and fall,
but we rise up and stand firm.

Psalm 20:7–8

On a handful of occasions Andy has had the opportunity to talk to a church or a Christian gathering about peak oil and its potential consequences. A few people seem to grasp the implications and become motivated about the issue, but most don't. After one such meeting, a man came up and reassured Andy that oil was 'a blessing from God, which wells up from the mantle of the earth and will continue to do so as long as we need it'. Despite this theory having no scientific evidence to back it up, it appears to be a widespread belief, for there seems to be very little concern about oil depletion among Christians. This could be because the facts are not widely known, but also I sense that many Christians simply feel that our modern, oil-dependent lifestyles are somehow God-ordained and normal (despite the fact that most people on the planet do not have the standard of living that we have). Neil has had a different response in his church. He showed a film about the Transition movement (which we explore in Chapter 9) on two separate occasions. In addition it also went around several house groups. It helped that the CEO of a major energy company (a member of Neil's church) mentioned peak oil as a serious concern when interviewed about his work by Neil's minister.

Peak oil in popular culture

Before we look at Christian attitudes to peak oil, what profile does the issue have in the wider culture? The leading sources of information to date have been a number of factual books written and published in the last few years. These books cover a range of different perspectives, but all share a common theme; that peak oil is a significant and imminent problem that humankind needs to wake up to. What they differ on is the scope for mitigating the problem and what steps we need to take. As well as books, a number of documentary films have been made about the issue over the years,[1] including a docudrama made by the BBC.[2] BBC television also made a political thriller in 2008 called *Burn up*, which dealt at least in part with the issue of peak oil. It has to be said that while these have created interest and comment among those concerned by peak oil, they have not impacted wider society.

Where potentially more impact has been made is when the issue has featured in world fiction, and there have been a number of examples of this. James Howard Kunstler, a journalist and writer who has also written a factual book on peak oil, has written two post-apocalyptic novels, *World Made by Hand* and *The Witch of Hebron*. Set in a small town in New York State after peak oil has led to societal collapse, these novels offer a view of the advantages and tensions present in community co-operation in such circumstances. In addition, for someone who does not claim to be a Christian, the author shows Christians (or what he perceives as Christianity) and the Church in a surprisingly positive light. Interviews with Kunstler and free-to-read excerpts can be found on his website.[3] Another fictional book, *Shut Down* by W. R. Flynn, was published in 2011. The plot concerns a woman fleeing Portland, Oregon, as society collapses, linking the financial crash and peak oil as the cause of the crisis. A sequel published in 2012 takes the story forward a couple of years. Sacii Lloyd (author of the Carbon Diaries series of books) has written a new book called *Momentum*, set in dystopian London in the near future, post peak oil.

Another fictional rendering of peak oil consequences is an Irish feature film, *One Hundred Mornings*, which was shown at various film festivals in 2009–11. After Irish society has collapsed due to

peak oil, two couples hide out in the countryside. The film is no
poorly made first feature, it uses actors who have been in well-
known films and the trailer looks enticing. Despite that, it seems to
have been shown only in festivals and has failed to get a distribution
deal. The left-wing comedian Robert Newman wrote a comedy
show, *A History of Oil*, based on peak oil. After a tour it was shown
on More 4 in 2005 and Neil found it funny. The only popular song
we know about with any mention of peak oil is by Canadian
singer-songwriter Bruce Cockburn, who said in an interview and
on the sleeve notes of his 2011 album *Small source of comfort* that the
song 'Iris of the World' is partly about peak oil.

Christian attitudes

Despite the potential effects on all areas of our lives, resource
constraints like peak oil tend to get pigeon-holed as 'environmental
issues' (probably because in the main it is people who are concerned
about the environment who have picked up on it). Unfortunately,
for various reasons the environment has not been high on the
agenda of most Christians and churches, though this may be starting
to change. Here in the UK there have been some excellent books,
articles and campaigns highlighting the need for Christians to take
creation care seriously. *Cherishing the Earth, How to care for God's
Creation* by Margot and Martin Hodson, and *Christianity, Climate
Change and Sustainable Living* by Nick Spencer and Robert White
are two recently published books. *Cherishing the Earth* combines the
perspectives of a scientist and a theologian to make a comprehensive
case, challenging Christians and churches to make environmental
concerns part of their core worship, prayer and outreach. *Christianity, Climate Change and Sustainable Living* is, as its title suggests, a
much more in-depth look at the theology and science of climate
change. (Neither of these books deals with peak oil issues except in
passing.)

Despite scepticism from some sections of the Church, the
Christian conservation charity A Rocha has prospered, and the
Eco-congregation organisation has encouraged churches to become
greener.[4] The Eco-congregation programme consists of 13 modules
for participating fellowships to work through; these cover every-

thing from the theology of creation care, looking after the church graveyard to measuring churches' carbon footprints. An increasing number of churches have signed up to this programme, which aims to introduce the concept of creation care into every area of a church's ministry. Despite Eco-congregation's success, it cannot be denied that in most churches in the UK and possibly worldwide concern for the environment is peripheral. It is rarely mentioned in sermons and then not always positively, with many church leaders not buying into it as an issue. Christians who are interested in environmental issues (although increasing in number) tend to be an isolated minority, found in only a few churches.

The reasons behind this are complicated, and a detailed analysis is beyond the scope of this book. However, it is worth having a brief look at five key points:[5]

- Christian indifference to environmental concerns at least partly dates right back to Genesis 1:28, where, in the King James translation, humankind is granted 'dominion' over the rest of creation. Some Christians see these verses as granting us power over the world to do as we see fit.[6] For their part, secular environmentalists have seen this traditional interpretation of Genesis 1, carried through the Enlightenment, as the root of the West's despoiling of the environment. This argument was first set out by Professor Lynn White of Princeton University back in 1966.[7] We explore this issue at greater depth later in the book.

- A further source of antagonism between the green movement and Evangelical Christians has been the fact that some early green campaigners espoused a pagan or pantheistic outlook on life.[8] With some green thinking also being influenced by James Lovelock's Gaia theory (which suggests the Earth should be regarded as consisting of a single living system), Christians have tended to shy away from environmental issues, viewing them as 'New Age' concerns.[9] This has ended up being a self-fulfilling prophecy; since few Christians are part of the green movement, it is not surprising that it doesn't reflect the Christian world-view![10] As Green parties have had electoral success in the UK and in other European countries and become more mainstream, the 'New Age fringe' of the environmental movement (such as David Icke, former Speaker of the Green party) has diminished in influence. However, many Christians and churches still carry a legacy of aversion to environmental concerns as a result of that past influence.

- Another reason why environmental issues receive low priority is that many Christians and churches value personal morality and the 'saving of souls' as of foremost importance, with everything else as secondary. This may be due in part to the fact that the Bible does not directly address the kind of environmental problems that we face today. After Andy spoke at his church in 2008 about the need for Christians to care for creation, several people questioned why, including one who contended that 'the size of our carbon footprint does not determine who gets into heaven'. While Christians may acknowledge the problems of climate change and environmental destruction, the impression given is that 'we don't think it matters to us. Hasn't God told us that this earth will pass away, and he will create a new heaven and a new earth?' This viewpoint, which sees redemption as being only about narrow personal salvation, is being increasingly challenged. Writer and emergent church leader Brian McLaren writes that:

> Christianity is a failed religion [when] it has specialized in dealing with 'spiritual needs' to the exclusion of physical and social needs. It has focused on 'me' and 'my eternal destiny,' but it has failed to address the dominant societal and global realities of their lifetime: systemic injustice, poverty, and dysfunction.[11]

He goes on to outline a holistic faith which encompasses care for creation and our fellow human beings alongside issues of redemption. Environmental degradation is often highlighted as a factor in many disasters around the world

– so love for our neighbour must surely include care for the environment on which he or she depends.

• Some churches in the UK, and many in the US, subscribe to a powerful 'end times' movement, interpreting biblical prophecy in a particular way in which history culminates in global turmoil, war and the collapse of society, leading to Jesus' return and the Earth's destruction. Despite this being only one among many interpretations of the relevant biblical texts, it has become a widespread belief in many Evangelical churches. Leading US exponents of this view are Tim LaHaye, an influential Evangelical and author of the Left Behind series of books, and Hal Lindsay, author of *The Late, Great Planet Earth* and several other books on the end times. LaHaye's books are a dramatic imagining of the end times based on this particular branch of end-times theology and, despite clearly being fiction, have had a big influence on US Christians.[12] In this interpretation, signs such as war in the Middle East, environmental destruction and climate change are signs of Christ's imminent arrival, and are to be welcomed by the faithful.[13] When we stop to consider the negative impacts that climate change is likely to have on poor and marginalised people around the world, it is difficult to see how welcoming global warming fits in with Jesus' teaching about loving our neighbour. Unfortunately, environmental concerns have become part of America's wider culture wars, largely opposed by the conservative, Evangelical Right. A further chapter in this story opened in February 2006 when 86 prominent American Evangelical leaders launched the Evangelical Climate Initiative, calling for Christians and churches to take urgent action to address the issue.[14] Among those launching this campaign were Rick Warren (leader of Saddleback Church in California and author of the Purpose Driven series of books), Bill Hybels (leader of Willow Creek Church in Illinois), together with the heads of 39 Evangelical colleges. Perhaps unsurprisingly, the campaign has been criticised by other Evangelicals and remains controversial.

- Last but not least, perhaps the foremost reason why Christians are ambivalent about environmental concerns is that we have bought fully into western materialism. While we may have different beliefs and morals, as far as consumption is concerned our lifestyles are almost entirely indistinguishable from non-Christians – and we don't see it as an issue. As we will see in later chapters of this book, the changes that peak oil and climate change will require of us will be difficult, and require substantial changes to our lifestyles. It may also mean a retreat from current levels of comfort and convenience, which will be a painful wrench for everyone, Christians included.

If the church and Christians are ambivalent about general environmental concerns, when we turn to peak oil the response is practically non-existent. (Having said that, in wider society the issue is hardly part of everyday conversation, although the rising price of petrol, gas and heating oil is increasingly a topic of debate.) The authors have very rarely heard peak oil or resource constraints mentioned in sermons. However, an internet search does throw up some interest, with sermons from theologically liberal churches on the issue.[15] In addition, there are is some thoughtful Christian Evangelical blogging on the subject.[16] Andy wrote a feature article on Peak oil for *Third Way* magazine in 2008, giving the background to the issue and highlighting some of the likely consequences for society and the Church. Emergent church leader Brian McLaren's book *Everything Must Change* does mention the issue in passing, as part of a section looking at how current society is using up the world's resources faster than they can be replaced. As mentioned previously, several other recent Christian environmental books do briefly mention resource constraints. There is one outstanding Christian response to peak oil we have found so far, and that is work done at Houghton College, an Evangelical Christian University in New York.[17] It made the issues around peak oil the focus of its Science Honors Program for 2009–10. Background information about Hubbert's peak oil theory was provided and the science programme majored on possible solutions to energy shortages.

The issues around the coming energy crisis lend themselves to apocalyptic viewpoints, and there is certainly plenty of cataclysmic secular material relating to peak oil on the internet, talking of a food crisis, energy shortages and even the third world war,[18] so it is surprising that so far very few apocalyptic religious ideas have surfaced – though a book has recently been published in the US linking the coming oil crisis into end-times prophecy.[19] Anecdotal evidence does suggest that peak oil is just starting to be thought about in Christian circles – with leaders such as the Archbishop of Canterbury mentioning oil depletion.[20] We have both come across a small but increasing number of people in our churches who have been thinking about this issue, sometimes for years, despite little coverage of peak oil in either the Christian or secular press.

There is no doubt that oil brings comfort and convenience to our lives today. However, our over-dependence on it has produced a way of living in which we are less dependent on one another and our relationship with creation is broken. Our energy-addicted lifestyles provide so many options and ways to be busy that we often have little time for God – arguably making our oil dependence a form of idolatry. Jesus' parable of the wise and foolish virgins in Matthew 25 has a micro-story of oil depletion as its theme – the foolish characters used up all their lamp-oil and were distracted when they should have been ready for the bridegroom's arrival. It is not difficult to extract from this story a relevant principle about our need to husband scarce resources carefully. Another biblical example of planning ahead and conserving supplies is the story of Joseph in Genesis 40—45. Rescued from prison because of his ability to interpret dreams, he is put in charge of Egypt's efforts to store up grain in seven good years, preparing ahead for the seven years of famine. In our analysis of the world today, we are still enjoying the years of plenty in an oil-fuelled bubble of prosperity. Are we ready to face the lean years to come?

In Chapter 1 we outlined the background to the coming oil crisis, and here in Chapter 2 we have looked briefly at some of the reasons why this is not on the agenda of most Christians and churches, and most of the wider population. Part of this lack of concern is because people believe that, if oil runs out, we can simply switch to other energy sources. In the next three chapters we explore the reasons why this will be problematic: Chapter 3 looks at the availability of other conventional energy – coal, gas and nuclear – and in Chapters 4 and 5 we examine the scope for switching to various types of renewable energy.

Notes

1   *A Crude Awakening: The Oil Crash* and *The End of Suburbia: Oil Depletion and the Collapse of the American Dream* being examples. These films are often used in transition unleashings (see later).
2   http://news.bbc.co.uk/1/hi/programmes/if/4989146.stm.
3   http://www.kunstler.com/index.php.
4   The late John Stott supported A Rocha from the outset and had a concern about the environment and climate change for many years. In the mid-1990s he refused to fly to Edinburgh to speak at St Paul's and St George's church, but came by train.
5   For a more detailed analysis, see by Revd Dave Bookless, *Planetwise: Dare to Care for God's World,* IVP, 2008.
6   Ann Coulter, a controversial Christian and Republican polemicist in the US, interprets the Genesis 1 verses as, 'God said, "Earth is yours. Take it. Rape it. It's yours." '
7   Professor White's case was first set out in a lecture entitled, 'The Historical Roots of our Ecological Crisis', later published in the journal *Science* in 1967.
8   http://en.wikipedia.org/wiki/David_Icke.
9   See www.gaiatheory.org.
10 By this we mean in a UK context Greenpeace, Friends of the Earth (FOI), or the Green parties in Scotland, England and Wales. However, the current director of FOI is a Christian (Andy Atkins).
11 B. D. McLaren, *Everything Must Change,* Thomas Nelson, 2009.
12 Dispensational premillenialism.
13 An example of this kind of teaching can be found here at http://www.despatch.cth.com.au/Main/index.htm.
14 www.christiansandclimate.org.
15 http://www.mnforsustain.org/oil_sermon_peak_oil_cook_p.htm.
    http://elizaphanian.blogspot.com/2007/03/peak-oil-and-slavery.html.
    http://makewealthhistory.org/2009/04/16/the-theology-of-peak-oil/.
    http://www.lyndaleucc.org/sample-sermons/dons-through-the-years/269-a-gallon-and-rising-hallelujah.html.
16 http://nothing-new-under-the-sun.blogspot.com/ is one example.
17 www.houghton.edu.
18 http://www.wolfatthedoor.org.uk/.

19 R. Rhodes, *The Coming Oil Storm*, Harvest House Publishers, 2011.
20 http://www.gci.org.uk/speeches/Williams.pdf.

Can't we just make do with coal, gas or nuclear power?

Since natural resources are finite, increased consumption must inevitably lead to depletion and scarcity.

Paul Ehrlich

Setting aside oil for this chapter, the other big conventional energy sources are coal, natural gas and nuclear energy. These are used in both the developed and developing worlds. But as oil starts to run short, what part will these other giants play? Can they step up to the mark and provide the world's needs in the decades ahead? We'll look at each in detail.

Coal

Coal was the original fossil fuel, hugely important in the past and still a critical power source today. Coal fuelled the Industrial Revolution, but now is used chiefly for electricity production, with large amounts also consumed in the production of steel and cement. To a limited extent, coal can be used as an alternative to oil as an energy source. A synthetic oil substitute can be produced from coal; this was used most famously by the Germans during the Second World War when they had little access to oil, but had plentiful coal.[1] The process is still in limited use today, notably in coal-rich but oil-poor South Africa.

Until recently the widespread belief has been that, at current rates of usage, the world has hundreds of years' worth of coal remaining. However, recent analysis of coal reserves data has undermined this view. Each year the world's governments are asked to send figures for their coal reserves to a small energy consultancy in Dorset, which collates this data for two authoritative reports, the BP Statistical Review and the World Energy Council triennial report.[2] These reports, taken together with the work of other analysts, have made surprising reading over the last few years, particularly for individuals who were worried about climate change (where coal plays a significant role), but more recently for those concerned about the global energy crisis.

The first thing to note is that global reserves have plummeted.[3] This is not because countries have mined the coal, but because the governments of coal-producing countries have decided there is not nearly as much extractable coal in the ground. Previous estimates have been recalculated downwards, and rigorous analysis has stripped away uncertain assumptions. In some cases there has been confusion between the terms coal *resources* (all that is in the ground in a particular country) and coal *reserves* (the amount of coal which is extractable at current prices with existing technology). The reductions in reported reserves are massive, with Germany 99 per cent lower, the UK more than 90 per cent lower and Poland 50 per cent down.[4] The US reserves have also been downsized. BP's analysis of how long coal reserves will last at current rates of use (known as the reserves to production ratio) has plunged downwards in the last few years; in 2000 they predicted the world had 277 years of coal left, 10 years later we apparently had only 119 years' worth (see Figure 1). The latest available data, for 2012, does show a smaller year-on-year fall; however, coal consumption was static due to the recession.

The second finding is that a lot of the officially reported data is dubious at best. China and Vietnam have reported no change in their stated reserves for many years, even though very extensive mining has taken place in both countries.[5] Also a massive amount of new coal-fired generating capacity has been built in China, India and other Asian countries, who seem to be depending on coal to fuel their economic development. Energy analyst and writer David Strahan reports that China built a massive 102 gigawatts of new coal-generating capacity in 2006 alone. (To put this in context, only around 50 gigawatts of new generating capacity was installed in the

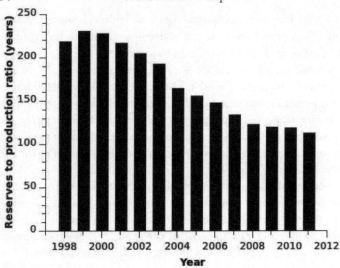

Figure 1: The fall in global coal reserves (source BP statistical energy review).

EU in 2010, of which about half was from renewable energy and only 4 gigawatts was new coal-fired generation.[6]) Professor David Rutledge of the California Institute of Technology has been study-ing past coal production figures and from these has extrapolated potential future production. He calculates that remaining global reserves are a staggering 50 per cent lower than previously reported.[7] The Energy Watch Group, an independent network of analysts, is equally pessimistic and predict a coal production peak in 2025.[8] This is disputed by the coal industry which claims that increases in the price of coal, together with improvements in mining technology, will make currently uneconomic seams worth extracting – increas-ing the reserves figures. However, this argument does not seem to stack up. The last few years have seen a substantial rise in the use and price of coal, and yet the reserves have fallen – suggesting that there is indeed less coal than previously thought. The third finding relates to demand. Up until the recent global recession, demand for coal had been rising, leading to higher prices for this fuel. The increased demand was in part due to coal substituting for increasingly expen-sive gas in electricity generation. In the short term, the slowdown in economic activity since 2008 has reduced electricity demand, and in the UK electricity company Eon has delayed plans for a new coal-fired power station. However, future demand is still predicted to increase significantly, some analysts predicting a rise of 70 per cent by 2030.[9]

If the 'coal pessimists' are correct and global coal reserves are much lower than previously thought, this has profound implications for both climate change and energy security. Professor Rutledge's contentious suggestion is that using the remaining coal will not have a significant effect on the climate, and that even if we burn all that can be extracted it would only increase atmospheric carbon dioxide to 450ppm *without any other intervention to limit CO_2 levels.*[10] It has to be said this view is extremely controversial. Other scientists, such as Pushker Kharecha, a researcher at the NASA Goddard Institute for Space Studies, argue that even lower levels of coal reserves still require curtailment of use to prevent climate change.[11] The implications for energy security are just as profound, because many governments are relying on 'clean coal' to help allow business as usual to continue as other energy supplies get tight. Clean coal is the phrase used to describe burning coal to produce electricity without allowing the carbon dioxide produced to reach the atmosphere. However, the process of carbon capture and storage (CCS) is untested on the large scale that is required, although a number of small-scale demonstration projects capturing carbon from different sources are in place. The description of these diverse technologies is beyond the scope of this book, except to say that the efficiency of the process is lowered both by the extraction of CO_2 and the energy used to pump it underground. Using CCS means that more coal is used to produce the same amount of electricity, effectively depleting reserves faster. Coal is expected by many to shoulder the burden of energy production as oil supplies tighten. However, as we have seen, there is a high degree of uncertainty about how much coal is left. We hope that some definitive data emerges in the next few years to allow sensible planning and use of coal. Burning large amounts of coal without capturing the carbon dioxide would be foolhardy, but if we take the most pessimistic coal-supply scenarios then the economic case for building CCS coal plants or any other coal-fired power station simply isn't there.

Natural gas

Considering our dependence on it today, it is amazing to think that gas was once a waste by-product of oil extraction. Often found over-lying oil fields, or dissolved in the oil, the gas coming up the oil wells was considered a nuisance rather than a resource, being flared off rather than being captured and used as it is today. In other places, gas is found in association with coal, or sometimes in large fields on its own. Today, around a quarter of the world's total energy needs are obtained from gas. From the 1940s in the US, and the late 1960s in the UK, natural gas replaced 'town gas' (gas produced from coal). With the provision of extensive distribution networks, gas has become the fuel of choice for heating in most urban areas in the western world. The other main use for gas is electricity production.

Natural gas is made up mostly of methane, together with a small proportion of other longer-chain hydrocarbon molecules such as ethane and butane, which are separated off before the gas enters the delivery network. The only products of gas when burnt are carbon dioxide and water vapour, and for each unit of energy produced, gas produces less carbon dioxide than coal or oil. The UK reduced its carbon dioxide emissions substantially during the late 1980s and 1990s simply by switching much of its electricity production from coal to gas. LNG (or liquefied natural gas) is methane that is liquefied by cooling to very low temperatures. This allows it to be compressed and transported by ship. LPG (liquid petroleum gas) is generally propane and butane, which are extracted from crude oil or natural gas and used either as a transport fuel, for camping stoves or for central heating systems off the gas grid. It is not a significant player in relation to future energy supplies because it only makes up 5 per cent or less of both of its sources.

While there has been much research, comment and forecasting on future oil production, there seems to be a lot less data available on the potential reserves of gas (a search of scientific journal websites produced many peer-reviewed papers on the term 'peak oil' but almost none on 'peak gas'). Like oil and coal, there is a finite amount of gas available; however, the physical nature of gas makes it more difficult to quantify reserves and accurately assess extraction and depletion rates.[12] There have also been problems with reserve data calculations because of misreporting of the same gas field under different names. Gas wells deplete differently to oil wells, with production building to a peak slower while dropping faster, but with a higher overall rate of recovery than oilfields (up to 80 per cent).[13] [14] Information sources on fossil fuels often combine information to produce a graph of potential future hydrocarbon supplies, including a significant component of gas, but do not give much detail.

One useful guide to future production is to look back at the figures for discoveries of gas fields, since these forecast extraction by some years. Harry J. Longwell, vice-president of the giant energy firm Exxon, published a paper showing that global gas *discovery* peaked in 1970 and declined sharply thereafter – lack of gas field discoveries inevitably leads on to a drop-off in gas production.[15] Dr Roger Bentley of Reading University is one academic who has studied the shape of future gas supplies. He predicts the peak in conventional gas supplies in about 2020.[16] Other analysts calculate an earlier date but forecast a broad plateau in production before a decline.[17] The annual BP Statistical Energy Review is the standard reference for energy data, and states that global gas reserves are sufficient for approximately 60 years at 2009 rates of consumption. However, the BP figures have been criticised for giving an inaccurate picture, particularly of reserve data.[18] It seems even the best-informed sources are in a guessing game as far as the remaining gas reserves are concerned. The UK energy regulator OFGEM has recently published a series of reports on the UK's energy security (OFGEM Project discovery 2009/10).[19] While OFGEM do not use the actual term 'peak gas', they are clearly worried about the security of supply and foresee very large price increases in the UK over the following decade (estimated between 7–61 per cent), due to more and more dependency on imported gas. Alarmingly, since their predictions were published, there has been an almost 30 per cent increase in gas prices in 2011 alone, as the uncertainties about future supply have become a factor in gas-trading calculations.

'Unconventional' gas

The potential for unlocking new sources of gas has excited scientists for many years, and has received a lot of publicity recently with some success, along with significant problems. 'Unconventional' gas is broadly speaking gas that is hard to extract. There are a number of different sources. The first is coal-bed methane, gas that is overlaid or in coal seams, formed by anaerobic decay. In certain instances (old mine workings) it makes sense to capture and use this methane (a much more potent greenhouse gas than carbon dioxide), rather than let it leach out. Another unconventional source of gas is methane hydrates, gas trapped in ice crystals formed by anaerobic bacterial digestion of organic matter.[20] These are found at the bottom of the seas, and mining these would present a huge technical challenge. Although there is a lot of research going on, to date no methane hydrate deposits have been commercially mined. There is also real concern about whether disturbing hydrates would destabilise them, releasing uncontrollable amounts of climate-change-inducing methane.[21] In any case the resource may be overstated, as in general they are found at low concentrations, but widely spread. At the time of writing, the likelihood of extracting significant amounts of gas from this source seems very low, and in fact energy analysts Professors Colin Campbell and Kjell Aleklett dismiss it completely.[22]

The final source is described as 'tight gas', meaning gas trapped in rock with very small pores. This is often in sandstone, but can be other types of geological strata such as shales – hence it is often called 'shale gas'. This gas is not easy to extract and has been considered uneconomic until recently. However, in the last couple of years there has been a lot of excitement, and also considerable controversy, as commercial extraction of shale gas has got under way, particularly in the US. The proponents of shale gas have talked up the potential of this resource so that it is perceived as a possible 'game changer' in the future energy arena.[23] Given the excitement, we need to examine shale gas and its implications in detail.

To extract shale gas, the rock containing the gas is accessed using vertical and horizontal drilling. The borehole created is lined with concrete. Since the gas is contained within or on the shale, this must be released. This is achieved by pumping a mixture of water, mud and chemicals down the borehole, creating pressure which shatters the rock, releasing the gas which is extracted through the borehole. This process is known as hydraulic fracturing, or 'fracking'. The controversy around shale gas is fourfold. These are contamination of the groundwater, carbon emissions, earthquakes and whether the resources are as big as some claim.

Contamination of the groundwater in the US has occurred in two ways. First, some of the chemicals used in the mixture used to shatter the shale are toxic or carcinogenic – one is benzene. These chemicals have been able to enter the groundwater around the drilling and then contaminate drinking or irrigation water. Second, the gas itself has been found to escape and enter the groundwater in rural areas. Evidence of this can be seen in the documentary film *Gaslands*, with the bizarre sight of tap water being 'set on fire' (search the web for videos). Despite these problems, the industry in the US denies responsibility. In France groups are being set up nationwide to fight exploration for the resource.[24] In the UK, exploratory drilling has taken place in Lancashire, but the company concerned claims that it is using mud rather than chemicals to create the rock-breaking pressure. It also claims that there is no chance of groundwater contamination due to the geology. During the initial exploratory drilling, two small earthquakes were recorded, caused by the extraction process, and drilling was suspended for a period. The company has announced that potentially huge reserves exist under Lancashire and expressed the desire to proceed.

The next controversy concerns that of the greenhouse effects of the extraction of the gas. All energy sources require some input of energy to extract them – but this is repaid by the energy yield from the coal, oil or gas recovered (we cover this in the next chapter). For conventional natural gas this energy return is surprisingly low, and for shale gas the net energy gain is likely to be even lower due to the amount of drilling required, although no verified figures are available yet. The quantity of drilling required can be seen in a presentation published by the US Energy Information Administration (USEIA) in 2010. It shows a map of Fort Worth, Texas, surrounded by more wells than it is possible to count, and what's most surprising is that many are in urban areas.[25] The opponents of shale gas argue that the CO_2 emissions are roughly equivalent to that of coal power.

The last area of controversy and the one most relevant to this book – is this a game-changer as far as the resource size is concerned? Could shale gas become a big provider of energy in the future? The wells deplete very fast (up to 65 per cent in the first year), with each well being exhausted in 5–10 years, hence the need for so much drilling.[26] This rapid depletion, together with the energy needed to extract the gas effectively puts a floor under the market price for shale gas (higher than conventional gas). According to the USEIA 2010 report shale gas will boost the global recoverable reserves of natural gas by 40 per cent.[27] However, while this report is conservative in terms of recoverable gas, it is probably optimistic on the size of the fields, basing its data in some cases on scant geological data. Recently one large shale gas field has had its reserves total lowered by 80 per cent.[28] Comments by Sam Laidlaw, the CEO of Centrica (formerly British Gas), reported on the *Guardian* website are cautious: he sees shale gas making little contribution outside the US in the medium term and thinks the rapid depletion of the fields may limit its effectiveness. The think-tank Chatham House have produced a report suggesting shale gas may even push up prices of gas after ten years since little exploration for conventional gas will take place while shale gas reserves are exploited in the intervening period.[29] As we are writing this book in early 2012, the rapid expansion of shale gas extraction in the US seems to have changed the energy picture as far as natural gas is concerned: stocks are up, prices are down, and the US has become a net exporter. It remains to be seen whether this change will be sustained over the longer term.

International gas trading

Unlike oil, for many years gas has been traded very little internationally and most gas trading has occurred within continents. This is because, unlike oil, gas is relatively expensive and hazardous to transport through pipelines or by liquefying it, although the costs of transportation have been falling. However, as indigenous production has declined (especially in Europe) some intercontinental trading has started. At the moment it makes up almost a third of global annual production and is rising fast, although most of this is accounted for by transfer of gas from Russia through pipelines to Europe.[30] At present, unlike oil, there is no global gas price. Prices are set regionally. In 2001, a number of major gas exporting countries set up the Gas Exporting Countries Forum. In 2008 they made a more formal arrangement attempting to set up a cartel like OPEC (GASPEC). The likely future effects of this organisation are unclear, but up until now it has had little effect on prices and appears rather disorganised.

Conclusions

Where does this leave us? It is very hard to come to definite conclusions about gas with so little data on reserves to draw on. One estimate of the total global conventional gas reserves is 10,000 trillion cubic feet, and it was calculated in 2003 that 73 per cent of this gas was remaining.[31] By 2010, the BP statistical energy review estimates remaining reserves at 62 per cent (a big drop in seven years). Very few commentators think that the gas peak is imminent.[31] And yet … conventional gas discoveries did peak in 1970 and peak oil theory (and indeed practice) suggests that if discovery does not keep pace with production/consumption then output will also peak and decline. In addition if conventional gas is so plentiful, why the sudden switch to shale gas which is more difficult and expensive to produce?

To complicate the issue there are a number of factors that could either enhance gas supplies or cause faster depletion. Many of the remaining reserves (possibly up to one-third) in conventional fields are 'stranded gas'.[33] That is, gas that is mixed with oil has too much CO_2 in it, or is physically stranded with no means of transportation to market. Much of this stranded gas is either flared off or re-injected into wells to force more oil out. Stranded gas means many remaining reserves may be unusable, at least in the medium term. While unconventional gas *may* enhance supplies, there are other factors that could lead to increasing rates of depletion. Consumption in India and China is one such reason. These countries have insufficient indigenous supplies to meet their fast-rising demand. While gas makes a small contribution to the overall energy supply in China, its use is rising very quickly, by 11.5 per cent in 2009 according to the *People's Daily* newspaper. The *People's Daily* also states that in 2008 the country became a net importer and is expanding its imports of LNG. The situation in India is similar.

Another factor is the use of gas to extract oil from tar sands (large deposits of sticky, thick tar found mainly in Canada). This process is not only very environmentally unfriendly in its pollution, use of water and sand, but is also extremely energy intensive, using natural gas.[34] While only approximately 0.5 per cent of daily world gas production is used for this process today, extraction of oil from tar sands is set to increase, which could have a significant effect on prices in a tightening supply market.

Lastly but very importantly, gas has other uses, being used to power some vehicles, to make plastics, chemicals, pharmaceuticals, fabric for clothing, packaging and fertilisers. Added to this, gas can substitute for about a quarter of oil's current uses. Of the four conventional energy sources we are examining, gas appears to have the best reserves, although these reserves, particularly unconventional ones, may be exaggerated. However, even large gas reserves will not delay a crisis if oil peaks soon, since the gas price is linked to that of oil for the reasons given above. It therefore seems likely that gas prices are going to keep rising. This is particularly true in western Europe where there could be actual shortages of supply due to depletion of indigenous reserves.

The morality of fossil fuels

The use of fossil fuels presents a number of moral issues for Christians. These fall into the following categories:

- First, pollution due to the extraction or mining of these resources. The BP disaster in the Gulf of Mexico had commentators in the rich world throwing up their hands in horror, and yet in Nigeria, the poverty-stricken inhabitants of the oil-rich Niger delta live with worse pollution from crude oil leakages and gas flaring every day. We cannot be sure that the petrol in our tanks comes from clean, safe production sites. Coal also causes widespread air pollution and environmental damage from its mining. As Christians, what responsibility do we have for the environmental cost of the energy we consume?

- Second, oil props up some extremely despotic Middle-Eastern regimes. The western world's tolerance of these regimes is highly influenced by its oil addiction. When Libya descends into turmoil we intervene, but Yemen and Syria are treated differently, and Bahrain with some oil and gas is mildly criticised when it shoots people. In buying oil from countries like Saudi Arabia we are not only supporting the regime, but also its extreme form of Islam. Many of the 9/11 hijackers were Saudi nationals.
- Third, our use of fossil fuels is one of the primary causes of human-made climate change, which has dire implications for everyone, in particular poor and marginalised people around the world.
- Another moral question arises from the technology of carbon capture and storage (assuming it works): is using this akin to sweeping dirt under the carpet, grasping an easy solution rather than dealing with the fundamental problem? While we have taken part in some discussion in Christian circles on the issue of climate change, and taken part in rallies and lobbied on the issue, we have never heard any discussion on these other moral questions. We think that Christians should be at the forefront of action, lobbying to break our fossil fuel addiction and setting an example by reducing our own dependence on fossil fuels.[/bl]

Nuclear power

Nuclear power, which uses uranium as an energy source, contrasts with the other energy sources we have discussed. The technology is different (in that it is not directly carbon based), and it also has military uses and a very long-term legacy issue. Most importantly, unlike oil/gas/coal where we can debate when production *will* peak, uranium production *has* already peaked years ago – a fact that is little known, or at least little recognised (not least by governments). We also know that there is insufficient uranium available to replace all current worldwide coal- and gas-generating capacity with nuclear power. The argument is about whether nuclear power could make a useful contribution in the years ahead.

There are a whole heap of issues that stick to nuclear like a bad smell. These include: safety; proliferation of nuclear weapons; terrorism; the environmental problems of the mining process; cost; inundation of new build by rising sea levels; and what to do with the waste. We will look at some of these issues, particularly since the recent Fukushima disaster has brought nuclear safety to the fore once again. However, in analysing the potential of nuclear power, we have concentrated on what we believe is the key issue – that of uranium supplies. For much of this section we are indebted to the late energy economist Dr David Fleming, who made a detailed and authoritative study of this issue (other sources are also cited). Readers who want to examine this in detail are directed to his webpage.[35] The BBC also has a very good summary of the process.[36] We think nuclear power raises a number of very tricky moral and ethical issues that Christians rarely consider, and we examine these at the end of this section.

An astonishing amount of political will, effort, commentary and controversy surrounds nuclear power, which is out of all proportion to the amount of *energy* it produces worldwide. For example, in the UK nuclear electricity provides slightly less than 20 per cent of electricity, but less than 4 per cent of *all* energy used in the economy. (The average person consumes most energy in domestic heating and transport, neither of which involve nuclear energy unless electricity is consumed.)

The energy involved in nuclear power

Nuclear power is an energy-intensive process. Uranium-containing rock (ore) has to be mined; this involves extracting a very large quantity of rock for an ultimately small quantity of uranium. Sulphuric acid is poured over the rock to extract the uranium from the rocks; this is known as 'yellowcake', one form of uranium oxide. This is then milled (large chunks broken up into smaller ones), and the resulting processed ore is then transported by land and sea to be enriched. This enrichment involves another chemical reaction so that the uranium can be transformed to a gas at relatively low temperatures. Most of the uranium in the ore is in the form of the isotopes uranium-234 and uranium-238, but what is required is another isotope, uranium-235, which is fissile.[37] By spinning the gaseous uranium very fast for a very long time in huge steel buckets, the uranium-235 can be enriched from the majority uranium-238. The process needs to carried out until the uranium-235 is about 3.5 per cent of the total. However, if you spin the centrifuges for longer, until the uranium-235 is in excess of 90 per cent of the total, you have weapons-grade material (hence the current controversy over Iran's nuclear programme – the same type of equipment can be used for both civilian and military purposes). For power generation, the uranium is converted back to a solid oxide form, packaged into ceramic pellets which are packed into alloy rods. These are then transported to the power stations for use.

After use in the power stations, the moderately radioactive uranium fuel has been converted to a whole series of highly radioactive elements. Some of these are very short- lived, such as Iodine-131 (which was released in large quantities at Fukushima), others are radioactive for millions of years. These waste materials have to be removed and cooled for a few decades under water, and then most countries plan to build repositories – where the material is buried deep beneath the earth in some kind of container for at least a hundred years, or even permanently. Ideas about what kind of burial in what kind of container and where vary – only Finland has actually gone ahead with construction of such a facility. Beyond that, no one knows what to do with the waste. Likewise, the power stations at the end of their life also have to be left to cool for several decades and then very carefully dismantled over a long period of time (probably about a hundred years, although it is claimed new reactor designs will take less time). Many parts of them are very radioactive and so contribute to the increasing stockpile of nuclear waste.

It is often claimed that nuclear power is a 'zero carbon' energy source, which has a big part to play in reducing our carbon dioxide emissions and therefore the effects of climate change. However, the extraction, processing and transport of the uranium fuel, the con-struction, eventual dismantling and clean-up of reactors all requires energy – which is provided by carbon fuels. (The very lengthy process of decommissioning has only recently started for the first generation of nuclear reactors, so until it has been fully completed we can only estimate how much energy this will take.) The only part of the process that is zero carbon is when the fuel rods are in the reactor, producing electricity.

Ore strength and energy return

Finding ore with a high percentage of the isotope uranium-235 in the rock, means that less energy will be expended in mining, milling and enrichment, and more is obtained back as electricity for a lower energy input. So when we examine the energy balance of nuclear power – and its potential contribution in the years ahead – the critical question is not only about *how much* uranium ore is left in the world, but also the *quality* of the ore. One study on the energy balance from nuclear power suggests that there is a critical cut-off point in ore strength: 0.01 per cent concentration of uranium for uranium ore derived from sandstone and 0.02 per cent of uranium for granite.[38] If the ore strength is below this it is not worth extracting – rather than expending energy on mining and processing, it would be better to use the energy to produce electricity directly.

Uranium supply

So how much ore is left and of what grade? Both the International Atomic Energy Agency (IAEA) and independent analysts Van Leeuwen and Smith pretty much agree about this, saying that we have enough for around 70 years at current rates of use. This looks encouraging until you dig around a bit (no pun intended). The first point to make is that this figure is undoubtedly optimistic. The figure of 70 years comes from the reserves to production ratio, a simple calculation where the currently known reserves are divided by annual usage. The problem is that geology doesn't work that way, production does not keep going at a maximal rate and then stop abruptly, instead it tails off. The second point is that uranium production has already peaked back in 1981 (see Figure 2), and the nature of the current supply is surprising.[39] [40]

While most of the uranium we use is mined, this has been insufficient to meet current demand for many years. The remainder

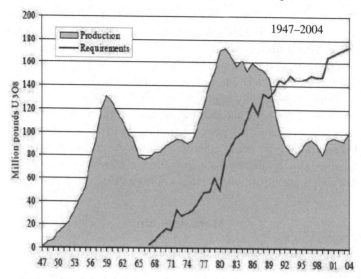

Figure 2: Uranium supply versus demand. Taken from the SDC report 'The role of nuclear power in a low carbon economy Paper 8: Uranium resource availability'.

comes from two sources: first, from stockpiles of previously mined ore, and, second, from material recycled from decommissioned nuclear weapons (resulting from the disarmament treaty between the US and Russia in the mid-1980s). The problem is that these additional sources of uranium are soon going to run out. Two new mines have been depended on to make about half the shortfall, but neither is anywhere near ready to do so: one is in the Australian desert with insufficient water supplies for an efficient mining operation; the other in Canada has repeatedly flooded.[41] There have also been recent reports of increased mining being planned in Namibia in a national park. Again this is in a desert area so the water would have to be pumped many miles. Currently almost all the power to do this would be from coal-fired power stations, although the mining company was insistent that they would use renewable energy.

There are other sources of analysis which give a similar picture. A report commissioned in 2006 by the UK Sustainable Development

Commission came up with a figure of 100 years Uranium supply remaining, but warned of a short-term supply crunch.[42] The Energy Watch Group from Germany are slightly more optimistic on immediate supply issues, but pessimistic on the long-term supply, predicting that by 2020 there will be severe supply constraints.[43]

Data on ore quality suggests that only Canada has good quality ore above 1 per cent, and that the other uranium-producing countries have ore below 0.1 per cent, putting them close to the energy balance limit. Is there any other way around the problem? (It should be noted that this uranium is required to fuel existing power stations, not cope with expansion.) Various solutions have been suggested.

More uranium

The most obvious solution is to find more uranium. There may be new sources of good quality uranium ore, however a lot of exploration took place in the 1970s when uranium was last valuable, before the accidents at Three Mile Island and Chernobyl. Since then geological surveying has been carried out looking for a whole range of minerals, and the geology of the planet is far better understood, making it unlikely that major new sources will be discovered. Even if a major new find emerges, opening a new mine is an expensive, time-consuming process. Also, any new sources are likely to be deep underground, requiring more energy to extract them. We cannot rely on this as an answer in the short term. In the longer term, the exploiting of any new uranium finds will depend on a complex calculation involving the quality of the ore and the energy required to get at it.

Other sources

Uranium is found in various other sources – in granite rock, phosphates and seawater – and there are potentially vast amounts available, but at very low concentrations, which makes recovery very challenging. Until some novel process comes along for retrieving these traces of uranium, the energy expended in extracting them would be far more than that gained.[44] Some academics have attempted to make a case for extracting uranium from seawater but their views on the issue have come under considerable challenge.[45] [46] With mined phosphates, again the uranium is at very low level (<0.01 per cent).[47] The process of extraction is dangerous and complicated and additionally phosphate production is generally accepted to have peaked (see later in this book).

New material from old weapons

On 2 February 2011 President Obama signed an arms limitation treaty with Russia. This limits each country to a maximum of 1550 *deployed* warheads. This is lower than the previous level of approximately 2200 warheads a side. If the uranium from these weapons was recycled into fuel for nuclear reactors, it would provide a useful boost to supplies. As discussed earlier, the weapons material is highly enriched and has to be diluted to a uranium-235 content of 3–4 per cent before it can fuel a reactor. Every warhead has 50kg of 90 per cent uranium-235 and this is equivalent to 7 tonnes of natural uranium. Thus 25 warheads will fuel an existing 1GWp reactor for 1 year.[48] (Making the assumption that all warheads will be retired from use and not stockpiled.) Then it is an easy calculation to work out that the fuel from these weapons is sufficient to fuel about 56 such reactors for 1 year – helpful, but not a game-changer.

Fast breeders

This is another type of nuclear reactor, several of which have been built around the world, though all have now been closed for safety reasons.[49] Though in theory this type of reactor should produce electricity *and* more fuel, in practice it has failed. Another similar idea uses the element thorium rather than uranium to fuel the process.[50] There is apparently a lot more thorium around than uranium and some experimental reactors were operated in the past.[51] These should breed uranium from the thorium fuel. One reactor was run for five years in the US at Shippingport, Pennsylvania. Careful analysis of the reports produced on this reactor indicates that it only managed to increase its uranium fuel by 8kg in five years of operation. Despite the fact that there are no such reactors currently in commercial use, India has put considerable effort into building a prototype, and has apparently proposed building 470 of them, but realistically it would be decades before enough reactors of this type were built to make any kind of useful contribution in an energy crisis.

Existing plutonium and recycling (MOX)

There is some weapons-grade material now intended for civilian use and in addition plutonium and uranium-235 in spent fuel. Current reactors are not set up for large-scale use of plutonium, which is a very hazardous material. In addition re-processing has been fraught with problems and has been unsuccessful; it has been banned in the US for many years, though both the Bush and Obama administrations have sought to change this.[52] One route is to reprocess the spent fuel into what are known as mixed oxides (MOX) by extracting leftover uranium-235 and plutonium-239 formed in current reactors. The plant to do this in the UK closed after a disastrous leak that wasn't discovered for nine months![53] At the time of writing it is unclear whether it will ever reopen.

Nuclear fusion

Unlike the conventional nuclear process of fission, nuclear fusion is a different technology without many of the drawbacks and is one that supposedly does not rely on uranium. Proponents talk of unlimited clean energy (once the technology is mastered). The physics of the process is complicated and will only be described very briefly. For a full explanation, seek online resources or read the chapter on it in *The Final Energy Crisis* by Sheila Newman.[54] If you take two isotopic forms of hydrogen (deuterium and tritium) and heat them to 100 million degrees centigrade they release an enormous amount of energy. Currently in all fusion experiments a small pellet of both of these hydrogen forms has either a very powerful laser fired at it (US), or is ionised then heated (Europe). Either way, no net return on the energy input has so far been obtained. Deuterium occurs naturally at a low concentration in water and is non-radioactive; tritium is radioactive with a half-life of 12.3 years.[55] Its short half-life means it does not occur in nature and has to be made. This is carried out in fission reactors from uranium (hence even fusion has a uranium dependency) and it is probably the most expensive isotopic element on earth.

There are a number of unsolved problems with fusion. Many of these are highly technical physics problems and will only be very briefly described. The first problem is the high temperatures generated. Obviously the heat is to be used to heat water to steam and drive turbines, cooling the core. However, no known material will withstand the temperatures generated. A second major problem is that of the intense neutron radiation generated as a by-product of the process. Neutron radiation already causes huge problems in conventional fission reactor cores since again there is no known material that is resistant to it. The last and perhaps greatest problem is that to make it sustainable tritium has to be bred in the reactor and recovered to breed new ones. Some physicists doubt this can be done.[56]

To produce energy, the fusion process has to run continuously (not just for a few seconds) at 100 million degrees. After decades of research and vast amounts of tax-payers cash this has not been achieved. An experimental reactor is under construction in France but is already over-budget and behind schedule and is not expected to start its first experiment until 2026![57] Once again it seems that claims are being made that in practice cannot be fulfilled. Even if the technical problems can be solved, not even fusion's most ardent adherents could legitimately claim it as the answer to peak oil – the generally accepted figure before a 1GW fusion reactor is up and running is 30 years (many would say this figure is optimistic).

The record of the nuclear industry (timing)

With peak oil imminent, can the nuclear industry deliver any kind of response on time? The most charitable way of describing the record of the nuclear industry worldwide is one of repeatedly making claims that it cannot deliver on. Up until now no nuclear power station has been built anywhere without some kind of government subsidy. In addition, no power stations have been built to time or cost or original design, probably anywhere, but certainly in the UK and the US. John Elkington lists some of the disasters that occurred in the 1960s and 70s in his (unfortunately) out of print book *Suntraps*. The construction mishaps and cost overruns were simply breathtaking. At the Diablo Canyon in California two reactors were under construction. While installing structural supports, the blueprints for reactor 2 were mistakenly used for reactor 1, and it was later discovered that the cooling system supports had been installed back to front.[58] It simply isn't credible that countries like the US, where no new reactors have been built for 40 years, can now construct a new fleet of reactors quickly without very considerable time delays and cost overruns. European experience also supports this; new reactors are under construction in Finland and France and again the same old problems of exaggerated claims both on cost and timescales are occurring. There are also problems over the supply of skilled personnel needed to build the reactors.[59] After Chernobyl it wasn't a great chat-up line at student parties to admit to studying nuclear engineering. Most university nuclear engineering departments in the UK (and elsewhere) closed and there is a shortage of inspectors to license new designs.

In addition, after having said they would manage a world first by building subsidy-free new reactors in the UK, there are rumours that the industry is once again asking for government money or getting multiple sources of subsidy revenue.[60] Unlike nuclear, the costs of renewables are falling continuously due to increased production and technological improvement.

We can only judge an industry by its past performance, and on this basis it is surprising that nuclear is even under consideration. The reasons for this 'renaissance' are simple. The nuclear industry has lobbied governments very successfully as a carbon-free way of solving a huge engineering problem (climate change), while allowing the electorate to continue to waste energy, fly and drive. It should be noted that the International Energy Agency 2006 World Energy Outlook report suggested that nuclear was the least efficient way to cut carbon emissions at 10 per cent of avoided emissions, slightly behind renewables and way behind energy efficiency. (However, this wasn't the spin put on the report by the agency.) Governments want to keep society pretty much moving along as it is at the moment. The drawback with this view is that climate change shouldn't, and peak oil won't, allow business as usual.

Fukushima

In early 2011 the nuclear industry worldwide was congratulating itself. With the twenty-fifth anniversary of Chernobyl approaching, many western governments had decided that worries about nuclear safety had been outweighed by climate and energy security concerns. Nuclear new-build was back, with most western governments planning new reactors. Then the massive earthquake and tsunami struck the eastern seaboard of Japan, killing a still unknown number of people and severely damaging four of the six reactors at the Fukushima nuclear plant. As we write this, the Japanese are still coping with the aftermath of both disasters. Precisely what occurred at Fukushima will only become apparent with time, and the implications will unfold over many years. However, even at this early stage after the disaster we think there are lessons we can learn.

The first is that the nuclear industry seems unable to stop a meltdown of the reactor core once it has started.[61] At Three Mile Island in Pennsylvania, 85 per cent meltdown took place, and in Japan partial meltdown has definitely occurred in some of the reactors. At Chernobyl the release of radioactivity was caused by an explosion rather than a meltdown, everything happened in minutes; but the other two disasters occurred over a longer timescale. At both, the companies concerned were left scrabbling around trying to work out what to do.

The second lesson is about the danger of storing spent fuel. Almost all reactors worldwide have large amounts of spent fuel stored on site in cooling 'ponds' due to a combination of government cowardice and an inability to work out what to with it. This is a huge vulnerability. At Fukushima, trying to stop the spent fuel rods catching fire, spreading plutonium and other radioactive elements up into the atmosphere and then downwind, was as big an issue as stopping meltdown. Safety at nuclear plants around the world remains a serious concern. The nuclear industry thinks it can engineer its way out of any safety issue. However, there is no way of completely eliminating human error from any complex engineering system. Thus we think there may well be more accidents, but a greater concern is that of terrorism. We can only speculate that terrorists may have seen what has happened in Japan, and noted the vulnerability of nuclear sites. Attacking and disabling the cooling system for the reactors or storage ponds could cause untold harm.[62]

The final lesson is that of cost. The operators of the Fukushima plant, the Tokyo Electric Power Company (TEPCO), cannot meet the cost of clean-up, decommissioning or even possibly buying alternative electricity to replace the lost capacity. Nuclear power plants are essentially uninsurable, and with clean-up costs from the Fukushima disaster initially estimated at US$133 billion, the Japanese tax-payer is learning about unlimited liability.

The implications of Fukushima are many, and what has happened probably raises more questions than answers. On the pages of the *Guardian* an increasingly acrimonious row has been played out between two of its columnists, George Monbiot, an environmental campaigner, and John Vidal, the paper's environment editor. George Monbiot's argument is that climate change is such a huge problem that we have to use nuclear; renewables are not up to the job and it's worth putting up with problems like Fukushima. John Vidal thinks the opposite. The argument then shifted to debating the numbers killed by nuclear power, particularly at Chernobyl. The problem is that proving death from cancers caused by irradiation is difficult in the long term when people die of other diseases, or even die of cancer (which could have other causes). This was particularly problematic in the Soviet Union when life expectancy was already short. While there seems little doubt that international bodies have played down the number of deaths, it appears to us that both the above commentators have missed the point. Probably few people will die directly of radiation poisoning from the disaster at Fukushima, but this is because very large numbers of people have been evacuated from a steadily expanding exclusion zone. It is this economic and social dislocation that has been the real cost of both Chernobyl and Fukushima.

Other questions Fukushima raises are that of political policy, the use and price of other fuels. Chancellor Merkel's Christian Democrats in Germany have suffered in regional elections in two Länder. In both, her support for nuclear power was a major issue, despite the fact that she had ordered the temporary closure of seven older power plants. Countries as diverse as Switzerland and China have imposed moratoria on building new reactors. The worldwide wholesale price of gas has risen, since Japan imports more to replace its lost nuclear generating capacity. Germany is continuing strongly down the renewable energy path it has started. Japan is unlikely to build new reactors (as was planned) but has introduced feed-in tariffs (see Chapter 4) for all forms of renewable energy, bridging the switch with gas. The country has a very large pumped storage electricity capacity[63] which would combine well with solar and wind output.[64] The US and UK governments seem determined even now to push ahead with new nuclear plants, but the problems of nuclear (cost, uranium supply and waste) remain. As we write this, it appears in the UK that companies that had committed to new-build are pulling out.[65] Increased safety costs may yet kill the whole idea off. China will build new reactors but there will be protests. The uranium supply issues mentioned above will be most likely unchanged in the short term since most of the world's existing fleet of reactors will continue operating.

Conclusions

There seems to be little scope for nuclear power making a significant contribution to the problem of peak oil due to the very long timescales involved in construction, and the uranium supply constraints. From the peak oil perspective, nuclear is arguably a huge distraction, since the very large amounts of energy and skills required to dismantle the power stations and deal with the waste legacy will be badly needed elsewhere. It seems certain that some countries are going to build new nuclear reactors, but the uranium supply is going to be an issue soon. In the near future it seems there won't be enough uranium to maintain the current fleet of reactors worldwide, much less expand their number.

Moral issues

Nuclear power raises some interesting moral issues for Christians, which they rarely confront. First, there is the legacy of the waste. Is it good stewardship to take something sitting in the ground, harming no one, and convert it to something that is deadly to human health for hundreds of generations? There is nothing in human history which has been looked after for anything like the time period that nuclear waste will require. Is it fair for us to load this problem on to future generations when they have had no say in the decision, and to do it with very little debate and no democratic vote?[66] Where to put the waste is a huge issue which governments (apart from in Finland) have so far ducked.

Another moral issue is the harm uranium extraction does both to the environment and those who mine it. While some uranium mining takes place in developed countries, much takes place in countries such as Niger and Kazakhstan where the rules will inevitably be less rigorous. Again this is not unique to uranium but is a problem for all mineral extraction. There are starting to be campaigns to change the mining industry and you can even buy fair-trade gold. However, we suspect fair-trade uranium is some way off.

There is also the long-standing link between nuclear weapons and nuclear energy. Throughout the cold war and beyond, Christians have taken widely differing views on nuclear disarmament – some apparently enthusiastic about nuclear weapons, others not so. The International Atomic Energy Agency attempts to police civilian nuclear power and stop countries developing weapons from it. Many countries, including the UK, have signed an international non-proliferation treaty, but this has not stopped the UK using civilian reactors to make weapons-grade material in the past. Some countries like Pakistan and Israel have not signed the treaty and are known to have nuclear weapons. Worse, a key nuclear scientist in Pakistan's weapon programme, Abdul Qadeer Khan, sold the technology on to other countries such as North Korea and Libya; he confessed but was pardoned by President Musharraf.[67] Iran is suspected of using its civilian nuclear programme to develop weapons. This has led some neighbouring Arab countries such as Saudi Arabia and the UAE to instigate nuclear programmes, the suspicion being that their interest is not entirely peaceful.

The final issue that must be addressed is that of honesty. The nuclear industry worldwide has a reputation for underplaying risks and costs, then when things do go wrong not being honest. This has happened again and again. We have seen this most recently in Japan when the public didn't believe TEPCO's assurances due to past problems at other nuclear installations. Tony Benn (who was UK energy minister in the early 1970s) recounted a story on BBC Radio 4 about being at a meeting and being asked by the Japanese energy minister about a fire at Sellafield that he knew nothing about! Officials had not told him.[68] Should we trust the industry or tolerate dishonesty?

In this chapter we have taken a detailed look at conventional energy sources. In the next two chapters we look at the potential for clean, renewable energy to meet future needs.

Notes

1   The Fischer-Tropsch process, named after the German inventors of the process.

2   Energy Data Associates of Bridport, Dorset.

3   B. Kavalov and S. D. Peteves of the Institute for Energy (IFE), *The Future of Coal*, prepared for European Commission Joint Research Centre, 2007.

4   D. Strahan, 'Peak coal – Coaled comfort', *Energy world*, April 2008.

5   *Ibid.*

6   From 'The Global Market Outlook for Photovoltaics Report', European Photovoltaic Industry Association, (2011.

7   Strahan, 'Peak coal – Coaled comfort', and http://rutledge.caltech.edu/.

8   *Coal: Resources and Future Production*, Energy Watch Group, 2007.

9   http://www.energybulletin.net/node/39236.

10   Strahan, 'Peak coal – Coaled comfort'.

11   P. Kharecha and J. Hansen, '*Implications of "peak oil" for atmospheric CO_2 and climate*', at http://arxiv.org/abs/0704.2782.

12   K. Aleklett and C. J. Campbell, 'The Peak and Decline of World Oil and Gas Production', *Minerals and Energy*, 2003.

13   *Ibid.*

14   R. W. Bentley, 'Global Oil and Gas Depletion: An Overview', *Energy Policy* 30, 2002, pp. 189–205.

15   'The Future of the Oil and Gas Industry: Past Approaches New Challenges', *World energy* 5.3, 2002.

16   Bentley, 'Global Oil and Gas Depletion', pp. 189–205.

17   Aleklett and Campbell, 'The Peak and Decline of World Oil and Gas Production'.

18   *Ibid.*

19   Office of the Gas and Electricity Markets; see www.ofgem.com.

20   http://marine.usgs.gov/fact-sheets/gas-hydrates/title.html.

21 http://www.energybulletin.net/node/47505. Methane has 20 times the climate-inducing effects of carbon dioxide.

22 Aleklett and Campbell, 'The Peak and Decline of World Oil and Gas Production'.

23 See *World Shale Gas Resources: An Initial Assessment of 14 Regions Outside the United States*, US Energy information service, 2011. This gives both good background information and technical geological information. The *Guardian* has also had a series of reports which can be accessed at its website.

24 http://www.guardian.co.uk/environment/2011/apr/20/southern-france-sarkozy-shale-gas.

25 R. G. Newell, 'Shale Gas – A Game Changer for U.S. and Global Gas Markets?', Flame 2010 Gas Conference.

26 *The Oil Crunch – A Wake-up Call for the UK Economy*, second report of the UK Industry Taskforce on Peak Oil and Energy Security (ITPOES), February 2010.

27 http://www.guardian.co.uk/environment/2011/apr/20/southern-france-sarkozy-shale-gas.

28 http://econintersect.com/b2evolution/blog1.php/2011/08/31/u-s-eia-slashes-marcellus-shale-estimates.

29 'The "Shale Gas Revolution": Hype and Reality', available at http://www.chathamhouse.org.uk/publications/papers/view/-/id/947/.

30 *Natural Gas in the World – 2009 Edition*, Cedigaz, 2009.

31 Aleklett and Campbell, 'The Peak and Decline of World Oil and Gas Production'.

32 Some more of these can be found on the excellent UK Parliament all-party peak oil and gas website, http://www.appgopo.org.uk/.

33 Aleklett and Campbell, 'The Peak and Decline of World Oil and Gas Production'.

34 http://www.moneyweek.com/investments/commodities/are-canadian-tar-sands-the-answer-to-our-oilneeds.aspx.

35 http://www.theleaneconomyconnection.net/index.html.

36 http://news.bbc.co.uk/1/hi/in_depth/world/2003/nuclear_fuel_cycle/mining/default.stm.

37 Fissile means an element, when bombarded by neutrons, is capable of releasing neutrons in turn rather than absorbing them. The numbers refer to the element's atomic mass. The atomic mass is the mass of the element due to the total number of protons and neutrons, electrons having negligible mass; the same elements with different mass numbers are known as isotopes. Note they have identical chemical properties.

38 J. W. S van Leeuwen and P. Smith, http://www.stormsmith.nl/. The site has a series of criticisms of their work made by the World Nuclear Association, and their rebuttals.

39 http://www.guardian.co.uk/society/2006/jun/07/
    guardiansocietysupplement2.

40 SDC, 'The role of nuclear power in a low carbon economy Paper 8:
    Uranium resource availability'.

41 See David Fleming's 'The Lean Economy' website; also, Googling various
    web-based investment sites confirms the truth in this.

42 SDC 'The role of nuclear power in a low carbon economy Paper 8:
    Uranium resource availability'.

43 Uranium Resources and Nuclear Energy EWG-Paper No 1/06, Energy
    Watch Group, 2006.

44 See 'The Lean Economy' website.

45 M. Tamada, Erice seminar 2009, 'Current status of technology for collec-
    tion of uranium from seawater'.

46 David MacKay, *Sustainable Energy – Without the Hot Air*, UIT, 2008.

47 See 'The Lean Economy' website.

48 http://www.technologyreview.com/blog/arxiv/24414/. 'The Future of
    Nuclear Energy: Facts and Fiction Chapter II: What is known about
    Secondary Uranium Resources?' Over 95 per cent of weapons are held by
    the Americans and Russians. While there are many good reasons for the
    UK, France and other countries to get rid of their weapons, energy is not
    one of them.

49 This is the reason given. In theory, since the plutonium is weapons-grade, a
    runaway chain reaction could occur and a nuclear explosion. However,
    there is a suspicion that the real reason is one of technical failure.

50 http://www.cosmosmagazine.com/features/print/348/new-age-
    nuclear?page=0%2C0.

51 http://www.technologyreview.com/blog/arxiv/24414/. 'The Future of
    Nuclear Energy: Facts and Fiction Chapter IV: Energy from Breeder
    Reactors and from Fusion?'

52 http://ecopolitology.org/2009/07/03/us-department-of-energy-cancels-
    nuclear-reprocessing-project/.

53 http://www.guardian.co.uk/society/2005/may/09/
    environment.nuclearindustry;
    http://en.wikipedia.org/wiki/Thermal_Oxide_Reprocessing_Plant.

54 See *Fusion Illusions* by M. Dittmar in *The Final Energy Crisis* edited by S.
    Newman. This is a nuclear physicist's (working at EPH and CERN)
    criticism of thermonuclear research.

55 This means if you have 1kg initially, after 12.3 years you will have half a kilo
    as the element decays to a completely different element.

56 M. E. Sawan and M. A. Abdou, 'Physics and Technology Conditions for
    Attaining Tritium Self-sufficiency for the DT Fuel Cycle', Abdou, *Fusion
    Engineering and Design*, 81:(8–14), 2006, pp. 1131–44.

57 http://news.bbc.co.uk/1/hi/sci/tech/6158040.stm and
    http://news.bbc.co.uk/1/hi/sci/tech/8103557.stm.

58 In addition, the electrical system related the plant's power supply was
    incorrectly installed. This plant led to the formation of Friends of the Earth.
    John Elkington, *Suntraps*, Pelican, 1984, pp. 112–13.

59 http://www.usnews.com/articles/education/2008/08/14/the-new-hot-
    job-nuclear-engineering.html;
    http://www.electric.co.uk/news/shortage-of-nuclear-engineers-
    expected-in-uk-1234333.html;
    http://www.publications.parliament.uk/pa/cm200809/cmselect/
    cmdius/0/5005.htm.

60 Details are still sketchy but apart from insurance there will be a carbon floor
    price which will penalise non-renewable and non-nuclear generation.
    These are known as contracts for difference. Their rates are being set in
    2013. The suspicion is they will be highest for nuclear.

61 Meltdown: nuclear material in the reactor reaches temperatures at which it
    becomes liquid and drops to the bottom of the containment vessel. There is
    then a danger of a breach of containment and a very bad leak. The reactor
    itself is unusable with partial meltdown. It is generally expressed as a
    percentage of the total fuel that melts.

62 http://www.ucsusa.org/nuclear_power/nuclear_power_risk/
    sabotage_and_attacks_on_reactors/impacts-of-aterrorist-attack.html.

63 Pumped storage is a way of 'storing' electricity when there is an excess of
    generation over demand. is pumped up to a reservoir. When power is
    required, the water is released down through pipes to drive a turbine and
    generate electricity. Japan has nearly 26GWp of capacity.

64 Apparently most of Japan's offshore wind turbines survived the tsunami, but
    many are out of use since their on-shore grid connections didn't.

65 http://www.guardian.co.uk/environment/2011/oct/07/rwe-uk-
    nuclear-power.

66 Italy (post-Chernobyl) voted to close all the power plants down, as did
    Sweden pre-Chernobyl. Italy was planning new-build recently (without a
    vote). However, a referendum took place in 2011, which the government
    lost. The state of Maine in the US voted in favour in the 1970s.

67 http://news.bbc.co.uk/1/hi/world/south_asia/3343621.stm and http://
    www.carnegieendowment.org/static/npp/Khan_Chronology.pdf.

68 This and other recollections can be found at http://www.tonybenn.com/
    nucl.html.

4

What about alternative energy?

Part 1: Renewable electricity

I'd put my money on the sun and solar energy. What a source of power! I hope we don't have to wait until oil and coal run out before we tackle that.

Thomas Edison, 1931

In the first three chapters, we examined the state of the world's current energy supplies and some of the concerns Christians may have about their use. We believe there are good reasons to be worried. As production of these fossil fuels peaks and declines, they are struggling to keep pace with current energy demands, let alone projected higher energy needs in the future. But are there other technologies that can help provide our energy needs in the years ahead? We hear a lot about renewable energy, but how does it measure up? In this chapter we look at these alternatives, and since both of us use a number of these different renewable technologies in our homes, we have working knowledge of their limitations and advantages. We will examine the costs and efficiencies of these domestic-scale renewables as well as larger schemes in this chapter, and look at heat and transport alternatives in the next. At the end of the next chapter we look at some of the moral and practical issues regarding all renewables. Specific energy conservation and efficiency measures are examined in a later chapter.

One of the problems with using alternative energy sources is that most of them suffer a comparative disadvantage in energy density when measured against our current, very energy-rich sources of power. Only a few centuries ago, humankind was burning only wood and dung for energy, and using hand-labour and draught animals to do work (and of course in many parts of the world people are still doing this). As populations increased, agriculture and demand for firewood cleared the forests and the resulting shortage of wood led to people burning coal. As development continued, the immense energy needs of industrialisation and urbanisation were met by the use of more and more coal, then oil, and more recently gas and nuclear fuel. Each change of energy supply has been to a more concentrated energy source, with the carbon and nuclear fuels we currently use having a very high energy density. The big disadvantage of renewable energy sources is that they are more diffuse – meaning that energy has to be harvested from a wider area, or from lower concentrations in order to be usable. However, in most cases the energy source itself is free. Wind turbines produce electricity 'out of thin air' – but only when the wind is blowing. Solar panels produce electricity from sunlight, but work best when the sun is shining directly on them.

Another issue is the net energy gain from renewables. Energy scientists use a measure called the Energy Return on Energy Invested (EROEI), which can be applied to any energy source. To obtain energy (from, for example, firewood) some energy has to be expended: in planting and growing the tree, making the tools to cut the tree down, the physical labour involved, and getting the fire-wood back to where it is used. This is fine when there is a net gain in energy, that is, the fire gives you more heat than all the energy you put into the process. If the firewood produced five times more energy than what had been expended, the net energy gain, or EROEI, would be 5:1. With concentrated forms of energy like oil, the EROEI ratio can be as high as 100:1, because even with all the effort of drilling, pumping and refining, there is still a colossal payback in terms of the energy recovered. With the alternatives the returns are usually much lower. If we take the example of a wind turbine, energy is used in the production of steel, concrete and other materials required for the manufacture of its components, transport-

ing them to site and the construction of the turbine. There will also
be an ongoing small energy input into maintenance, spare parts, and
some more energy required for taking down the turbine at the end
of its working life. Even though the source of energy (wind) is free,
all of those energy inputs have to be 'repaid' before the turbine
produces a net energy gain. For some technologies (both conventional and alternative) when all the inputs of energy have been taken
into account, there is only a small net energy gain. Clearly any
energy source where the EROEI scores less than 1:1 (i.e. more
energy has to be put in than is returned) is not worth pursuing. Yet
some come close to this figure – a poorly sited wind turbine or solar
panel could take years to repay the energy used in its production.
Some conventional energy sources – for example producing oil
from tar sands – also produce only a small net energy gain.

So before we start examining alternative technologies, how do
conventional resources fare? The EROEI figures for each technology (where we have been able to obtain figures) are shown in two
tables below: Table 1 compares conventional energy sources and
Table 2 the renewable or alternative energies.

Type	Net Energy Gain (EROEI)	Comments
Oil and gas	100:1	1930
Oil and gas	30:1	1970
Oil and gas	11-18:1	2005
Natural gas	10:1	2007, with carbon capture 2:1
Tar sands	2-4:1	
Coal	80:1	1930 (at mine mouth)
Coal	30:1	1970 (at mine mouth)
Coal	5-11:1	Prof. Cleveland, 2006
Nuclear	2-50:1	

Table 1: Energy return of 'conventional energy sources'.

The figures in Table 2 come from a variety of sources.[1] This data
highlights the fact that the net energy gain for any given technology
depends on a number of factors, such as where something is
mined/made/used, the energy efficiency used to make it and the
suitability of its location etc. For oil, the EROEI has been steadily
falling over the last century, from when 'gushers' have given way to
increasingly hard-to-extract oil (from deep water, for example).

Recent research also found a worrying drop between 1999 and 2006 when the EROEI for oil almost halved from 35:1 to 18:1; this suggests that the trend is accelerating.[2] Oil produced from tar sands is even lower. For coal, the references we found came up with two completely different EROEI figures, leaving us with a vast range of 80:1 down to 5:1. The higher figure is probably coal from open-cast mines, produced close to the power station, with the lower figure representing deep-mined coal which has been shipped long distances. As we examined earlier in Chapter 3, the easy-to-mine coal is largely gone, so the average EROEI figure for coal is falling towards the low end of that range. The EROEI for coal using Carbon Capture and Storage (CCS) has been estimated at only 2:1.[3] Natural gas has a surprisingly low EROEI of 10:1, and unconventional gas is likely to have an even lower figure than this, being harder to extract. Figures quoted for nuclear power range from 50:1 down to 2:1. Proponents of nuclear power often cite higher figures than this, but these are based on the thermal output, not electricity output of the stations. As described in the last chapter, the net energy gain from nuclear power is highly dependent on the ore strength used. So overall with a falling EROEI for conventional energy sources, we are putting more energy into the extraction processes in order to merely maintain our current levels of energy output. An analogy is that of someone on a treadmill having to run faster just to maintain their current position.

Turning to the renewable technologies, we anticipate that the EROEI ratio for many of these given below in Table 2 will improve in the future as we learn to use less energy in their manufacture, make them near to where they will be deployed, and benefit from economies of scale as the renewable industry grows. Alongside efficiency, another factor also merits attention. We are used to energy provision taking up very little land area: coal mines are mostly deep underground, oil and gas wells are out at sea or in arid countries where they don't conflict with agriculture. However, many proposed alternative energy sources are likely to require large areas of land to produce the amounts of energy we need in the future. Here in the UK, the arguments over putting up wind turbines close to homes or in picturesque countryside are an early sign that this may be problematic.

Type	Net Energy Gain (EROEI)	Comments
Hydro-power	>100:1, 6-17:1	Figures reflect different studies.
Wind (large-scale)	18:1, 25:1	This average figure masks improving trend over a long timescale up to 123:1.
Micro-wind	29:1	
Tidal range	116:1	Guess at this stage.
Tidal stream	17:1	Guess at this stage.
Wave	12:1	Guess at this stage.
Wood	24-35:1	Based on several studies.
Heat pump	3:1	Ecologist magazine.
Solar hot water	1.9-17:1	Based on several studies.
PV	2-8:1	
Thin film PV	7-40:1	
Biogas	8:1	Can depend on feedstock.
Biofuels	1-3:1	

Table 2: Energy return of renewable energy sources.

Energy conservation and efficiency

Before looking at new energy sources, it has to be emphasised that we could massively reduce our demand for energy if we conserved it, and used it much more efficiently. A simple example of energy *conservation* would be switching a light off when not required. Energy *efficiency* would be improved by switching to either a compact fluorescent or an LED (light-emitting diode) bulb, which use much less power. Improvements in conservation and efficiency can be driven by encouraging behavioural change, by legislation (taxation, energy ratings on houses and appliances, action on the stand-by function on appliances), or more controversially by (major) building refurbishment or demolition of buildings that cannot be made sufficiently energy efficient.

Unfortunately these relatively cheap and easy reductions in energy use are often overlooked. At a Scottish Parliament cross-party renewable energy group meeting that Neil attended in the early 2000s, a representative from Scottish Power outlined how they ran a pilot scheme where they offered to provide and fit insulation in customers' houses for free. They could get no uptake at all![4] Some reasons for this are a lack of trust in energy companies (why would they help to reduce consumption?), inertia, a lack of knowledge on energy conservation and worries about the cost.[5]

It is not as though the UK does not have a problem with leaky old buildings; our housing stock is generally poorly insulated compared to other parts of northern Europe (particularly Scandinavia where many buildings are so well insulated they require minimal or no heating systems). Old houses can be improved by insulation measures; we outline these in Chapter 11. New homes are built to higher efficiency standards, but the UK still lags behind some of our European neighbours.[6] Energy conservation reduces our carbon emissions and lessens our dependence on fossil fuels as a nation and also as individual households – and it saves us money. In 2006 those households in the UK defined as fuel poor (households which spend more than 10 per cent of their income on gas and electricity) was numbered at 3.5 million. The latest figures (based on data from 2008/09) suggest a total UK level of roughly 5.2 million households in fuel poverty, showing a substantial increase over 3 years as energy costs have risen.[7]

One final but important point should be made about energy efficiency, which is the law of unintended consequences, otherwise known as the 'Jevon's paradox' or the ''Khazzoom-Brookes postulate' after the economists who produced this theory. Essentially it means an increase in energy *efficiency* does not necessarily lead to a decrease in energy *use*. A good example of this is cars. Recently there have been car scrappage schemes throughout Europe, encouraging people to trade in their old car for a more efficient model. In the US, President Obama has ordered vehicle fuel-efficiency standards to be raised. The paradox is that people who buy a more fuel-efficient car, thus saving money, sometimes then use it more, thereby wiping out any efficiency gains made. This is not to argue against raising energy efficiency, but simply to warn that without lifestyle change it is not enough.

Renewables

So what are the alternatives to conventional energy sources? As you will read below, renewables are a very diverse group of technologies. Due to controversy over the best known renewable, large-scale wind power, their characteristics tend to be unfairly lumped together. There is an excellent website that gives a fair and detailed background on all forms of energy including renewables, and the reader with internet access is encouraged to visit it.[8]

Renewable electricity

Solar photovoltaics

Photovoltaic (PV) is where energy from sunlight is converted directly into usable electricity. The photovoltaic effect has been known for over a century but the first proper silicon-based solar cell was made by Bell laboratories in 1954. Bell discovered that by treating two pieces of silicon with different elements, joining them together and exposing one side to the light, current could be made to flow in an external circuit. The first manufactured cells were astronomically expensive and were used in the space programme and for off-grid applications, but with manufacturing scale and development the cost has come down substantially. Solar PV panels are now a common sight on the roofs of houses. Usually several panels are linked together and the current is passed through an inverter to produce normal alternating current for use in the building, with any excess exported into the national grid. Until 2009 there were grants available to encourage the installation of PV panels, but in 2010 the government replaced these with a system of feed-in tariffs (FITs) which pay producers a premium for generating electricity from renewable sources, as well as a small payment for each unit exported to the grid. As in other countries where feed-in tariffs have been used, it has massively increased the installation of PV panels and also cut their cost – so much so that since 2011 several cuts in the FIT rates have been made. Recently production of panels has been increasing very fast at almost 50 per cent a year. Installed on-grid capacity worldwide is approximately 70GW (2011).[9]

The biggest advantage of PV is its low land usage. Panels can be installed anywhere, but ideally are retrofitted to the roofs of buildings where the technology does not compete with other land uses such as growing food. Installation is usually easy and quick. The disadvantages are that there is no power produced at night and little produced during the winter months when electricity demand in the UK and other high- and low-latitude countries is highest. Preferably PV needs an un-shaded roof which faces as near to south as possible. It is interesting to note that many traditional churches meet these criteria. Planning permission on historic buildings can be an issue, but there are instances where it has been obtained.

Criticism of PV technology falls into three areas: utility (they don't work or only produce small amounts of energy), energy payback (they don't ever repay the energy used to make them) and cost (they are nice to have, but currently economically non-viable). On utility, the solar resource of the UK has been calculated at approximately 460 terrawatt hours each year – more than our current total electricity demand.[10] Use of energy in homes amounts to about 30 per cent of the UK's total energy demand – and this is where most solar panels have so far been fitted. (Neil's home PV system produces about one-third of the electricity his family use, hardly negligible. Another couple of kilowatts of installed capacity would make his house a net exporter to the grid.) Another 40 per cent of energy is used in offices and factories, where PV could also be used to produce some of the electricity required. A report produced by the Energy Saving Trust for the UK Government Department of Trade and Industry (DTI) stated that micro-generation could contribute 40 per cent of electricity demand by 2050, which would mainly be PV. The latest official government line in the UK is an expectation of 22GW of installed capacity by 2020.[11] At the beginning of 2012 solar PV is being taken very seriously as an energy source, with a forecast for 1.6GW to be installed every year in the UK from now on until 2016, then increasing.[12]

The economics of PV is somewhat clouded by the various financial incentives that have been used to promote installation. It is probably fair to say that few of those who have had panels installed recently would have done so without the feed-in tariffs. The cost of installing PV panels is high; however, once the extended life of the panel is factored in, it doesn't look like expensive electricity. In addition, the cost of the systems is falling very fast. Since the start of the feed-in-tariff scheme in the UK the cost of systems has fallen 30–40 per cent in its first year.[13] This is being replicated in other countries. In a diverse range of countries from Brazil to Denmark, solar PV is at or close to grid parity (the cost of conventional energy). The suggestion in the UK is that PV will be cheaper than onshore wind generation next year and at grid parity within four years. A report from the consultancy McKinseys out in April 2012 says solar PV will be cost competitive with coal and nuclear by 2020.[14]

The final criticism is that of energy payback. A study by Bath University, which calculates a net energy gain ratio of 6:1 in the UK, also calculates that a typical system would take less than 4 years to repay the energy to make it. These figures assume a 25-year life for the system as is the usual guarantee, although many systems are expected to work well for 40 years, improving the EROEI further. New types of solar panels are in development which use a thin film instead of individual cells joined together in modules. In experiments these have achieved a far higher energy payback ratio (7–40:1), although these PV types have other disadvantages at the moment.[15]

Andy had a 2.15kW PV system fitted to his house in early 2011 which has so far reduced his electricity bill by 40 per cent. The initial cost of the system was £8,000, but the savings in electricity use together with the feed-in tariff and export payments totalled up to over £1,400 in the first year alone. He found that the best savings are made by, where possible, tailoring household use of electricity to when the panels are producing – so electricity use that is time-flexible, such as the washing machine or dishwasher, is switched on once the sun is on the panels in the morning, hence using home-produced electricity rather than imported. Neil tries to do the same by using his bread-maker during peak sun hours. There are now systems available that will automatically switch on appliances when your panels are producing electricity.

Conclusion

Solar PV cannot supply all our energy needs, being limited to daylight hours and having output varying with the sun's strength. However, it can significantly reduce our consumption of fossil fuels by helping households to import less electricity. Many houses and other buildings with southerly facing roofs could be fitted with panels which produce electricity right at the place (home, office etc.) where it is needed. This technology is going to be ubiquitous.

Microwind

These are small wind turbines fitted to a building, or mounted on a tower. Defined by the British wind energy association as less than 50kWp output, the UK is the largest manufacturer. Microwind turbines are best fitted in country areas, since they work best with a lack of turbulence and obstacles around them. In cities, buildings produce turbulence and reduce the power of the wind, which lessens the power a small turbine can produce. Neil measured the urban wind resource on his house in Edinburgh using an anemometer that automatically recorded the data. The results were disappointing, meaning that he will not be fitting a turbine on his roof. By contrast, almost any open country area in the UK is potentially suitable. The British Wind Energy Association website has a UK Wind Speed Database which can give you the potential wind resource in your area from a six-figure OS map reference. This does not take into account local obstacles such as trees or buildings. Wind systems have the advantage of producing most output in the winter months when more electricity is required. Installed capacity in the UK was 7.4MWp in 2008 and by 2011 had risen to just under 50MWp. The EROEI depends partly on the size of the turbine, according to Professor Cleveland, small turbines of 5kW having a net energy gain of about 3:1.[16] The Bath University study mentioned above gave a very much higher figure. Even without comparing it to its displacement of conventional 'dirty' energy systems, the Bath study showed that for a 600W turbine, it only took 18 months to repay the energy used in construction.

Conclusion

In the UK, the government's 2050 analysis report stated that microwind could provide 8.6TWh per year of electricity.[17] To put this in context, this would be around 2.5 per cent of the total UK electricity production of about 350TWh per year. So this technology could make a small but important contribution. The UK is a windy country so other countries may find the contribution this technology could make is more limited.

Hydroelectricity (large, small and pico)

Go to almost any town or village in the UK with a river or sizeable stream flowing through it, and you will find a road called 'Mill Lane'. While most of the water mills are gone, the ubiquitous legacy of road names gives an indication of how much we harvested energy from water in the past. Nowadays the water could be used to generate electricity rather than for grinding grain. The potential for any site depends on several factors – the volume and speed of water flow, and the topography of the site. If you are lucky enough to have a river flowing through your property, you may be able to generate some electricity from it by installing a pico or micro-hydro system. Otherwise, there is potential for communities or commercial inter-ests to develop medium- or large-scale schemes.

The UK already has some large hydro schemes; most are in Scotland with some in Wales and a few in England. Some of these are for simple energy generation; others are pumped storage schemes where off-peak electricity is used to pump water up to reservoirs, effectively 'storing' the electricity. At times of peak demand the flow is reversed and the water flowing back down can have the generating equipment working at full capacity within seconds.

The large hydro schemes in Scotland were built after the war for social reasons, to create employment and in their time were as controversial as wind farms are today.

Even in the Scottish highlands, with its excellent hydro poten-tial, water has to be harvested in many schemes through a network of tunnels from small lochs to give sufficient power. Due to contro-versy over flooding of valleys it is hard to see many more large schemes being built. However, a 100MWp hydro generation project has recently opened at Glendoe, Loch Ness, built by Scottish and Southern Energy.

Clearly there are many places across the country where water power could be exploited to produce electricity; however, it is difficult to obtain reliable estimates for the size of this resource. The

Scottish government commissioned a report published in 2008 on Scotland's hydro potential.[18] There the potential capacity in Scotland was given as 657MWp. The report also suggested an additional potential of 2593MWp from power schemes that have not been financially viable previously. The new feed-in electricity tariff will now make many of these schemes viable, since the power output limit for a single technology or any mix of technologies is 5MWp. Indeed an updated report in 2010 has raised the potential to double the 657MWp referred to above, due to the feed-in tariff.[19] An Environment Agency report on the hydro potential in England and Wales gives a theoretical capacity of about 1200MWp.[20] This report may underestimate the resource somewhat since it seems to mainly refer to where there are weirs and existing manmade structures. In the US, it seems some large schemes may be built as part of the Obama administration's economic stimulus package.

A common problem preventing small-scale hydro schemes is that the watercourses are often not near connections to the grid (i.e. buildings). One possible way round this is for local energy co-operatives to form and work together to connect up micro-generation to the grid. This has been done in Wales in the Brecon Beacons by a social enterprise company, 'The Green Valleys'. They offer a complete package of feasibility study, through installation to maintenance. Payback can be very fast; one of the farmers involved in a Welsh scheme estimated that the cost of his 12kW system was repaid within two years, with just under 14p a unit paid for his power.

Harnessing water power often involves blocking a watercourse so that the water can pass through a water wheel or turbine. This can cause problems for wildlife, particularly birds and migrating fish. There are ways of operating schemes to mitigate or avoid these issues; the Scotland hydro-potential report describes how, with examples of good practice. The EROEI given in the 2006 paper by Cleveland seems a bit low being in the range of 6–17:1; in the 2008 study it is given as 20–40:1, which, given the longevity of hydro-power kit and dams, seems more realistic. Another reference gives it a ratio of greater than 100:1. Unlike wind there is no information on the relative energy payback in relation to the size in output.

Conclusion

Hydropower can make a small but important contribution to our future energy needs since it can provide relatively predictable, steady base-load electricity production. For the lucky households or communities with good sites for small-scale schemes, hydro could provide most or all of their electricity.[21] In addition, pumped storage schemes allow power companies to 'store' electricity, and so contribute to the overall functioning and efficiency of the national power network. The government's 2050 analysis report suggests if all UK water resources were used we could triple hydro power production to nearly 14TWh of electricity per year (around 4 per cent of our total electricity needs).

Large-scale wind

This is the best known of renewable technologies, the cheapest, biggest installed capacity and the most controversial. There is now almost 239GWp installed capacity worldwide.[22] The UK, surrounded as we are by the sea, has vast wind resources both on and offshore. However, large-scale wind power has attracted large-scale criticism. Similarly to PV, critics argue that it simply doesn't work, and there are also concerns about noise, shadow flicker, interference with television reception and air traffic control radar. Above all is the concern about visual intrusion, particularly since the parts of our country with the best potential, such as upland areas and coasts, are highly cherished landscapes.

In a similar manner to PV, the 'does it work?' arguments hinge on four issues: capacity factor, load factor, network integration and energy payback. Criticisms sometimes betray a lack of knowledge of the way the grid functions and even basic engineering principles. One journalist in a national newspaper even wrote that wind turbines don't work because the blades were turning slowly, obviously not having the vaguest understanding of the concept of gears! However, within the context of peak oil these issues do require examination.

Load factor is how much conventional plant is displaced by the wind power. Capacity factor is the ratio of actual power output to the theoretical maximum power output over the same time period.[23] Network integration or balancing is the issue of how the grid can cope with power coming in (often at short notice) from different locations and at different output capacities.

Taking the load factor issue first, the argument put by wind power critics is that wind power is adding to carbon emissions since conventional plant has to be kept running just in case the wind stops blowing. Currently backup capacity (known as spinning reserve) is provided largely by gas-powered power stations with some pumped-storage hydro, the former run but don't send power to the grid.[24] The wind critics ignore the fact that backup capacity is required for all forms of generation since some power stations will always fail at short notice. Very occasionally this leads to large-scale power cuts. The sustainable development commission estimates if wind supplied 20 per cent of total generating capacity the spinning reserve required is 4–8 per cent of the wind capacity. This is however outweighed by the additional conventional plant retired. In fact, examination of the national electricity trading homepage shows how surprisingly pre-dictable wind power is.[25]

The capacity factor is the weakest argument put forward by critics of wind power. Wind power has been growing steadily over the last thirty years and very rapidly over the last four years. Globally, over this time hundreds of billions of pounds have been invested in it by both large businesses and community groups. If the technology doesn't work, why do these groups continue to invest in it? Espe-cially since no subsidy worldwide is not linked to power output, so no generation, no money. The Environmental Change Institute, having studied the weather records over the last forty years, found just one hour over that period where there was insufficient wind to turn a turbine. Critics of wind power also state that the turbines never pay back their energy used to make them, but in fact most do so within months of becoming operational.[26]

Integrating wind into the grid is not regarded as an insurmount-able obstacle.[27] A study by Edinburgh University for the Scottish executive examined various scenarios using a mix of renewable generating technologies with a very high proportion of wind power.[28] The aim was to model the 2020 Scottish 40 per cent renewables target and to see what the generating shortfall would be. With up to 6GWp installed capacity (mainly onshore wind) the shortfall was just over 10 per cent. This led the authors of the report to conclude the 40 per cent target was achievable and indeed it has since been raised to 50 per cent.

The SDC report suggests noise levels are about the same as in a quiet bedroom. Logic suggests that if the wind is blowing you hear the wind, unless you are very close to the turbine. Neil's own experience having been right beneath several working turbines is that all he could hear was a gentle 'swoosh' with nothing further away. In fact, Neil was cycling around the fields in a summer fog in France searching for them. They were turning, but he could not locate them by sound. When he eventually did find one, standing beneath it with the rotating blades looming out of the fog was a very eerie experience.

However, people living near to some turbines report consider-able problems with constant pulsing noise, sleep disturbance etc. when the wind is from a certain direction or the turbine is turning at a particular speed. These complaints have been enough to make many communities antagonistic to new wind farms planned near them. The UK government is now considering introducing a minimum distance between homes and any new wind turbines. Another option is simply to site turbines offshore, well away from homes, and where the wind resource tends to be better anyway. In fact this seems to be the way government policy is going, with plans for huge numbers of turbines to be installed in the North Sea and other areas. The problem with offshore wind is that the installation and maintenance costs are much more expensive than for turbines built on land – possibly 50 per cent higher. Turbine foundations have to be seated on the sea bed, and any repairs or other access is by boat and is weather dependent.

The final question is, how much of our power could wind provide? The Zero Carbon Britain report mentioned earlier envis-ages wind producing 50 per cent of the UK's electricity by 2027, albeit combined with an overall 50 per cent cut in electricity demand. The UK renewable energy strategy consultation (2008) set a potential target of 13GW on land and 33GW offshore, although it admits this may not be achieved by 2020. A recent valuation of offshore wind power reported the potential for much higher gener-ating capacity.[29] The net energy gain from wind power is very good compared to other renewable technologies. The figure shown in Table 2 also hides an improving trend with recent larger turbines, one new turbine giving a ratio of 132:1. This good ratio is influenced by the 'cube' law which states that wind turbine power output rises as a cube of increased wind speed, thus large wind turbines in a good location give a very high return on the energy used to make them.

Conclusion

Wind power is the largest renewable contributor after hydropower, although PV is rapidly catching up. There is no doubt that large-scale wind will become a huge source of renewable electricity in the medium term. Offshore wind farms may have better wind resources but are more expensive to build and run. Onshore wind faces opposition around noise and visual issues. However, we are likely to see many more turbines being built in suitable sites (away from homes and where landscape concerns are not a big factor).

Wave and tidal power

Wave and tidal power are two forms of energy completely dissimilar in their characteristics, but are covered here together since they both involve the sea. In the long term they may displace wind as the largest renewable player in countries like the UK. There are many small developments planned and taking place worldwide in both technologies. The potential resource is huge. Estimates of the potential of wave power worldwide are in the same order as current global electricity demand. Tidal streams are thought to be lower in resource size, but estimates put the potential contributions to UK electricity output at anywhere between 3 and 34 per cent of our needs.

Wave power involves a device bobbing about on the sea's surface or built into the shoreline. The best known (and one of the few devices in use), the British Pelamis device, uses wave energy to compress air, the release of which drives a turbine.

Tidal power can be harnessed in two ways. Tidal ranges (the difference between high and low tide) can be exploited by capturing the high tide behind a barrage, and then releasing the water through turbines – an example of this at La Rance in Brittany has been operational since 1966. A more recent development is the tidal stream generator, an underwater device similar to a wind turbine, which captures energy from tidal flows. Since water is denser than air the turbine blades turn more slowly, but capture more power.[30] While energy from waves, like the wind, is likely to be variable, as any sailor will tell you tides are entirely predictable in advance, meaning that if energy is harvested from tidal flows the output is also predictable, so with sufficient geographical spread, tidal energy could supply some base-load electricity. The world's first commercial tidal stream generator was installed at the entrance to Strangford Lough, Northern Ireland, in 2008, and has been generating electricity for 18–20 hours each day ever since. There has been some debate in the UK about the potential for building a tidal barrage across the River Severn estuary, to harness energy from what is the world's second highest tidal range (14m). Such a development would be extremely costly and provide a complex engineering challenge, but could potentially supply 5 per cent of the whole country's electricity. A number of feasibility studies have been carried out over the years, but so far there are no definite plans and the coalition government has shelved the idea. With the development of tidal stream generators, there is the possibility of harnessing the tides flowing in and out of the Bristol Channel by installing a large number of these devices rather than building a fixed barrage – a solution likely to be more acceptable to environmentalists concerned about the loss of habitats that a barrage would cause.

The main problems with both wave and tidal energy are the lack of grid connections and the costs of engineering the devices to withstand corrosive saltwater and winter storms, but they have an advantage that they don't occupy land humans use. These technologies are too new to have much efficiency data; there is a suggestion that the Pelamis wave device has a net energy gain of 15:1 over its lifetime, and a recent report puts wave power at 12:1.[31] The same report gives a net energy gain for tidal range at 116:1 and tidal stream at 17:1. Since wave-power production closely matches wind but the energy density of waves and currents is higher, we would expect the EROEI to be higher than wind, although the devices are more complicated to manufacture. Also critical to the energy return will be the reliability of these systems.

Conclusion

Wave power has huge potential but so far the technology is immature. Tidal energy has potential for supplying predictable energy but requires government support for the large-scale engineering required. In the current economic climate this looks unlikely. Neither of these technologies looks like supplying a significant proportion of our energy in the near future, though they will become more important in the longer term.

Niche players

There are number of renewable and non-renewable technologies that might make a minor contribution to the problem, but are definitely not the solution. One of these is landfill and coal gas. Both are non-renewable. Landfill gas is derived by anaerobic digestion from waste. Since methane is a potent greenhouse gas it has been recognised for some years that waste landfills should be capped and the gas captured. Usually this is burnt for electricity generation. Most sites have probably been exploited in the UK and it is non-renewable, in that the bacteria will exhaust their carbon source and die off. Mine (or coal) gas was mentioned in Chapter 3.

Energy from waste includes the production of biogas, but also some other technologies. The first and most controversial is incineration. This is simply burning the waste and then using the heat to generate electricity. In most cases it makes more ecological sense to recycle the waste, although sludge from anaerobic digestion could be burnt. Burning other waste materials is highly controversial due to the perceived release of polychlorinated biphenyls (PCBs) and dioxins into the locality around plants. Although incineration technology has reputedly improved so that these chemicals are not released into the air, there still remains the problem of toxic ash which requires disposal. The probability is that a lack of public acceptance makes this a tiny niche player.

Another energy technology is that of microbial fuel cells. Some bacteria can respire using metals, reducing them chemically in the process. Bacteria that can reduce metals such as iron also have the potential to directly transfer electrons from an organic carbon source to the anode (conductor) in a fuel cell. There are indirect methods of transfer but they are less efficient. The electrons can flow through an external circuit doing useful work and combine at the cathode with oxygen and protons from the anode side to form water. Carbon dioxide is produced at the anode side. This is how a conventional fuel cell works, only the 'fuel' and catalyst are different. The two sides can be separated in different compartments or exist within the same compartment. What makes these devices the focus of quite a lot of research worldwide is the uniquely high energy conversion efficiencies, greater than 80 per cent. The probable niche that this technology occupies is that of waste disposal (they do not produce heat). Until recently, microbial fuel cells have existed only in the laboratory or in pilot scale in sediments, but one at a pilot scale has been constructed at a Fosters brewery in Queensland, Australia.[32] There is another enormous resource, which is that of sediment at the bottom of the sea or lakes, the oceans being one of the planet's major carbon sinks. This is, in our opinion, a problem. In harvesting the various organic molecules, carbon dioxide would be released. EROEI unknown, but the use of these technologies is likely to be very limited.

Conclusion

These experimental technologies may have some limited role but they are not our salvation! As we have seen in this chapter, there is a lot of scope for renewable energy generation. Each technology has both merits and problems. What would be most effective is a combination of different energy sources working together and complementing each other: tidal and hydro energy to supply pre-dictable base-load power, solar PV maximising capture of the sun's energy during daylight hours, and wind power playing a significant role. The UK is blessed with abundant wind resources as well as huge potential for wave and tidal energy. But even taking all this into account, the biggest impact we could make in this area is by drastically reducing our demand for electricity.

Notes

1   http://www.theoildrum.com/story/2006/10/17/18478/085;
     www.theoildrum.com/node/3810; S. R. Allen et al., 'Integrated Appraisal

of Micro-Generators: Methods and Applications', Proceedings of the Institute of Civil Engineers, Energy 161, EN2 (2010), pp. 73–86; Offshore evaluation report, A report produced by DECC, UK devolved governments, Scottish and Southern etc.; N. Gagnon et al., 'A Preliminary Investigation of Energy Return on Energy Investment for Global Oil and Gas Production', Energies 2 (2009), pp. 490–503; C. A. S. Hall et al., 'What is the Minimum EROI that a Sustainable Society Must Have?', Energies 2 (2009), pp. 25–47.

2   Gagnon et al., 'A Preliminary Investigation'.

3   Offshore evaluation report.

4   Judging by this report, despite energy price increases nothing much has changed:
    http://www.consumerfocus.org.uk/files/2011/03/Green-deal-or-no-deal.pdf.

5   Ibid.

6   The reasons for this are probably lobbying by the building industry and the fact it is less cold than these countries.

7   Ibid. 7.

8   http://www.window.state.tx.us/specialrpt/energy/renewable/index.php.

9   http://files.epia.org/files/Global-Market-Outlook-2016.pdf.

10 http://www.guardian.co.uk/environment/2009/may/14/feed-in-tariff-solar-power and pathways-analysis-report.pdf.

11 Bloomberg New Energy Finance White Paper UK power forecasts, February 2012.

12 Ibid 11.

13 Source DECC FIT review, since the FIT reduction prices of less than £2/watt installed can be found in 2012. This should be compared with £6/watt in 2004 and about £4/watt at the start of 2011.

14 http://www.businessgreen.com/bg/news/2168375/mckinsey-solar-cost-competitive-decade.

15 http://energycrisis.com/aspo-usa/2005/.

16 http://www.theoildrum.com/story/2006/10/17/18478/085.

17 http://www.decc.gov.uk/assets/decc/What%20we%20do/A%20low%20carbon%20UK/2050/216–2050-pathways-analysis-report.pdf.

18 http://www.scotland.gov.uk/News/Releases/2008/09/02084203.

19 'The Employment Potential of Scotland's Hydro Resource', Nick Forrest Associates, www.scotland.gov.uk/Resource/Doc/299322/0093327.pdf.

20 'Opportunity and Environmental Sensitivity Mapping for Hydropower in England and Wales', March 2010, www.environment-agency.gov.uk/shell/hydropowerswf.html.

21 The feed-in-tariff in the UK assumes 75 per cent export to the grid from hydro systems.

22 BP Statistical Review of World Energy, 2012.

23 SDC, 'Wind power in the UK', 2005. The capacity factor depends on the engineering of an individual turbine model. This makes comparisons difficult.

24 'The Costs and Impacts of Intermittency: An assessment of the evidence on the costs and impacts of intermittent generation on the British electricity network', UKERC report 2006.

25 http://www.bmreports.com/bsp/bsp_home.htm.

26 http://www.theoildrum.com/story/2006/10/17/18478/085.

27 http://www.bmreports.com/bsp/bsp_home.htm.

28 'Academic Study: Matching Renewable Electricity Generation with Demand', Edinburgh University report for the Scottish Executive, 2006.

29 Offshore evaluation report.

30 'Future Marine Energy', Carbon Trust, 2006.

31 http://www.theoildrum.com/node/3949 and Offshore evaluation report, 2010.

32 See http://www.microbialfuelcell.org.

5

What about alternative energy?

Part 2: Renewable heat and transport

Because we are now running out of gas and oil, we must prepare quickly for a third change, to strict conservation and to the use of coal and permanent renewable energy sources, like solar power.

US President Jimmy Carter, speaking in 1977

One of the biggest problems we face is the decline in natural gas. This was essentially a waste product of oil extraction and we have become very highly dependent on it, with most of us now accustomed to living in homes warmed by gas central heating. In this chapter we will examine technologies that have some potential to substitute for gas. We also look at alternatives to oil as transport fuel.

Solar hot water (SHW)

In some ways this is a very basic technology. Water is passed through narrow pipes in a box exposed to the sun, and is heated by the infrared end of the electromagnetic spectrum. It has been known for centuries that something encased in glass heats to increased temperatures in the sun and that dark material gets hotter than light material. In 1891 one Clarence Kemp, based in California, patented a basic solar water heating device and gave it the unfortunate name of 'The Climax'.[1] In 1909 William J. Bailey went one better and patented a recognisably modern solar water heater.[2] This consisted of a flat plate with narrow pipes and a separate storage tank. He also gave it a rather strange name, 'the day and night'. What happened next is one of the object lessons in how big businesses can damage the environment. His invention sold in its thousands in California until natural gas was found which decimated its sales there. Then it sold well in Florida until after the war when the power company in Florida destroyed it by offering cheap electricity. After this, the solar hot water scene went quiet until the 1973 oil shock. Then collectors started to sell all over the world; they were made mandatory in Israel and there were 3 million installed in Japan by 1981. In the UK sales took off but there was a reputation (which persists to this day) of cowboy installers making implausible payback claims. These and falling energy prices meant the idea disappeared until the late 1990s – there are now at least 90,000 solar hot water installations in the UK.

There are number of different variants of solar hot water technology including flat plate with antifreeze and without antifreeze, also a type with vacuum tubes. In this latter type antifreeze solution is passed through tubes with a vacuum surrounding them like a Thermos flask. This keeps in the captured heat and allows them to warm water in cloudy weather and even in winter by means of diffuse light. The disadvantages of vacuum tubes are higher cost, and the vacuum is gradually lost over time. Most solar hot water systems use sophisticated controllers which measure the temperature difference between the hot water tank and the collector and switch a pump on when the difference between the two is a certain pre-set value. The pump requires electricity, but there are now some totally solar powered models on the market. The panels generally take up 3–5m^2 of roof space on an average house, although they don't have to be on a roof, just catch the maximum amount of sunlight. They work best facing as near south as possible. Solar hot water does work in our climate; friends of Neil's achieve temperatures in the order of 70°C in April in the north of Scotland with their flat plate antifreeze systems. Neil has a less effective system but has still heated water to over 40°C in early March in some years and 60°C in May 2009. Andy's evacuated tube system heats most of the hot water his household needs through the summer months, and still does well on sunny days at other times of year.

There are a number of problems with solar hot water. First, if you are already connected to mains gas and so getting relatively cheap heating, it is only just becoming economic to install SHW. Second, you have to work at saving money, that is, use your heating controller/timer to switch the boiler off when the sun is due to shine otherwise you will see no savings (of course this can go wrong if the weather changes). Third, antifreeze systems are complicated, requiring special hot water tanks with heat exchangers in, adding to the cost. Fourth, not all systems are compatible with combi-boilers or pressurised heating systems, though many are. Lastly, sometimes you have more hot water than you can use. With a PV system you can automatically send excess electricity to the grid and now get paid for it, not so with hot water. There are grants which can help with the cost of installation, but in 2013 these will be replaced by a renewable heat incentive – a payment made to the household for each unit of heat produced from solar panels and other renewable heat technologies. Seventy-five per cent of homes in the UK could benefit from having SHW fitted; most house roofs have space for these and some PV too.[3] Flats are more of a problem due to the shared ownership of the roof, but Changeworks in Edinburgh has been involved in pilot projects on retrofitting solar hot water to tenement roofs.

Unfortunately the published net energy gain figures are low for this technology. No details are given on the methodology, but we can think of two factors that may affect the outcome negatively. The first is that most systems use mains electricity to work a pump, which lowers the efficiency; a comparison by the UK government of eight different systems put this difference at about 20 per cent of the systems efficiency compared with a totally solar-powered system. Secondly, any study should take into account the gas displaced by the system, not merely the energy produced. The Bath University study quoted in the previous chapter used this method for assessing a solar-powered system and calculated an EROEI of 17:1. Logically we would expect solar hot water systems to have a better EROEI than photovoltaics since they are more efficient in capturing the sun's energy and take less energy to produce in the first place.

Conclusion

Solar hot water systems are a tried and tested technology that continues to improve. Used carefully they can reduce a household's energy consumption and therefore reduce dependence on fossil fuels. If installed more widely, they would reduce the UK's dependence on imported gas. There is some competition for roof space with photovoltaics, although most suitable roofs could take both.

Air solar heating

There is a variant on solar hot water panels, which are panels that heat air – which is then fed into a living area to provide space heating. Fife council have fitted these to some council housing. Difficult to score since we have not heard about their effectiveness, they would certainly require a very well-insulated building for space heating. There are some systems in use in Japan of this type.[4] As regards the net energy gain, there are no published figures available, but it is probably about the same as SHW.

Biomass heating

Biomass heating includes wood-burning stoves and boilers. Wood stoves have been selling so rapidly that there is reported to be a waiting list for some models, as well as a shortage of seasoned hardwood in some parts of the country. This interest in wood for heating has been stoked mainly by the increased cost of gas and oil. Also, a wood-burner is perhaps the only piece of renewable energy kit you would buy because it looks great and is romantic. Of the three renewable technologies Neil has fitted to his house, this is the best by far in terms of economic payback. Most wood-burners on the market have the facility to heat water; this may require the fitting of a pump if the burner is not near enough to the water tank to transfer heat by convection. There are a whole range of wood-burning devices, from the very basic stove which requires lots of manual attention, regular feeding with logs, stoking, clearing out of ash etc. and just heats the room it is in. At the other end of the scale are fully automated boilers burning wood pellets, which will run your central heating and heat water at the touch of a button. These models are more functional in appearance, but they have the benefit of not requiring you to pop downstairs at four in the morning with matches and newspaper to get them going. Any wood-burning device is far more efficient than burning wood on an open fire, where a significant proportion of the heat is lost up the chimney.

Still, there are a variety of minor problems with this technology. The room where the wood-burner is sited is slightly dustier, as inevitably some ash escapes the stove when the door is opened. Not all stoves have self-cleaning glass. In built-up areas you need a stove or boiler that is exempted from the Clean Air Act (in the UK). You also need a dry area to store wood or pellets, quite a considerable area if you're using wood as a source of central heating. Biomass boilers can be fitted with hoppers for automatic feeding. However, these are very expensive and require space on the outside of the building on the other side of the wall from the boiler. Power outputs of 6kWp and above for both technologies require an external air supply to the room where it is sited. Lastly, obviously a stove needs feeding with wood now and again; this keeps you fit and warm running in and out of the house, as does collecting it and chopping it up!

The main problem is that of wood supply. There simply isn't enough wood produced indigenously to allow every British household to provide their space heating in this way. The UK government reckons there may be the available land to provide 6 per cent (100TWh) of the UK's total energy demand.[5] From a peak oil context this has to be questionable since it involves using a total of 17 per cent of UK arable land to grow energy crops, land that may be required to grow food (see later). The total also involves an additional 2 million tonnes of wood coming on to the market by 2020 (enough to heat 250,000 homes) from better management of England's woodlands – this is more plausible.[6] Another interesting fact is that around 7–10 million tonnes of wood is sent to landfill every year.[7] The wood sent to landfill falls into two types: some has been chemically treated, or is covered in paint and varnish and so should not be burnt. However, much untreated wood, joinery off-cuts or mistakes, are also thrown away – and this could be burnt. (Neil's experience of scavenging skips suggests the great majority is the latter). However, even assuming the entire 6 million tonnes is combustible, this is only sufficient for another 1.5 million homes.[8]

There are a couple of potential additional sources of wood supply. The first is of waste wood from tree surgery. This tends to be shredded on the spot and composted by local authorities. The second is the upland moorland areas of Britain which are mainly used for shooting.[9] These used to be almost all forested two thousand years ago. While not all areas should be turned over to trees since moorland is an ecosystem in its own right, many areas could be. The potential from both these sources of wood is unknown, although it is unlikely to make this the majority option for space heating in the UK. There is also competition from large-scale biomass power (see below). We see biomass heating as a supplemental form of space heating. In terms of the net energy gain from biomass, Professor Cleveland's second study gives firewood an EROEI of about 25–35:1, which isn't bad; the EROEI rises the more the device is used, and wood-burners have a very long lifetime. Wood-burning boilers will be eligible for the forthcoming renewable heat incentive in the UK.

Conclusion

Wood can provide energy for heating homes and water. In rural areas, where firewood can be obtained at a reasonable price, it is already widely used, and is coming into greater use in other areas as heating from other sources has risen steeply in cost. Better management of woodland, planting more trees and diverting useful wood from landfill will all boost firewood supplies, so that more homes could use wood for heating; however the numbers will always be limited.

Geothermal energy

This falls into two types. The first is naturally occurring hot water or hot rocks, into which water is pumped underground through one borehole, and the resulting steam collected through another borehole. (This is not strictly speaking renewable energy since the water gradually removes the heat from the hot strata.) In UK terms this is a minor energy source, although there is a district heating scheme in the centre of Southampton using this technology. The main UK resource, which has been under consideration for many years, is in Cornwall, though only a few test boreholes have ever been tried. This seems to be about to change with the Eden Project being involved in a geothermal project. More recently the UK government's 2050 pathway analysis suggests a reasonable resource under Northumbria and some parts of Scotland. There is a larger resource in other countries. Iceland gets much of its energy this way, the US has some large geothermal electricity generating plants and there may be expansion in countries with good natural resources such as Italy, Indonesia and parts of Africa. However, in general energy terms this will be a fairly minor player.

The second type of geothermal energy is heat pumps, which in fact are a completely different technology. They work on the same principle as your fridge or freezer. You extract heat from the inside of the fridge and that heat emerges from the grill at the back. With heat pumps the process works in reverse – you get heat for your house by extracting heat from the ground or air around the building in which the pump is installed. Ground-source heat pumps take heat energy from the ground near the surface, even though the average ground temperature is low, typically 8°C; strangely enough there is still heat energy to be extracted from it. Air-source heat pumps take their energy from the air around the building they are installed in. At first glance a heat pump appears to break the first law of thermodynamics, since you get three to four times as much heat out as the electricity you put into the pump.[10] In actual fact if you put in 2kW of electricity and 4kW of heat from the ground you get a total of 6kW of heat, meaning conventional scientific theory is intact! This heat transfer is accomplished by means of a very efficient heat exchanger. These systems are very common in Scandinavia and the technology works well up to a point. The Zero Carbon Britain report predicts very heavy use of them for domestic heating, as does the UK government in its renewable energy 2020 target.[11] The Scottish government has been installing them to heat houses off the mains gas grid, where insulation alone is not enough to bring bills down to reasonable levels.

There are a number of drawbacks with this technology. The first is that they use electricity, and so widespread adoption would therefore require more electricity generation – would this come from renewable sources? One way round the problem is to use on-site generation to displace imported power (wind power is obviously better placed than PV to match higher winter use). Another problem with heat pumps is that the claimed performance has often not been found in practice. The ratio of heat output to electricity input is known as the Coefficient of Performance (COP). Many advocates of such systems quote a COP value of 4:1, however, in practice, figures of 3:1 or even 2:1 are more common.[12] Another issue is that to run a reasonably sized heat-pump system requires a three-phase electricity supply – which is not usually fitted in a domestic setting. This is due to a momentary but very large power spike when the system and the pump start up. This happens with any pump (e.g. fridges), but heat-pump systems pose a particular chal-lenge due to the larger pump size. In addition widespread deploy-ment in an area might require grid reinforcement, since the grid must allow for the (admittedly) worst-case scenario when all the heat pumps in an area start at the same instant!

Another problem is that ground-source heat pumps are very disruptive to fit. They require either a long length of thin pipe (slinky) to be buried under a wide area of ground (probably an area bigger than an average UK garden to heat an average-sized house) or a borehole. The boreholes need to be quite deep and usually multiple boreholes are required. The disruption doesn't stop on the outside. These systems work best as low-temperature systems with special radiators or under-floor heating – which is difficult to retrofit in old buildings and therefore expensive. Air-source heat pumps don't have the disruption factor associated with ground-source heat pumps, but they are less effective. The problem is you are trying to extract heat from something (air) that is cooler than the ground and is at its coldest when you need the heat the most. They are similar to an air-conditioning type unit fitted to the outside of the building – and can be noisy.

The final issue is the high initial cost. This seems a problem at first glance, since these systems cost much more than a conventional boiler. However, since they have few moving parts and don't require annual maintenance, they are more cost effective over their lifetime. A typical ground-source heat pump is expected to last for fifty years; in that time you would have replaced a gas boiler three times (possibly four). This and the maintenance/parts savings means they would end up being cheaper. In addition, they will be eligible for the UK government renewable heat incentive.

Conclusion

For pure geothermal systems, a net energy gain of 2:1 up to 39:1 is reported.[13] As for heat pumps, *The Transition Handbook* reports an EROEI of 3:1.[14] While we have concerns about their efficacy this figure seems low due to their longevity. Bearing in mind their drawbacks we cannot see these systems making a huge contribution in a post-peak oil world, particularly because of their electricity consumption. Despite these drawbacks we have managed to find a church that is heated by a ground-source heat pump and this is covered as a case study in a later chapter. Geothermal energy using hot rocks is continuing to expand particularly in the US and some developing countries such as Kenya. Even in the UK it could make a useful contribution to base-load power.[15]

Heat storage

Most heat energy in the form of infrared radiation falls on buildings in summer, which is not when we need it most. There are a number of systems in Europe which capture heat in summer and store it for winter use, known as 'inter-seasonal heat transfer'.[16] Most of these systems are district heating systems, although a school in Hertford-shire is heated this way.[17] This could be done on a household scale using either a solar collector or a conservatory. A rough calculation suggests that to heat an average-sized house would require a $9m^2$ solar collector, heating a 750-litre water tank.[18] This is obviously a crude approximation, but does suggest it *might* be possible to heat a house or even a church. As with other renewable heating systems, this method would be a low-temperature system and therefore require very good building insulation. The system could be disrup-tive to fit, the obvious place to put a large well-insulated tank of water being underground. You could use materials other than water, such as some chemical salts or broken glass, but these have a lower heat-storage capacity. Most of the existing systems in Europe are district heating systems in the countryside, where there is room for a field of solar collectors. This is less applicable in city areas although individual buildings' solar collectors could be combined together in a network sharing heat. We have raised it as an idea due to the lack of ready renewable heat alternatives. Probably like many of the suggestions for renewable heat it will not be the sole means of heating the building. The net energy gain is likely to be better than solar thermal; the systems are relatively simple so would last many years, raising the EROEI.

Large-scale biomass (electricity production and district heating)

As discussed previously, wood or other biomass can be used for small-scale heating, to heat a church or a house. It can also be used on a larger scale either to produce electricity only as a conventional power plant, or both heat and electricity simultaneously (known as combined heat and power or CHP) in some form of neighbour-hood heating plan. CHP is much more efficient than making electricity alone, since nearly 100 per cent of the energy is captured for use either as heat or electricity. Conventional power plants using wood are becoming more common. There is a large one planned for Port Talbot in Wales (350MWp). In addition a number of smaller plants are working at Lockerbie and Eccleshall and a number of others are planned.[19]

In Sweden district systems supply heat to millions of buildings. In the UK there are a few small-scale CHP projects up and running, mostly to heat social housing.[20] The electricity is not directly used by the tenants but is sold to the grid. The advantages of biomass power plants are that as an electricity source they provide predict-able, base-load power. The problem is finding enough material to burn, as described above. The wood for the Lockerbie plant is 80 per cent sourced from a wood products factory next door (pellets are also made on site). The remainder comes from short rotation willow coppice.

The wood for the Port Talbot plant is due to come from Canada, and while the developers claim this is sustainable we feel it would not be. It also would seem better to use wood for local CHP schemes where the heat is used as well and transmission losses are minimised. The net energy gain is probably lower than for using wood directly for heating, due to electricity transmission losses in biomass power plants, but better for CHP where the heat produced is used locally.

Conclusion

Plants which use local biomass resources to provide both heat and power offer a step-up in efficiency compared to conventional power distribution and individual home heating, great for those lucky enough to benefit. Otherwise biomass can make a small contribution to (base-load) electricity generation. Concerns remain about the source of wood.

Biogas

Bacteria belonging to the *Archaea* class can produce methane gas through anaerobic digestion. They exist naturally in marshes, peat-bogs, lake and ocean sediments, and in the rumen and intestinal system of animals. Anaerobic digestion has been known about for over a millennium but the world's first anaerobic digester was built in India in 1859. Today, millions of people in Asia and East Africa use this process to provide methane for cooking, usually from animal dung. There are a number of different digester technologies but in practical terms a feedstock such as dung or food waste is placed in a sealed vessel, and through a series of bacterial processes, the material is broken down and methane is produced. A useful by-product of the process is the digestate which is used as fertiliser. This technology works well at a simple, household level in the developing world, but is also in widespread use on a larger scale in Europe, where farm and food waste is used to produce gas for electricity generation. In the UK some biogas is produced from sewage.

Until recently this would have been described as a potential niche source of base-load electricity and no more. However, the UK government's 'Meeting the EU 2020 Renewables Target' consultation suggested an interesting idea – taking biogas and injecting it into the gas grid and mixing it with natural gas. This has been tried on a small scale in Germany and other countries. The consultation document came up with some figures which, although useful in meeting the 2020 EU renewables target, were still small compared to demand. However, when the National Grid commissioned analysts Ernst and Young to investigate the potential biogas resource in the UK, they estimated that it could provide a staggering 50 per cent of the gas required for homes (about 25 per cent of total gas demand).[21] These predictions would require the use of huge quantities of various wastes: sewage, animal manures and other farm waste, domestic and food waste, as well as some woody biomass. Feeding biogas into the gas grid so that it can be used in individual homes is a more efficient use of the resource than burning it to produce electricity. Any country doing this could make its natural gas go further and reduce its need for imports. Unlike hydrogen (see below) none of the existing gas infrastructure would require replacement, though building the numbers of digesters required would require a huge investment. The sludge that is left can either be dried and burnt or used as fertiliser. The latest news is that the renewable heat incentive will provide a payment for every unit of biogas pumped into the grid, and the green energy company Ecotricity are planning soon to start producing biogas for this purpose.

There are some problems with biogas. First, not many people would want to live next door to a digester. With such a high proportion of biogas suggested, the number of digesters would have to be large and widely dispersed – and moving material to them would increase road traffic. In addition, some energy would be required to raise the pressure from that of a low-pressure digester to the high-pressure gas grid. The EROEI for biogas is quite low (see Table 2) and the transfer of gas on to the grid would lower this still further.[22] The net energy gain is highly dependent on the feedstock, with some materials giving more gas than others.

Conclusion

Given the huge potential identified, it is clear that biogas could make a substantial difference in providing future energy, using the existing gas distribution network. It would, however, require a huge amount of money to build the infrastructure required – about £30 billion according to the National Grid report.

Biofuels

One of the most controversial renewable technologies in recent years, biofuels, are mainly for use as transport fuels. Much has been made of their potential to substitute for conventional oil. However, there are a number of challenges – some ethical, others technical or logistical. To put the problem in perspective, Virgin Atlantic ran a much publicised biofuel test flight from London to Amsterdam, using a fuel processed from coconuts. While the biofuel was only 5 per cent of the fuel mix, it still required the equivalent of 150,000 coconuts for the one short flight! The term biofuel covers a range of different processes and products, and we look briefly at each of them below.

Bioethanol

This is made by the process of fermentation, using yeast and a source of glucose or other simple sugars. Sugar beet, sugar cane, wheat and maize are commonly used. Wheat has to be germinated so that enzymes can break down the starch into its glucose monomers. With maize this breakdown is done by using a combination of chemicals, enzymes and heat.[23] The end product of fermentation is one many of us are aware of and has been known for thousands of years! To make a usable fuel the alcohol is distilled and all water is removed. The ethanol can then be used at low concentration in normal internal combustion engines, or at high purity in adapted engines. Brazil has used bioethanol produced from sugar cane for many years. Pure ethanol is highly toxic (yes really!) and flammable. Since it is infinitely soluble in water it also reabsorbs some moisture almost instantly from the atmosphere, and this can lead to engine damage.

The main issues with this fuel are the land area required in competition with food crops, and the net energy gain. The land area problem is common to all biofuels and will be covered at the end of the section. The energy balance of ethanol production is also a critical issue. Does the process of producing the ethanol consume more energy than the fuel returns? This has been debated for many years and there are too many reports to cite here, reaching diametrically opposite conclusions. What is certainly true is that the comparison between the energy inputs and output is finely balanced, at best it is only marginally positive. As well as the energy used in growing the crop and transporting it to the processing plant, the production process requires heat for two parts of the process and this is the fundamental problem. The great hope of ethanol proponents is next-generation ethanol production (covered below), this may also make a minor contribution to the energy balance issue.

Next-generation biofuels

One of the problems with biofuels is that they are mostly derived from the edible parts of crops – thereby setting up a competition between their use for food or fuel. But what if you could use structural parts of the plants that humans tend not to eat – stems, straw or wood? These parts of the plants are made of polymers called cellulose and lignocelluloses. Unfortunately (but not surprisingly) these do not easily break down, and so production of fuel from them provides a complex challenge. However, lots of research and experimentation is being done in this area, and enzymes have been identified that will break down these compounds to glucose, but pre-treatment of a chemical or even physical nature is still required. Even then the enzymes are repressed by the products of their breakdown. The way round this is to combine breakdown and fermentation, so that the glucose is utilised as soon as it is produced. This requires modest amounts of heat, but less than required for production of bioethanol. Recently researchers have been looking at new sources of enzymes, such as bacteria found in termite guts and in reed beds.[24] By using these heat and other pre-treatments described above would not be required, so improving the energy balance. It appears that this has been achieved in trials, and the biotechnology company Zymetis claim a net energy gain of 8:1 for their process.[25] If this is true, this is very significantly better than conventional bioethanol.

Another potential liquid fuel is biobutanol, which is produced from *Clostridia* bacteria using fermentation. It has a higher energy density than ethanol, is less soluble in water and can be mixed at any ratio with petrol. It is also possible to use it in diesel engines. There is now a company claiming to make it from plant waste or woody materials.[26]

To understand what contribution these second-generation biofuels could make to our energy needs, we need to know both the amount of fuel that could be produced from cellulosic material and the quantity of that material available. This information is not easy to find, but sufficient data is available to make a ballpark calculation. A US government report gives a yield of 122 litres of fuel from a dry tonne of biomass, and suggests that the US could supply 30 per cent of its current petrol requirement by the middle of the century from sustainable sources (75 per cent from crop residues, the remainder from wood) with no impact on food production. A similar ballpark calculation for the UK suggests that if the nonedible crop residues from the 2008 grain harvest could be turned into fuel, it would make only a 5 per cent contribution to replacing current petrol requirements. At a Society for General Microbiology meeting, in a talk on biofuels, the speaker gave comparative land areas and driving ranges for different fuels. So biodiesel/bioethanol derived from food crops would allow 11,500km per hectare (Ha) compared with 32,200km/Ha from cellulosic material derived from ryegrass. This last figure sounds great, but under questioning the speaker admitted it would take 80 per cent of the UK *total* land area to provide enough fuel for our current driving needs.[27] Clearly there is still a work to be done before commercial-scale fuel production from straw and wood is possible; however, these second generation biofuels have some potential.

Biodiesel and SVO (straight vegetable oil)

Biodiesel is made by a process which involves reacting a plant-derived oil with an alcohol. The reaction requires some heat (50–60°C) and a catalyst. The energy balance of the process is less controversial than for bioethanol; the net energy gain is generally accepted at being about 8:1, although some studies report a lower figure. Biodiesel can be derived from a number of sources including used cooking oil and tallow, oilseed rape and palm oil. Recycling used oil from chip shops into fuel is great, but the supplies are limited. Since vegetable oils are a significant food crop, using rape or palm oil presents a moral issue which is discussed further below.

Biodiesel can be used in unmodified engines. In some older diesel engines straight vegetable oil (SVO) can be used, but there can be problems due to the viscosity of the oil compared to mineral diesel. Engine components can seize up or be blocked if vegetable oil is used at high concentrations. Cars require modification, either using separate tanks so that the engine switches to the vegetable oil when the engine is warmed up (this lowers the viscosity) or a device that pre-heats the oil.

The land use issue

The common feature of all biofuels is their use of land. Producing the fossil fuels that currently drive our society require very little land area; they are also a very concentrated source of energy which we use in huge quantities. Thus their replacements start from these two comparative disadvantages.

Using land to produce fuel might be fine if that land were not required for other purposes. In our current circumstances with a growing world population and pressure on agriculture, biofuel production inevitably conflicts with food production. The steep food commodity price rises seen in 2008 and 2011 have been partly caused by supply constraints, as large amounts of maize and other grains are being used for bioethanol production, particularly in the US.[28] Another particularly worrying area is the production of biodiesel from palm oil. Neil has seen the consequences of this in terms of rainforest destruction in South East Asia to make way for palm oil plantations. Oil palms have the highest yield per hectare of any of the oil-yielding plants, but there is no question that it would be highly immoral to clear ancient primary forest to plant palm oil trees, so that we could continue to fly and drive. However, so much palm oil is used in our industrialised food system in everything from biscuits to margarine that it is difficult to pin ecological destruction just on to driving. It is difficult to say where most of the vegetable oil used to make biodiesel is derived from, but even if it is made from locally grown oilseed rape it is still displacing land used for food production. The proponents of biodiesel have suggested several alternatives. The first of these is *Jatropha curcas*. This is an oil-bearing plant that has the advantage of growing on very arid, marginal land. However, it also grows in better soils and so could displace food crops or rainforest.[29] While growing this plant on marginal land in India or Africa makes sense for local production of transport fuel in these areas, shipping it across continents would not, due to the energy balance. If fuel was to be produced in quantity from *Jatropha*, it would require a colossal area of land to keep the world's cars moving. In addition, how could we be sure that the oil used to fill our tanks has come from marginal land with no other use?

Algae

As the use of *Jatropha* has been questioned, the next great hope of biodiesel has loomed into view – algae. Some forms of algae use photosynthesis to produce an oil-like substance, and a huge amount of research is going on in this area to develop a commercial process for harvesting the algal oil and producing usable fuel. In theory algae has significant advantages over other sources of oil for production of biodiesel. Being photosynthetic, its carbon source for growth is carbon dioxide and its energy source is light. It therefore doesn't require any valuable crop or energy input for its growth stage. The process of production is to some extent established, having been used on a small scale for many years.[30] Algae also (in theory) overcomes some of the land area substitution concerns, since the output per hectare is much higher even than palm oil. The challenges of algae include how and where to grow it? The 'how' is whether to grow the algae in sealed tanks or, as most is at the moment, in open ponds. (Growing the algae in open ponds has the disadvantage that less productive strains colonise the tanks, outcompeting the preferred strains.) The 'where' is physically where to carry out the growth process: one suggestion is at sea in the tropics, temperate regions not having enough light. This overcomes the land area/food issue, but building open structures, for example, that could survive tropical storms would be a challenge. Another suggestion is in the world's deserts (opening up parts of the US and southern Europe as production centres). However, this throws up the issue of water supply. Although algal-derived oil offers huge potential, until these logistical and technical challenges have been overcome, it remains unclear what contribution it could make to future fuel supplies.

Other fuels

In 2007 a letter to the scientific journal *Nature* described a process involving the production of a chemical fuel called 2,5-dimethyfuran from the sugar fructose.[31] The process is complicated, involving heat for the multi-stage reaction process and for the final separation process of the fuel. The derived fuel is very insoluble in water (good) and has 40 per cent more energy density than ethanol (making it about the same as petrol and better than diesel). It is also toxic. However, a more efficient process needs to be developed with reduced energy input (using enzymes) before this could be considered worthwhile, and the land area issue would still arise.

Other researchers are working on a variety of 'branched' alcohols used in food flavourings. These compounds are very immiscible with water. Various bacterial pathways are being added or tweaked in bacteria to allow the bugs to make these compounds.[32] Another alternative is to make a synthetic fuel by using the Fischer-Tropsch process. German chemists Franz Fischer and Hans Tropsch invented this process in the 1920s. Carbon monoxide and hydrogen are combined at a temperature between 400 and 500°C to form a variety of hydrocarbons, from methane to diesel to waxes. Traditionally coal has been used as the feedstock for this process, though gas and wood can also be used. In an era where all these energy sources are depleting, it is difficult to see how this process can help, beyond its usefulness in converting a solid energy source into a liquid. It also requires large amounts of energy, so the net energy gain for Fischer-Tropsch is less than 1:1.

Conclusion

Although it is possible to make liquid fuels from a variety of materials, there are problems with almost all the processes and products. First-generation bioethanol, together with biodiesel made from vegetable oil or palm oil all face the same challenge: in an increasingly hungry world with rapidly rising food commodity prices, diverting food or food-producing land into fuel production should not be seriously entertained. Producing oil by planting *Jatropha curcas* on marginal land is an attractive idea, but it is difficult to see how this would not also displace food crops. Algal fuel production and other novel ideas offer huge potential, but all have many technical hurdles to overcome. Perhaps the one area of hope is the production of next-generation bioethanol or biobutanol from wood or plant waste. If the success of laboratory trials can be scaled up to a commercial process, this could be a significant player in the future. However, overall there is no renewable or alternative technology that will do what oil does for us today. Not one of the technologies we have examined can replace the expected shortfall in conventional oil supplies in the years ahead. The bottom line here is that we will have to manage with less.

Electric cars

Electric cars have been around in very small numbers for nearly thirty years. There is even a documentary film called *Who Killed the Electric Car?* This gives the clue that until now they have failed to make a market breakthrough. This all changed when Toyota brought out the Prius. This is a 'hybrid' car that uses battery power at low speed, and a petrol engine when going faster and to charge the batteries. Despite not being fully electric, it has raised the profile of electric vehicles and led to some cost reductions and improvements in battery technology. Nissan has recently started production of the Leaf, an electric five-seater slightly bigger than the Prius, and BMW have plans for an electric Mini. With other car companies bringing out electric cars, they seem likely to take a larger share of the market. Electric lorries and vans are made by Smith Electric Vehicles in the UK; they have sold vehicles into the fleets of the delivery companies TNT and DHL.

Electric vehicles raise a number of issues both environmental and practical. The first is that of electricity. Obviously mass use of electric vehicles will raise electricity consumption. By how much is so far unclear. The government in its 'Meeting the EU 2020 Renewables Target' consultation cited above, suggest it will increase overall demand, but decline to give a figure. The Institute of Mechanical Engineers suggest that electrifying *all* transport in the UK (this includes road transport and rail) would require a doubling of the country's generating capacity.[33] The Zero Carbon Britain report comes up with an even larger figure, and there is every reason to believe the problem would be as substantial in other countries. Turning our transport electric would only make sense if the electricity used came from clean, renewable sources. Since we are already struggling to replace our existing polluting generating sources, the idea of a higher target for renewable electricity is a stretch at best, unrealistic at worst. There are also some practical issues. Pure electric cars still don't have much range between charges – currently about 100 miles (160 km). This isn't so much of a problem most of the time since most car journeys in the UK and US are much shorter than this. But it does mean that charging points will have to be put everywhere, including potentially along main roads and motorways. There is also the problem that charging is not instantaneous. We are all used to the short time it takes to refuel our cars, but charging an electric car will take a lot longer. Nissan suggest that the Leaf will have two charging rates, but the fastest will still take 40 minutes to reach 80 per cent charge and it's possible this may shorten the battery life. One solution to this that has been suggested is that the batteries themselves are swapped. The driver would drive into a filling station and the staff would whip out the battery pack and replace it with a fully charged one. Renault suggest that the driver may own the car and rent the batteries, possibly from them or from a utility.

At the moment electric vehicles cost more to buy than conventional ones, but are much cheaper to run. To take the example of the Nissan Leaf, with a £5000 UK government grant it costs just under £26,000.[34] This is in the middle of the cost range; some of its rivals are a bit cheaper (Mitsubishi i-MiEV), others more expensive (Peugeot Ion). The problem is these are all small family cars and their fossil-fuel rivals are cheaper. The nearest car to these in our view is a VW Golf hatchback which can be picked up new for about £9000 cheaper. The cost of running a conventional car, assuming 50mpg with diesel at £1.41 a litre, would be 12.7p per mile. The Leaf has a range of 100 miles on a 24kWh charge at 15p a unit, hence would cost 3.6p a mile. This means the extra cost of the Leaf will be recouped in about 10 years assuming an average mileage of 10,000 miles a year. If pump prices doubled this would obviously be a more reasonable 5 years. Whilse the trend in fuel prices is relentlessly up, 67 per cent in 10 years according to the AA, the trend is still not high enough to double in the short term without some kind of oil shock.[35] Another factor works against electric car economics, that is, that conventional car consumption is improving – for example there is a Golf that can achieve over 70mpg. It costs extra money to buy but is still cheaper than the electric alternatives. The economics and 'range anxiety' mean that so far sales of electric cars have been underwhelming.

The greatest concern may not be the issue of electricity, but that of lithium and neodymium supply. Currently all electric cars use lithium batteries and the electric motors require elements known as 'rare earths' (especially neodymium) to make powerful permanent magnets. There are 27 million cars in the UK and around 600 million worldwide. It seems to us that replacing all these with electric cars with lithium batteries, let alone increasing the number, may not be possible. There is also an ethical issue which Christians should be concerned about, which is where the lithium comes from and how it is mined. At the moment most lithium is mined in South America and the largest potential reserves are in high-altitude desert in Bolivia, which is a unique ecosystem. There has to be concern that we may exchange one problem of damage to the environment caused by our driving for another. Bolivia also wants a cut of the action, that is, to add value to the supply chain by getting fairly paid for the materials it sells us and preferably making the batteries there. Neodymium raises similar issues. In addition there is a suspicion that China, the largest source, is controlling the market, although new mines are opening outside China.[36]

There are counter arguments to the above issues. The first, on electricity supply, is the obvious one that replacing petrol cars with electric ones will happen gradually, allowing time for the electricity supply to increase. This is true, but we would still contend that this supply will have to be increased many times over our current requirements of electricity. On the lithium supply, Nissan claim to have looked into this and argue it is sufficient for batteries and other uses. It also should be noted that lithium battery technology is said to be in the early stages of development, so that improvements in technology can be expected, reducing the need for lithium. Lithium batteries are also recyclable. As to mining and exploitation, it is up to consumers to press companies and governments involved to make sure as little damage is done to people and planet as possible. Electric cars probably take broadly the same amount of energy as a conventional car to produce, but are 90 per cent efficient to run compared with conventional petrol or diesel cars which can barely manage 50 per cent. Professor David MacKay, in his book *Sustainable Energy –Without the Hot Air*, suggests a car takes 76,000kWh of energy to produce. If it is replaced even just every 15 years this is still the equivalent of 14kWh per person per day (in the UK).

Conclusion

Electric cars may be feasible in terms of energy consumption when in use (especially with improvements in battery technology), although to simply transfer all fossil fuel vehicles to electric is going to require a lot of extra generating capacity. However, the authors question whether this is desirable. While in recent years interest has been in what comes out of the exhaust, there are many other problems caused by car use. These include road safety, traffic jams, road building and car parks, out-of-town shopping and all the dreadful architecture that goes with it. The dominance of the car has had a profound negative effect on many of our towns and cities. It would be nice to see car use in the UK and US come into line with that in many European countries such as Holland, Switzerland and Sweden where car ownership is high, but everyday commuting use is much lower. Another big issue is the sheer amount of energy needed to build a new car, and whether once energy supplies tighten, this kind of energy will be available.

Fuel cells

The microbial fuel cells described previously, although clearly a niche player, are capable of running on renewable waste materials.

This is a harder claim to make for chemical fuel cells, although some could use bioethanol. There are many different types and the reader is directed to sites such as www.fuelcells.org for a more complete description, but fuel cells are regarded as continually cycling batteries that work as long as fuel is provided. Hydrogen is the preferred energy source for most fuel cells. They convert the chemical energy from the fuel into electricity by a chemical reaction. The process (although not combustion) is about 50 per cent efficient and produces waste heat – (if this heat is also used the efficiency is about 85 per cent). Fuel cells have been used in a wide range of applications, from the Apollo space missions to submarines. Their primary uses today are to provide CHP (combined heat and power), or for transport. London and other cities have experimented with fuel-cell buses, and a lot of work is going into developing a practical fuel cell car. While progress has been made, even within the industry there is caution. Recently the chairman of General Motors, Daniel Akerson, stated that the technology is 'still too expensive and probably won't be practical until the 2020-plus period'.[37] As we have described many times in this book, the problems are not just technological, but also logistical – where does the fuel come from?

Hydrogen

Hydrogen is often promoted as the ultimate clean fuel. Combustion of hydrogen produces only heat and water – not even any CO_2! The problem is that unlike gas or oil, there are no deposits of hydrogen lying around waiting to be used. Hydrogen does in fact exist in nature; it is produced in very limited quantities by certain bacteria and algae and is part of the water cycle. However, potential biological production, as we have seen with other renewable fuels above, is limited for the same reasons (feedstock and land area). The obvious source of hydrogen is fresh water, which if you electrolyse it using platinum will split into hydrogen and oxygen. (There are other methods, but none of them offer compelling advantages.[38]) The drawback is plain – this takes electricity. This means that producing hydrogen is simply an energy transfer from one type (electricity) to another (hydrogen) – with about 50 per cent of the energy being lost as heat in the process. Another 50 per cent would be lost converting the hydrogen back into usable energy. Hydrogen is not an energy source, it is an energy carrier – and not a particularly efficient one. It cannot be compressed easily for storage or transport.[39] Compressing hydrogen and piping it around takes a lot more energy than methane and would require a whole new infrastructure, as the existing gas pipes are not suitable.

While a hydrogen-powered vehicle (either a fuel-cell vehicle or an adapted internal combustion engine) would produce no emissions at the exhaust, the electricity used to make the hydrogen could still be producing CO_2 and other pollutants at the power station. If we were to use renewable energy to make hydrogen for use in vehicles, it would require a massive up-scaling from current levels of renewable electricity generation. Regions such as California and South Wales in the UK are attempting to build hydrogen economies; the success or otherwise of these will help prove whether the idea has any merit. A rough calculation shows that to run all our existing transport on hydrogen fuel cells would require enormous amounts of electricity.[40]

Hydrogen could have a role in localised energy storage, despite the conversion losses when turning electricity into hydrogen and back again. We think it is possible to envisage hydrogen being used to store excess output from very large wind farms, such as at night when the wind is blowing but there is low power demand. This spare electricity would generate hydrogen from water, which would be stored – possibly in empty gas fields. At times of higher electricity demand, conventional gas plant or fuel cells would then generate electricity from the stored hydrogen. Some advocate making hydrogen and then combining it with carbon dioxide to make methane, which has the advantage that methane has more embodied energy per unit of volume, so can be transported further while getting a return on the energy. It also uses existing energy infrastructure.

Conclusion

In our opinion the idea of a future 'hydrogen economy' is a fantasy. The inefficiencies inherent in producing hydrogen and then converting back into usable energy means that the net energy gain is lower than 1:1. It is likely that hydrogen will occupy a niche, but no more in a post-oil world.

Frequently asked questions about renewables

Here we attempt to sum up these chapters by answering some of the questions that come up when renewables are discussed.

Q: Aren't renewables intermittent?

We would prefer to say variable, but however you look at it, the sun doesn't always shine nor the wind blow, and hydro systems sometimes dry up. Are there any ways around this? A number of solutions have been proposed which we will briefly describe.

Balancing one technology against another. By linking together a variety of different technology types with a wide geographical spread, the variable nature of some of the technologies can be balanced against each other and shortages overcome. This has been modelled successfully in Germany on a small scale and works in Woking, although many of the power sources used in the latter are not renewable. It seems common sense not to rely on one technology alone.

Smart grids. The flow of electricity in the future will be a two-way flow between consumers and the grid. It is very likely that almost everyone will have to fit some form of micro-generation (most likely PV). Thus power flow will be a complex process with electricity flowing in multiple directions around the grid. Computer technology monitoring production and demand in real time will allow the most efficient use of this electricity. This will be aided by –

Smart metering. This is a technology used in buildings to monitor total energy consumption in real time and predict and manage trends. It has been trialled on a limited basis in some countries. By 2019 all meters in the UK for every supply point will be changed over to smart meters, the largest such programme in the world. If this is just metering in a cupboard that aids the power companies by doing away with meter readers then it would be a waste of time; consumers need to be able to see and interact with the devices easily. Trials have shown smart meters cut consumption of gas and electricity although the amounts have varied. This makes maximum sense when used with –

Smart devices. Individual consumer devices, mainly 'white goods' and probably electric cars, would be fitted with chips which tell them when to use power, for example at night when there is an excess and it's cheapest. We might have to live with our washing machine switching itself on in the middle of the night.

Energy storage. A vast number of energy-storage systems have been mooted. Many of these are chemical and we don't think there will be enough of the earth's resources to make sufficient systems to meet all demand. There are however mechanical systems that exist, such as flywheels and compressed-air systems. With localised energy storage the grid could be broken up into a series of semi-autonomous micro-grids, making for very efficient use of local electricity. One possibility is to use electric cars as a means of energy storage, although it might be difficult to get car owners to sell the electricity back to the grid.

Direct current transmission technology. This is an extension of the balancing idea above but on a continental or even inter-continental scale. A series of connections would make what is effectively a massive renewable electricity grid. Wind farms in Scotland and the North Sea could be linked to geothermal and hydropower in Iceland and Norway and solar power in southern Europe or North Africa. When there is excess electricity being produced in one part of Europe and not another then the power is first fed to those parts that need it. If no one needs it the power is sent to Norway, Iceland and other parts of Europe with pumped storage. At times of high demand when there is no wind, the pumped storage hydropower systems cut in. In the longer term, wave, tidal and a high penetration of micro-generation could be added to the mix. Some elements of this grid are already built or planned. There are some issues to be resolved such as who pays for it, who decides who gets the power and how do the producers get paid? Additionally, do we put large amounts of solar power generation in North Africa, making ourselves partially dependent on countries outside Europe, and is this another form of colonialism?

Q: Can we afford to switch to renewables?

A strange question when it seems we don't have much choice. All the elements described above are costly, and with many renewable technologies the cost is largely upfront and the savings come over the longer term. However, we have just been through the biggest financial crisis since the 1930s. A combination of another financial shock and peak oil is not something we would like to contemplate.

Q: Have we got time to switch to renewable power?

No. We are too close to the oil production peak and energy crunch to mitigate it completely. It seems highly unlikely that enough renewable capacity will be in place to substitute for losses in conventional supplies.

Q: Can renewables match the energy supply we have today?

This depends. Figure 1 below all too clearly shows our addiction to a high-energy lifestyle today, and how much less energy will be available in 2050, even with a switch to 100 per cent renewable as detailed here. It will be much easier to meet our basic needs if we get serious about energy conservation and lifestyle change; this is detailed in later chapters of this book. A combination of different renewable technologies, together with a substantial reduction in energy demand would make life easier. The one area where we will struggle is provision of liquid fuels for transport.

Q: Can we run a globalised economy on renewables?

In our opinion, resource constraints will force globalisation into reverse, to be replaced by extreme localisation. There is no simple substitute for the oil which keeps the ships, planes and lorries moving goods around our globalised economy. (See page 105.)

Moral issues facing Christians

In some ways it is difficult to think of renewable energy causing moral concerns for Christians. But even with a non-polluting energy source there are still issues we need to consider. No energy

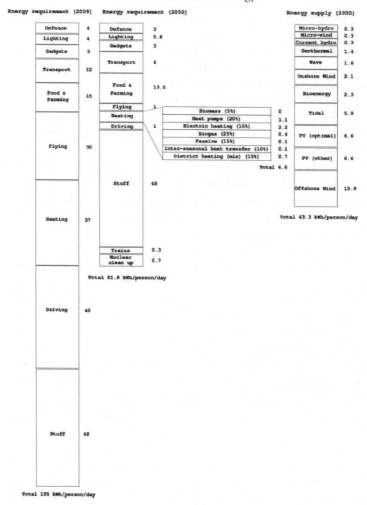

Figure 1: Energy supply 2010 alongside possible future demand and supply. All energy used in the UK economy is expressed as kWh/day/person; population 60 million now and 70 million in 2050. Energy demand now is taken from David Mackay, *Sustainable Energy – Without the Hot Air*. Future energy supply is calculated by the authors using the UK Department of Energy and Climate Change 2050 pathway analysis background information. For details, see extra documents on our website (http://www.theoillamp.co.uk/).

system can be made without causing some pollution. As we have seen above, many renewables pay back the energy used to make them pretty quickly and give reasonable (in some cases good) energy returns, increasingly comparable with our current sources of energy which are falling. However, even with efficient technologies there can be disadvantages. One example of a negative impact from moving to renewable energy is the proposed tidal barrage across the Severn estuary, which would damage an area of habitat important for birds and other species.

Another problem with renewables is the impact of wind turbines and other devices on the people who live nearby. The ethical issue arises when something which is good for society and the climate is detrimental to a household or community that is directly affected – for example, by noise or visual intrusion from a wind turbine. The problem extends not only to the devices themselves, but also to the other support energy infrastructure required, such as power lines and large substations. In Scotland the Beaully-Denny transmission upgrade provides a classic case of the problems caused by this. To support the increased production of electricity from wind farms, new hydropower in the highlands, wave and tidal power off the north coast of Scotland, and transfer the energy to where it's needed (the central belt of Scotland and England), the power lines along this route are being upgraded. Essentially this means building taller pylons in an area of the Highlands that is both beautiful and close to a national park. Replacing much of our conventional energy generation with renewables would inevitably require more pylons and power lines linking to where the renewable resource is greatest – in rural and coastal areas. The question is, how much 'industrialisation' of the countryside is desirable? Wind farm opponents stress this point (among others), although it can be argued that the countryside has changed radically over recent centuries, with deforestation, enclosure in England, the clearances in Scotland and the industrialisation of agriculture. Lastly, it should be noted some parts of our energy infrastructure such as the pylons of the national grid and Scottish Hydro schemes were bitterly opposed when they were built. While pylons would never be described as pretty, we hardly notice them today. Polls have suggested that wind farms follow the same pattern of acceptance.

Our view is that a number of guidelines should be followed. First, any potential renewable resource should be carefully and honestly analysed, so that resources are not wasted. Second, developers should work closely with the communities that are directly affected. Third, there should be a strong element of community benefit rather than pure profit. The positioning of wind turbines, in particular, should be carefully planned, and minimum distances to homes should be established. Micro-generation doesn't have such aesthetic drawbacks – it is unlikely large numbers of people will be offended by PV panels on your roof, although we await the first neighbourly dispute over system shading due to trees or development.

Alternative means of transport also offer the thoughtful Christian some moral issues. For example electric or fuel-cell cars only solve *some* problems related to conventional transport. Localised pollution out of the tailpipe and carbon emissions are reduced.[41] The other problems caused by cars described above are not altered one bit by what powers the car. These problems will only be reduced when we become less dependent on our cars, and walk, cycle or take public transport where possible.

The most challenging question is, should we use renewable energy to continue our current, highly energy-dependent lifestyle? Our view is that we should not. The reasons for this are very simple. Access to cheap energy has allowed us to do great ecological and social damage to ourselves. It has made us more insular, being increasingly cut-off from our fellow human beings (despite or perhaps because of easy foreign travel and electronic communications), disconnected from nature and materialistic. Even if we had plentiful cheap renewable energy we would use this to do other harm to our shared planet. We realise this is an unpalatable message (perhaps impossible for a politician to voice). But at the same time it is one that fits in very well with many passages in scripture, one example being Matthew 6:19–20: 'Do not lay up for yourselves treasures on earth, where moth and rust destroy and where thieves break in and steal, but lay up for yourselves treasures in heaven, where neither moth nor rust destroys and where thieves do not break in and steal.'

In the remainder of this book, we examine how Christians can face the challenges and opportunities that will come our way in the next few years, as the energy crunch starts to take hold. The next chapter looks at how this will affect the production of something important to everyone on the planet – food.

Notes

1   http://www.californiasolarcenter.org/history_solarthermal.html.
2   *Ibid.*
3   http://www.eci.ox.ac.uk/research/energy/40house.php.
4   S. Roaf *et al.*, *Ecohouse: A Design Guide'*, Architectural Press, 2001.
5   UK government EU renewables 2020 target consultation.
6   http://www.forestry.gov.uk/england-woodfuel.
7   UK government EU renewables 2020 target consultation.
8   This is taking the Forestry Commission's figure of 4 tonnes of wood a year figure to heat a house, which seems too low to us in any case.
9   http://www.guardian.co.uk/business/2010/jan/20/moorlands-and-biomass-crops.
10 The first law states energy types are interchangeable and can neither be created or destroyed, or that the energy in a closed system is constant.
11 UK government EU renewables 2020 target consultation.
12 See John Cantor at www.Heatpumps.co.uk.
13 http://www.theoildrum.com/node/3949.
14 R. Hopkins, *The Transition Handbook*, Green Books, 2008.
15 http://www.decc.gov.uk/en/content/cms/tackling/2050/2050.aspx.
16 http://www.rehau.co.uk/files/2._Interseasonal_Heat_Transfer.pdf.
17 http://www.icax.co.uk/.
18 Carried out using data from an on-line European database of such systems which no longer exists.
19 http://www.decc.gov.uk/en/content/cms/news/pn11_114/pn11_114.aspx and http://www.worldarchitecturenews.com/index.php?fuseaction=wanappln.projectview&upload_id=13717.
20 http://www.chpa.co.uk/.
21 http://www.nationalgrid.com/uk/Media+Centre/Documents/biogas.htm.
22 For example, http://www.lrrd.org/lrrd21/11/pres21195.htm.
23 A. Scragg, *Environmental Biotechnology'*, 2nd edn, Oxford University Press, 2005.
24 http://www.technologyreview.com/Energy/19745/; http://www.zymetis.com/.
25 http://www.zymetis.com.

26 http://www.rsc.org/chemistryworld/Issues/2008/February/ BiobutanolEntersBattleAlcohols.asp.

27 Source: talks given at SGM Autumn Meeting Edinburgh Conference Centre Heriot-Watt University, 7–10 September 2009.

28 http://www.guardian.co.uk/environment/2008/jul/03/ biofuels.renewableenergy.

29 http://www.ecoworld.com/features/2005/08/21/jatropha-in-africa/ gives a very honest revue of the history of this story.

30 http://www.renewableenergyworld.com/rea/news/article/2009/06/is-the-future-of-biofuels-in-algae?cmpid=WNL-Wednesday-June17–2009.

31 Y. R-Leshkov *et al.*, 'Production of Dimethylfuran for Liquid Fuels from Biomass-derived Carbohydrates', *Nature* 447, 7147 (2007), p. 982.

32 Source: talks given at SGM Autumn Meeting Edinburgh Conference Centre Heriot-Watt University, 7–10 September 2009.

33 *Nuclear Build: A Vote of No Confidence?*, Institute of Mechanical Engineers, 2010.

34 http://www.autoexpress.co.uk/motorshows/tokyo-motor-show/ 275803/nissan_leaf_price_to_drop.html.

35 http://www.theaa.com/motoring_advice/fuel/.

36 http://www.reuters.com/article/2009/08/31/us-mining-toyota-idUSTRE57U02B20090831.

37 D. Shepardson, 'GM CEO: Fuel Cell Vehicles Not Yet Practical', *The Detroit News*, 30 July 2011.

38 http://en.wikipedia.org/wiki/Hydrogen_economy.

39 U. Bossel *et al.*, 'The Future of the Hydrogen Economy: Bright or Bleak?', 2003.

40 http://www2.warwick.ac.uk/fac/soc/economics/staff/academic/ oswald/windaccountancy04.pdf.

41 Even when using 'dirty' energy, electric cars at current ranges and electricity production mix offer significant carbon emission cuts. The reader can work this out using their electricity suppliers declared CO_2 production per kWh, their mileage per year and the range between charges given by manufacturers such as Nissan.

But we don't *eat* oil, do we?

He makes grass grow for the cattle, and plants for people to
cultivate – bringing forth food from the earth:
Wine that gladdens their hearts, oil to make their faces shine,
and bread that sustains their hearts.

Psalm 104:14–15

Following the oil crisis of 1973, a book titled *Eating Oil* was published, which warned about how our food supply was dependent on fossil fuels. A more recent report by the environmental group Sustain, looking at the same issue, concluded: 'If anything has changed since the 1970s it is that the food system is now even more dependent on cheap crude oil. Every time we eat, we are all essentially "eating oil" '.[1] Oil plays a significant part in modern food production because it provides fuel for tractors, combine harvesters and all the other machines used in modern food production. Oil also provides the feedstock for agrochemical production, and natural gas is used in the production of fertiliser. Beyond the farm gate, the storage, processing, transportation and presentation of food all involve substantial inputs of oil to get it on to the store shelf. Given this dependence, the expected peaking and decline in world energy supplies will inevitably have profound effects for food production and food security around the world.

The modern food production systems which developed over the course of the twentieth century are only part of the story of agricultural development that has taken place over millennia, as human beings have learnt how to make land, crops and animals more and more productive. However, what took place from the around the Second World War onwards was a remarkable leap forward, as science was rigorously applied to the task of raising food production after the shortages of the war years. Improved varieties of crops and superior strains of animals together with new agricultural techniques increased crop yields and productivity substantially, and enabled swelling populations to be fed. The impact of these changes was felt first in developed countries, but in later decades the uptake of these new technologies, particularly irrigation, in parts of the developing world led to the so-called 'green revolution' where food production was also raised substantially.

Though much of this development can be put down to improved plant and animal breeding and improvements in farming skills and practice, there is a significant underpinning provided by sources of energy. To understand this, we need to look back at the significance of soil fertility to food production. The earliest farmers would simply move on when their soil became unproductive – leaving the land fallow for several years allowed its fertility to slowly rebuild. As populations grew, there was less room to leave land fallow, and other methods came into use. In the not-too-distant past, the only way to improve soil fertility was by using the wastes from animals in the form of manure; in some parts of the world human excreta was (and still is) used for this purpose. Farmers also made use of leguminous crops which fix nitrogen from the air through symbiotic relationships with bacteria attached to their roots. A productive system could be maintained by rotating nitrogen-fixing and nitrogen-using crops, and incorporating animals into the system as well. This all changed with the introduction of fertiliser in the nineteenth century. Initially this came from natural sources such as guano (vast deposits of seabird and other animal droppings) which were mined, transported and spread on the land. The mineral content of these fertilisers was high, particularly in nitrogen, potash and phosphates, the three key minerals needed for plant growth, and the effects could be clearly seen in improved crop growth and increased yields. But as the guano began to be used up, farmers had to look elsewhere for sources of fertility.

In the early years of the twentieth century two German chemists developed a method to do what the legumes and bacteria had been doing naturally – fixing nitrogen out of the air into a usable form. Fritz Haber and Carl Bosch were both rewarded with Nobel prizes for developing the process to produce ammonia in quantity. Simplified, the Haber-Bosch process uses methane from natural gas, nitrogen from the atmosphere, and a great deal of energy to produce ammonia, this can then be converted into a usable form, as ammonium nitrate or urea. Although this process was first used on an industrial scale less than a hundred years ago, it now underpins much of the world's food production. One hundred million tonnes of nitrogen fertiliser is produced per year, using up to 5 per cent of the world's natural gas supply.[2] At least a third of the planet's population is directly sustained by modern, fertiliser-dependent farming. Fertiliser use is not limited to developed countries; Andy's experience of working in Nigeria and Malawi is that many small-scale farmers have become dependent on it to boost crop yields. The future peak and decline of gas supplies will therefore have serious consequences for fertiliser users, as does the possible peaking of phosphate production which are very important to agriculture.[3] Some hints of this have already been seen, with fertiliser prices fluctuating wildly over the last couple of years. Sustained high prices or actual shortages of fertiliser would inevitably lead to a significant drop in food production. When this scenario was outlined to a group of farmers here in the UK, one succinct response was, 'If they can't give us fertiliser, we can't give them food.'

The modern food industry is not just dependent on fertiliser; it is also a significant user of oil and other energy inputs. This is not only on the farm, where diesel fuels machinery. Energy is used to store food, to transport it by ship, air or road, to refine and process food, and to produce and transport food packaging. A study of the American food system showed that 10 calories of energy input is used to produce 1 calorie of actual food energy.[4] Some foods use even more energy: growing asparagus in Chile and air-freighting it to the UK uses a staggering 97 calories of energy input for every 1 calorie of energy in the food.[5] Such an energy-hungry system will inevitably struggle to cope with energy shortages once oil supplies get tight. A foretaste of this came in the UK in the year 2000, when protesters briefly blockaded oil refineries in a dispute over high fuel prices. Though the resulting shortage of fuel was artificial and short-lived, within a couple of days the effects could be clearly seen in emptying supermarket shelves as the distribution system started to fail. Sir Peter Davis, the head of supermarket giant Sainsbury's, contacted Prime Minister Tony Blair to say that food would run out in days rather than weeks. While that crisis was resolved and has passed into history, food production and distribution remains extremely vulnerable to such shocks, being highly energy dependent and lacking resilience, a fact that the British government acknowledged in a report on food security produced by its agriculture ministry in 2009.[6] Our current system involves food travelling long distances from the field or factory to the fork, and produces some peculiar anomalies. Research by the New Economics Foundation found that, in 2004, the UK imported 17,200 tonnes of chocolate-covered waffles and wafers, and exported 17,600 tonnes; we imported 10,200 tonnes of milk and cream from France, and exported 9,900 tonnes to them.[7] We imported 44,000 tonnes of frozen boneless chicken, and exported 51,000 tonnes of fresh boneless chicken. This kind of global food trading clearly makes some kind of economic sense when fuel prices and transport costs are relatively low. But once we make the paradigm shift into thinking of oil as a depleting commodity that we need to conserve, then the vast amount of food transport starts to look like collective madness. This is not really about whether or not we would like to eat a particular type of Swiss chocolate biscuit, the wider concern is how we can continue to feed the world.

The United Nations Food and Agriculture Organisation's definition of food security is 'when all people, at all times, have access to sufficient, safe and nutritious food to meet their dietary needs and food preferences for an active and healthy life'.[8] Clearly this aim is not being met everywhere in the world at present, and in fact over the last five or six years there have been some worrying developments which have made the world arguably less food secure, and have caused global food prices to surge upwards:

- a significant amount of grain (20 per cent of the US maize crop[9]) being used to make biofuels rather than being used for food;

- more meat consumption by increasingly affluent populations in China and other developing countries is causing
rising demand for animal feed;
- poor harvests and export restrictions in countries which
usually export grain;
- increasing areas of productive soil becoming degraded by
unsustainable farming practices;
- input costs, particularly fertilisers, rising as oil and gas
prices have risen;
- historically low global food reserve stocks and increased
amounts of commodity price speculation.

The UK government's chief scientist Professor John Beddington
warned in 2009 that the world faced a 'perfect storm' by 2030 when
shortages of energy, water and food would start to really bite
(although problems may show up a lot sooner than that). The huge
price rises in basic food commodities in 2008 led to protests and
riots in several countries, as people found their staple foods increasingly unaffordable.

Food production systems vary widely around the world, and not
everyone is fed by the industrialised productions systems which
supply our supermarkets. There are still many places where much of
people's diet is produced locally by sustainable small-scale farming
and household-scale food production. Even in developed countries
there are organic farmers who are producing food sustainably
without artificial fertilisers (though even they would struggle without any oil). One example of a country that has come through an oil
shock is Cuba, which was forced to re-model its food production
when the collapse of the Soviet Union cut off its previously
subsidised supply of oil. While still struggling to feed its people,
significant steps forward have been made by a focus on small-scale
organic production and by the development of productive urban
gardens. Another example is Russia, where at times when the Soviet
system failed to provide for people's basic needs, many people
managed to feed themselves from their gardens and even produced
enough to barter.

Examples like this, together with the resurgence of gardening
and allotment use here in the UK, provide some kind of template for

what *some parts* of a sustainable food system might look like in an energy-constrained future. But could such systems feed the world? There seem to be two basic choices for the way ahead. One is a model of intensive agriculture producing food for the globalised marketplace, which maximises the yield from crops and animals and uses increasingly hi-tech methods to achieve this. Advocates of this approach point to the advances made over the last 50 years, and look to the potential of technologies such as genetically modified crops. Yet the productivity of intensive agriculture has come at a cost – large areas of land has become degraded, non-renewing aquifers are being pumped dry for irrigation, and many thousands of farm workers suffer from exposure to pesticides. Imbalances in global trade and consumption mean that, while millions go hungry, in developed countries there is an epidemic of obesity and related health problems. Crucially, this food system is hugely dependent on energy inputs which are looking increasingly uncertain in the future. Even the UK government has admitted that 'existing patterns of food production are not fit for a low-carbon, more resource-constrained future'.[10] A recent report from the UK Parliament's Environmental Audit Committee reinforces many of the concerns above.[11] Among its recommendations are fair prices for food producers and that the planning system should have a presumption to provide land for local people to grow food.

The alternative to this is to work towards a more sustainable, resilient global food system. This would mean more food being produced and consumed locally rather than being transported long distances. Farmers would be encouraged to produce for local needs rather than the global commodity markets. Soil fertility would be maintained by crop rotations using nitrogen-fixing crops and applying animal manures and even treated human waste. Patterns of consumption would have to change. Less pork and poultry meat would be produced as this involves high feed inputs, but there could be more grass-fed beef and lamb production. Alternative farming techniques such as agroforestry and permaculture could play a much bigger role in providing resilient food production. Agroforestry is where productive trees are incorporated into the farming landscape. The combination of perennial and annual crops makes more efficient use of the available sunlight and produces a greater overall yield

than growing trees and crops separately. Permaculture (a combination of the words permanent + agriculture) uses principles from
nature to design highly productive landscapes, combining different
species for a high level of synergy.

In a sense some parts of this new system are already in place.
Organic farming, often derided as 'pesticide-free food for affluent
foodies' is in fact a decent attempt at creating a sustainable farming
system. Although yields can be lower, it uses far less energy per unit
of production than conventional farming. The choice between
large-scale agri-business and small-scale sustainability is not really a
straight choice. The resource constraints that the world is facing will
mean that industrial agriculture in its present form will inevitably
falter and fail – and in fact it never did feed the world adequately
anyway. We are all likely to be eating more locally in the future. But
if we don't plan for the changes that will happen, many of us will
have to eat less.

Another area for concern – chemicals

Many people make the mistake of thinking that peak oil is an energy
issue alone. As we have seen, it is also a transport issue, and a food
issue. While 95 per cent of oil is used for transport the other
5 per cent is forgotten about. This is made up of volatile fractions
separated from heavier components such as petrol and diesel. In the
early days of the oil industry no one knew what to do with these
refinery left overs. Then it was discovered that they could be used to
make something useful – plastic. Nowadays oil is used to make so
many different products and it is hard to imagine life without them.
Inevitably future oil shortages will have significant effect on the
production of plastic and other chemicals. This is a serious issue that
no one seems to have foreseen.

There are two challenges. The first is that of 'embedded energy'.
For example, household bleach is not directly made from oil but uses
oil-derived energy for its manufacture and transport. However,
many of the products we use every day, such as plastics or pharmaceuticals, not only have embedded energy in them but are also
manufactured from a series of oil derived chemical building blocks.
Even toothpaste has oil-derived components. A quick look around

any room will find many items that are produced from oil: CDs, lipstick, carpets, contact lenses, shoe polish and aspirins to name a few among many thousands. Currently how the chemical industry works is that oil-derived feed-stocks are converted through a whole series of chemical reactions to the end product. Many of these reactions involve high temperatures and metal catalysts (a catalyst is something that speeds a chemical reaction up). While chemical engineers are superb at capturing the heat and reusing it, the processes are by necessity very energy intensive.

The alternative to using oil is to start with a different set of chemical building blocks derived from living organisms (be it plants or bacteria) and use the natural catalysts that these organisms use themselves (enzymes) to produce useful products. Enzymes have a whole series of advantages over conventional catalysts, but one is that they work at low temperatures, saving very large amounts of energy. The British government has done some research on this, which indicated very considerable energy savings (along with waste and resource savings).[12] In the case of one chemical (acrylic acid), the biological-based manufacture cut the energy use by over 90 per cent. The report admitted these figures were uncertain because the bio-based processes are so new. Some bio processes are already in use. The company DuPont produce a chemical used to make plastics and paints biologically from glycerol. Glycerol is a by-product of soap and biodiesel manufacture (described above) and there has been a glut of it on the world market for many years. Other products are less easy to produce. The problem that this example does not illustrate well is the same as biofuels, land area. The plants and (indirectly) the micro-organisms used in biological processes require land (since the bacteria would mostly grow on plant-derived feedstocks). The current idea in many chemical engineering circles is that of the 'biorefinery'. In a manner similar to the petrochemical industry, the waste by-products of making biofuels could be used to make useful commodity chemicals using micro-organisms. These in turn could then be used to make a range of plastics, chemicals and drugs using enzymes. As we discussed in the last chapter, biofuels cannot fully meet our transport needs, and so it seems unlikely that their by-products will meet our chemical needs. We think it is inevitable that we will have to steeply reduce our use of plastics, chemicals and other synthetic products. The problem in this case is not energy, but resource limitations.

Other materials

As has been alluded to elsewhere in the book, there are early signs that we are using up a variety of other non-renewable resources. For example the prices of all metals have soared over the last few years. So much so that we often hear about theft of copper and other metals from the railway system and even metal plaques in war memorials. A number of reports looking at metal resources have been commissioned by the UK, US and EU.[13] Their findings have profound implications for the subjects we are discussing in the book. First, as we discussed concerning uranium, as ore strength declines the amount of energy to extract anything useful from it rises. Copper ores being mined now contain 0.3 per cent copper, at the beginning of the twentieth century they contained 3 per cent.[14] There is an estimate that 40 per cent of global energy might be required to extract metals by 2050.[15] The second problem is that many of these metals are required to build the new green energy economy (neodymium is used to make permanent magnets used in electric cars and wind turbines, for example).

Moral issues

Like many areas, the material covered in this chapter raises issues that we as Christians often ignore. There is the whole question of how we produce our food and distribute it and whether the producers (wherever they are) get a fair price for it in a system dominated by big supermarkets. There is also the issue of why so many of us live with the results of over-eating when so many starve. Finally, we have grown used to living in a throw-away culture where both food and non-renewable materials are sent to land fill. Many Christians are involved in farming, business and productive industries. In all these areas we need to consider how we can make changes that move us in the direction of more sustainable living, where our lives, our businesses, our farms are using less precious energy, using less *resources*, and giving greater consideration to the limits of creation.

Notes

1   Andy Jones, *Eating Oil: Food Supply in a Changing Climate'*, Sustain/EFRC, 2001.

2   http://www.fertilizer.org/ifa/statistics/indicators/ind_reserves.asp.

3   *A Rock and a Hard Place: Peak Phosphorus and the Threat to our Food Security*, Soil Association, 2010.

4   D. Pimental and M. Giampietro, *Food, Land, Population and the US Economy*, Report prepared for Carrying Capacity Network, Washington DC, 1994.

5   Jones, *Eating Oil*.

6   *UK Food Security Assessment: Our Approach*, DEFRA, 2009.

7   Andrew Simms *et al.*, *The UK Interdependence Report*, NEF, 2006.

8   *Rome Declaration on World Food Security*, FAO, 1996.

9   *Biofuels: Prospects, Risks and Opportunities*, FAO, 2008.

10 *Food: An Analysis of the Issues*, Cabinet Office Strategy Unit, 2008.

11 *Sustainable Food: Eleventh Report of Session 2010–12'*, Environmental Audit Committee.

12 'Study into the Potential Energy and Greenhouse Gas Savings of Renewable Chemicals and Biocatalysts', 2008. See BERR website at www.berr.gov.uk/files/file51240.pdf.

13 *Reinventing the Wheel: A Circular Economy for Resource Security*, Green alliance, 2011. This report summarises very neatly the findings and the potential problems using a number of sources.

14 *Reinventing the Wheel*.

15 *Reinventing the Wheel*.

Surely the market will provide? The economics of resource depletion

I see in the near future a crisis approaching that unnerves me and causes me to tremble for the safety of my country … Corporations have been enthroned, an era of corruption in high places will follow, and the money-power of the country will endeavour to prolong its reign by working upon the prejudices of the people until the wealth is aggregated in a few hands.

Abraham Lincoln, 1864

In the book so far we have examined the consequences of a looming energy crisis. Our use of and dependence on energy is linked to the value we attribute to it, which leads us to another problem, economics. A brief critique of current thinking is justified since energy use underpins the dominant model, that of market economics, growth and globalisation. Also pertinent is a quick review of alternative ideas and recent opinion on a potential new economic model.

We are currently locked into a neo-liberal economic system that operates under what has become known as the 'Washington consensus'.[1] Under this system, broadly speaking, markets are good, delivering what we need, and the state is bad (with government intervention frowned upon). Free movement of goods, money and (within limits) people is encouraged. Very large amounts of money are traded in commodities, futures and other financial instruments, which move around the globe electronically.

Mainstream economic thinking has come under severe pressure since the credit crisis of 2008, and rightly so. This period of turmoil has exposed deep-seated problems with the present system, which include rich individuals and big businesses, particularly in banking and investment, benefiting greatly from the present system while real incomes for ordinary people fall, widening the gap between rich and poor to record levels and lowering the tax base.[2] This is done in many cases by the perfectly legal use of tax avoidance and offshore tax havens. The classic case is that of the UK retail magnate Sir Philip Green. He was appointed to help the new UK coalition government cut spending, but pays almost no tax in the UK. This is because, it is alleged, all his money is held in the name of his wife, who is resident in Monaco.[3] It has recently come to light that the internet retailer Amazon is being investigated by the tax authorities in the US and UK for paying almost no tax in these jurisdictions. Some of the money that ends up in these tax havens is from the proceeds of organised crime.[4]

As we saw in 2008, the current financial arrangements are a highly interlinked system that fails even under its own rules. Consider that when Lehman Brothers and other large institutions went bust it caused such a market reaction that many of the world's banks had to be supported by the taxpayer. Free market dogma suggests that these banks should have been allowed to go bankrupt. They had to be bailed out for the simple reason that banks are also utilities that millions of people use every day, if they had been allowed to fail the world economy would have gone into a severe downward spiral. As it was, disaster was only narrowly averted. The events of 2008 presented an opportunity to move towards a different type of system but politicians flunked it.

To add to this, conventional economics with its expectation of continual economic growth seems to ignore the fact that humanity exists within a closed, finite system. Our way of life, our expectations, our economic models are built on the presumption that the resources humanity draws on (such as energy) are unlimited – and that business as usual can continue *ad infinitum*.[5] A typical comment about the relationship between the economy and the planet was made recently by the UK Chancellor of the Exchequer, George Osborne, when he said, 'we're not going to save the planet by putting our country out of business' – perhaps forgetting, like many politicians, that the economy has to live within the ecology. Resource depletion or actual resource limits present a fundamental challenge to the accepted economic wisdom, which treats resources like oil as consumables, when they should be considered (natural) capital.

The counter argument to these criticisms is that market-based capitalism has lifted more people out of poverty than any other development effort, and that alternatives such as the centrally planned economy have been tried and failed.

Current thinking

Historically, classical economics has not taken very much account of environmental or resource factors.[6] [7] [8] Where it does, it assumes a 'technofix' can sort out every problem.[9] There is a concept in economics called 'elasticity of substitution' which assumes a balance between 'capital' (machinery, factories etc.) and environmental resources.[10] When one of these (environmental resources) diminishes, the other increases to make up.[11] [12] Classical economists also argue that productivity, skills and knowledge can also make up any environmental/resource shortfall for a very long time.[13] They also believe that as commodity prices rise it becomes economically viable to extract resources that were previously considered too difficult and expensive to exploit.[14]

Green growth

Part of the problem in trying to critique the conventional economic view is that it is very dominant and few people work outside its current strictures. However, the growing realisation that climate change might threaten this world view has led to some new thinking on economics. Perhaps the best known is Sir Nicolas Stern who was chief economist at the World Bank. The UK government asked him to write a report on the economics of climate change, which he did in 2006.[15] The *Stern Review on the Economics of Climate Change* was published predominately to get the world (and in particular the US) to sign a binding treaty on climate change and has to be seen that context. The review had verbal brickbats thrown at it by all sides of the argument. While it has much that is useful in it, the Stern Review does have some shortcomings. Stern seems to have over-looked resource constraints like peak oil as an issue. His headline recommendation was that we could head off the problem of climate change by spending only 1 per cent of gross domestic product on measures to reduce emissions – a figure that seems absurdly low (if so, why aren't we doing this?). But its overarching conclusion was that 'green growth' (i.e. growth that does not damage the environ-ment) was possible; this was reiterated in his book.[16] In 2012 the World Bank published a report saying the same thing.[17] Criticism of this general view rests on the following points from a paper written by Professor Cleveland of Boston University. We have covered each point briefly and attempt to explain them by means of examples.[18]

- *Limits of the market and technology.* How much technological substitution is really possible? If some natural resources are depleting they may not be replaceable.
- *The role of energy in technical change.* The review paper by Cleveland makes a very interesting point that of all the technologies humans have developed or discovered, two have had more impact than any others – fire and the heat engine (this is a technical way of saying a steam engine or an internal combustion engine). The heat engine provides more excess energy than fire, allows us to do more with this energy, and we get dependent on this excess. How-ever, this excess energy is now in decline (this is covered in more detail at the start of Chapter 4).
- *Do rising incomes improve environmental quality?* There is an assumption in classical economics that rising incomes lead to less pollution and environmental damage, but this has been proven only in the case of a few pollutants where the cost of mitigation was low.[19] Overall the theory is unproven, and in fact the opposite may be true. In any case it takes no account of something running out.

- *Countervailing forces: rising affluence and the rebound effect.* We mentioned this in Chapter 4. The principle here is that, human nature being what it is, if you save money by for example buying a less polluting car, chances are you will spend that money on something else that inevitably depletes and/or pollutes, so undoing the good you might have done.

- *Thermodynamics limits substitution.* This criticism focuses in on the fact that there are physical limits on the efficiency of energy conversion, and these reduce our options for substituting one technology with another. The classic example of this is the idea of the hydrogen economy (see Chapter 5).

- *Complementarity limits substitution.* Manufactured capital (e.g. an oil refinery) and natural capital (e.g. crude oil) are complementary, the two together produce a flow of useful product. However, without crude, the refinery on its own is useless – it can't substitute for the oil.

- *Physical interdependence and scale limits substitution.* An example of this is that, in a household, putting in extra insulation can reduce heating fuel use: the insulation effectively substitutes for the oil. However, at the national level, if everyone is using insulation, this has to be manufactured using energy – that is, there is a complicated interdependency between the manufactured and natural capital. Thus, producing more of the 'substitute' – manufactured capital – requires more of the thing that it is supposed to substitute for.

- *Irreversibility limits substitution.* If you degrade an ecosystem too far (e.g. forests), then you may have no wood left to use. This is one theory about what happened to the inhabitants of Easter Island.

- *Market signals aren't always a reliable compass.* Market prices aren't always reliable. For example with wave and tidal power, these technologies are years away from being cost-effective and deployed in the seas on a large scale, but the potential energy resource is huge. At present they need subsidy since energy companies would never invest in them without that.

- *Uncertainty, ignorance and the unintended side-effects of technology.* Technology can have downsides. There are numerous examples of where technology has produced a different result to that intended. Nuclear power, which was predicted to be 'too cheap to meter', has been abandoned by many countries because of uncertainties over cost, reliability and waste. Technology has brought massive benefits to humankind; however, the negative effects must also be included in any analysis.

Before we give up completely and decide that green growth is an oxymoron, there is one bit of research that does give some credence to the opposite view. Chris Goodall, a businessman and former Green Party candidate in England has done some private research using UK government statistics on what are called the UK material flow accounts (these measure the physical resources such as energy and waste used by a country). What he found surprised him.[20] For the UK, all of these had peaked, that is, we are using less oil, producing less waste etc. But what was more surprising was when these flows had peaked, it was all well before the global slump, when the economy was growing fast.[21] Could it be that economic growth can be decoupled from use of resources?

The static economy and other alternative economic models

If the jury is still out on Chris Goodall's findings (for instance what about other countries?), are there any economic models that take into account peak oil? There are few economists who have thought about the limits of resources and economic growth. Christian economist Herman Daly is one of this select group, as is another Christian, the late Dr David Fleming. Other individuals and groups described below have also been involved in this field for some of their work.

In 2008 Daly wrote a short paper summarising his work, entitled 'A Steady State Economy.'[22] A steady state is one that has no overall change but is not at rest or equilibrium. What Daly is suggesting in our reading of the report is an economy that runs very, very slowly.

Goods are designed to be extremely durable (and presumably highly recyclable, although he doesn't say this). The population shows no growth (low birth and death rates) and there is very high income redistribution with both a minimum and maximum wage. The only growth part of the economy would be action to combat poverty. Trade between nations would be substantially reduced, with only countries that have agreed the same economic model being allowed to trade (otherwise ones that hadn't would gain an economic advantage). Taxation would shift from income to those things that are bad for the environment or are non-renewable. The economy would be measured not just by its growth but by a measurement of how bad that growth could be for it. Daly does not claim to have all the answers; for example he is unsure whether such an economy could support full employment (his counter argument is that he doesn't think the current globalised one can either). Daly also thinks that such an economy could not support, as he puts it, an 'enormous pyramid of debt that is precariously balanced atop the real economy, threatening to crash' (written before the 2008 crash).

Another economist, Tim Jackson, wrote a report in 2009 for the Sustainable Development Commission called 'Prosperity Without Growth'; he later wrote a book with the same title.[23] He called for government intervention and spending on infrastructure (particularly renewable infrastructure) and regulation of markets concerning lending and financial instruments. In addition, he wanted green bonds and community bonds to encourage saving, new ways of measuring GDP to take into account social needs, sharing work more equally by altering the work–life balance through lower working hours and tackling inequality. Finally, he suggested using happiness indicators to measure prosperity, localisation on a Transition model (see Chapter 9), a carbon ration or some other such alternative, and technology transfer of low-carbon technologies to developing countries.[24]

Dr David Fleming wanted localisation of the economy down to a parish level and tradable energy quotas (see in Chapter 9).[25] He wanted almost all energy to be produced locally and operate the economy almost as some kind of closed system.

In 2010 the New Economics Foundation think-tank published a report called the *The Great Transition*. This takes many of the ideas above under seven headings linking the financial crash, peak oil and climate change. 'Great Revaluing' calls for environmental and social goals to be the central goal of policy-making; it uses some of Herman Daly's ideas on taxation (the UK government's happiness index is a small step in this direction). The 'Great Redistribution' redistributes wealth and assets over 10–20 years in five different waves, it also envisages redistributing time (working hours) and carbon emissions (this latter point implies tradable energy quotas although they are not mentioned). The 'Great Rebalancing' envisages markets being regulated to take into account social and ecological goals. 'Great Localisation' uses some of David Fleming's and the Transition movement's ideas concerning local businesses, co-operatives, local control of the economy and local currencies. The next idea, 'Great Reskilling', is classic Transition movement territory, and also covers local energy co-ops. The 'Great Irrigation' envisages using taxation to bring about these aims; it also suggests setting up a green bank (we note that this has been in done in the UK although it will start with limited capital). Finally, the 'Great Interdependence' looks forward to the UK taking part in international treaties on carbon emissions but conversely importing less, particularly less energy.

In 2012 the Royal Society published a report, *People and the Planet*, which looks at the whole area of sustainability, natural ecosystems, finite resources and economic growth. It makes a number of general recommendations which fit in with much of what is written above (alternative ways of measuring GDP, alternative economic models such as that suggested by Herman Daly, consumers paying the currently externalised costs of pollution, and the need for the rich developed countries to reduce consumption to allow others to increase theirs). There are two recommendations that have not featured elsewhere. The first is the idea of a circular economy, which is one where almost everything is recycled.[26] The second is that of addressing population growth.

We do not have space to cover all their arguments on population but we would recommend the reader looks at the Royal Society report, because it is an excellent primer on this issue.[27] Most environmentalists have avoided the issue of population until recently for a variety of reasons.[28] In recent years this has changed, with two

high-profile thinkers, Jonathan Porritt and George Monbiot, taking
diametrically opposite views.[29] These are summarised by Monbiot's
'Population growth is not a problem – it's among those who
consume the least', and Jonathan Porritt's belief that the earth has a
finite 'carrying capacity'. The global population currently is in the
order of 7 billion, with projected future growth in a range of 8.1 to
10.6 billion people, although there are some estimates that it could
go far higher. No one really knows what population the Earth could
support ('carrying capacity') and estimates of this figure tend to
depend on which side of the argument above you are on.[30] However, the rate of population increase has declined since its peak in the
1960s, as has mortality.[31] [32] This fertility drop has largely been
achieved by the education of women, alongside the increased
availability of contraception, also more controversially by sterilisa-
tion and abortion.[33] The Royal Society essentially side with
Jonathan Porritt. The problem is that both sides are partly correct.
We need to reduce the global population for environmental and
resource reasons. However, given the urgency of climate change and
resource depletion, the policy levers are extremely limited.

Lastly, the Transition movement, which we examine in its own
chapter, has started to think about what a new economy might look
like.[34] Their initiatives feature many of the ideas discussed above.
Their definition of localisation is worth reading. It is more about
economic activity at an appropriate scale: 'In some cases national and
globalised systems will be the best approach'.

Conclusions

Clearly the dominant economic model has produced huge benefits
for much of humankind. Yet its problems, and in particular its
inability to value creation and its resources in a way that is sustainable, fundamentally undermine the progress it has produced. But
what is the alternative? Green economics has some strengths, in that
it starts to take the environment into account, but also has obvious
shortcomings in that it still seems to assume that there are limitless
resources and therefore that conventional growth is possible.

Christians view economics essentially depending on their political viewpoint. The Bible (especially the New Testament) says little

about how an economic system should operate. One approach is found in the book of Isaiah. In this passage, the prophet Isaiah instructs on true and false worship. True worship is seen in the following manner:

> 'This is the kind of fast day I'm after:
>   to break the chains of injustice,
>   get rid of exploitation in the workplace,
>   free the oppressed, cancel debts.
>
> What I'm interested in seeing you do is:
>   sharing your food with the hungry,
>   inviting the homeless poor into your homes,
>   putting clothes on the shivering ill-clad,
>   being available to your own families.'

> (Isaiah 58:6,7, The Message Bible)

These and other verses in this chapter suggest that charity is required, but also the need to break structural economic sin. In the various ideas we discussed above, we saw that some people are starting to feel around for an alternative economics. For free market-ers reading this book there is both good news and bad news. The good news is that all the people we quoted above see a role for markets. No one wants Marxism or centrally planned economies (which were mostly not good for the environment too). The bad news is that they want a lot more government intervention, control of markets, localisation (with trade mostly within countries), ration-ing and/or taxation of non-renewable resources, and redistribution of wealth. They consider this last point important not only because countries with better equality of wealth are happier places, with lower crime and better health outcomes, but also because the current economic system works on the basis of envy.[35] (As we discuss later, reducing materialism may be more difficult than we think, even with less material goods.) They all want new ways of measuring progress beyond GDP, measures which take into account happiness or ecological constraints. We think these general charac-teristics of a new economy fit with Isaiah's challenge, and are points that Christians should support. Isaiah goes on to say that building a more just society will make us fully human again.

> 'Your lives will begin to glow in the darkness,
>   your shadowed lives will be bathed in sunlight.
> I will always show you where to go.
> I'll give you a full life in the emptiest of places—
>   firm muscles, strong bones.
> You'll be like a well-watered garden,
>   a gurgling spring that never runs dry.
> You'll use the old rubble of past lives to build anew,
>   rebuild the foundations from out of your past.
> You'll be known as those who can fix anything,
>   restore old ruins, rebuild and renovate,
>   make the community livable again.'

(Isaiah 58:10–12, The Message Bible)

An alternative economic system is inevitable. Precisely what kind it will be we cannot say. The current system is like a merry-go-round going faster and faster, which no one wants to jump off first. The problem is the longer we delay the bigger the fall will be. We should start discussing and planning this new economy now rather than when it is forced upon us by events. Christians, though they may have differing views on economics, should be at the centre of this debate. Our value system should challenge that of the world as we seek God's Kingdom first.[36] We will leave the last word on this issue to Dr Fleming, with a telling comment on one part of the solution: 'Localisation stands, at best, at the limits of practical possibility, but it has the decisive argument in its favour that there will be no alternative.'

Notes

1   http://www.cid.harvard.edu/cidtrade/issues/washington.html. The originator of the term has tried to distance himself from the outcomes. It could be argued that for millions of people in China and India and now parts of Africa the system is working in that it has lifted them out of absolute poverty.

2   http://www.businessweek.com/news/2011-09-14/decline-in-u-s-income-raises-stakes-in-2012-presidentialrace;   html   and   http://www.businessweek.com/news/2012-03-28/u-dot-k-dot-economy-shrinks-more-than-firstestimated-on-services .

3   http://www.guardian.co.uk/business/2010/aug/19/philip-green-liberal-democrats-tax.

4   http://www.guardian.co.uk/commentisfree/2009/mar/08/comment-tax-avoidance. Also, Googling 'tax haven' and 'organised crime' brings up a lot of material.

5   *People and the Planet*, a report by the Royal Society, 2012.

6   *Ibid.*

7   H. Daly, 'Economics in a Full World', *Scientific American*, 2005.

8   *Inclusive Green Growth: The Pathway to Sustainable Development*, World Bank, 2012.

9   C. J. Cleveland, 'Biophysical Constraints to Economic Growth' in D. A. Gobaisi, editor-in-chief, *Encyclopedia of Life Support Systems*, EOLSS Publishers Co., 2003. This paper is essentially a review of this issue.

10   *People and the Planet*, a report by the Royal Society .

11   Cleveland, 'Biophysical Constraints to Economic Growth'.

12   *Inclusive Green Growth* .

13   Daly, 'Economics in a Full World'.

14   *People and the Planet*.

15   http://www.hm-treasury.gov.uk.

16   N. Stern, *A Blueprint for a Safer Planet: How to Manage Climate Change and Create a New Era of Progress and Prosperity*, The Bodley Head, 2009. The clue is the title really …

17   *Inclusive Green Growth*.

18   Cleveland, 'Biophysical Constraints to Economic Growth'.

19   *Ibid.*

20   http://www.guardian.co.uk/environment/2011/oct/31/consumption-of-goods-falling.

21   http://www.carboncommentary.com/wp-content/uploads/2011/10/Peak_Stuff_17.10.11.pdf.

22   H. Daly, *A Steady-State Economy*, SDC, 2008.

23   http://www.sd-commission.org.uk/publications.php?id=914.

24   Tim Jackson, *Prosperity without Growth? Transition to a Low Carbon Economy*, SDC, 2009.

25   http://www.theleaneconomyconnection.net/.

26   *Reinventing the Wheel: A Circular Economy for Resource Security*, Green alliance, 2011. This report gives a full description of what this term means.

27   Another   is   the   Christian   Medical   Fellowship.   See   http://www.cmf.org.uk/publications/cmf-files/ no.33.

28   http://www.jonathonporritt.com/blog/population-1. One reason is its

tendency to degenerate into eugenics. The view is poorer, less-educated and non-white people shouldn't be allowed to breed. This idea is totally at variance with scripture. God loves everyone equally without favour and died for all.

29   http://www.guardian.co.uk/commentisfree/cif-green/2009/sep/28/ population-growth-super-rich.

30   *People and the Planet.*

31   www.un.org/esa/population/publications/sixbillion/sixbilpart1.pdf.

32   *People and the Planet.*

33   *People and the Planet.*

34   http://www.reconomyproject.org/?p=1409.

35   P. Hanlon and G. McCartney, 'Peak Oil: Will it be Public Health's Greatest Challenge?', *Public Health* 122, 2008, pp. 647–52. Also see *The Great Transition* by the NEF, 2010.

36   John 15:19; 17:14; Matthew 6:33.

What are the consequences if we just carry on?

re·sil·ience
1. the power or ability to return to the original form, position,
etc., after being bent, compressed, or stretched; elasticity.
2. ability to recover readily from illness, depression, adversity, or
the like; buoyancy.

With a world that seems largely unaware that oil is a finite resource, what might the future look like if we continue living as we do now? We have argued in earlier chapters that there will be an energy shortfall in the years ahead, but what are the likely impacts? There are now many books on peak oil and its consequences, mostly published in the last decade. These provide a range of viewpoints, from the optimistic to the apocalyptic. There are also many well-researched reports by academics, task forces, policy institutes and industry analysts, which tend to be more circumspect in their predictions. All these have something to say and add to the broader view, but it can be tricky to reconcile the different opinions and come up with a coherent picture.

It is important to state that predicting the future can be a mug's game. It's been said that history is a record of the unexpected. A detailed prediction can become a hostage to fortune as events veer off in an unexpected direction. In the area of peak oil, unfortunately there have been many times when specific forecasts about the timing and impacts of energy depletion have turned out to be just plain wrong. For example, Andy recently read a book by a US writer on these issues.[1] Published in 2009, the book confidently outlined imminent energy shortages and the beginning of societal break-down within months. As I am writing this, three years later in early 2012, his predictions seem to have been unduly pessimistic, (though of course it is possible that only his timing is out!). Flawed predic-tions of this kind can seem to undermine the case that is being made, and there are even websites which collate and ridicule these mis-takes, accusing the writers of 'crying wolf'.[2] However, as well as getting things wrong, peak oil futurologists have got many facts right, including correctly predicting price spikes of the kind experi-enced in 2008 and since. Given that detailed predictions are danger-ous territory, what can we be confident about?

- *Global oil production will begin to decline.* This is likely to happen in the next few years, though (as discussed in Chapter 1) the exact timing is uncertain.
- *Shortages (or anticipation of shortages) produce high prices and hardship.* The economics of supply and demand determine the price of oil, with oil traders intensely analysing every piece of information as they speculate on what will happen to prices. In the past, even the perception of a tightening of supply has been enough to increase prices. Clearly actual shortages would be damaging for households and coun-tries that were unprepared.
- *High prices stimulate energy production, but reduce demand.* Back in 2008, the oil price reached a high of US$147 per barrel. High prices mean that prospecting and developing oil wells in difficult environments becomes economically viable. Expensive new technology which can recover more oil from old fields is justified. Mining tar sands in Canada and using steam to wash out the oil suddenly makes economic sense. Additionally high prices give a massive boost to the development of alternatives to oil. Another effect of high oil prices is to reduce consumption. Following the 2008 price spike, the global economy went into recession, and many people chose to use less oil. They drove less, they flew less, they turned down their heating to save money, and factories used less oil because they were

making fewer products. This 'demand destruction' had its effect – the price of oil fell back sharply to US$35 per barrel only a few months later.

- *Energy futures are complex and impacts are difficult to predict.* There is a relationship between energy supply, energy price and economic activity: High prices (as seen in 2008) cause a massive shock to the economy, oil demand is reduced and its price falls. As economic recovery takes place, demand recovers and prices rise. Some analysts predict that we are likely to see the oil price 'yoyo-ing' up and down over the next few years, with each price spike followed by an economic slowdown – potentially creating enormous hardship. However, energy supply, price and their effect on the world are incredibly difficult to predict, particularly where they interact with the human factor. Things could turn out very differently if the human race decided to change its behaviour.

People thinking about the future come up with a range of scenarios. At the optimistic end of the spectrum is the belief that things will pretty much continue as they have done before, with business as usual and a general trend of rising living standards. Given the technological advances that have occurred over previous decades, it's a reasonable world-view, based on past experience. Problems may occur, but solutions will be found. A combination of technology and human ingenuity will see us through. Our expectations are coloured by the dazzling technological success, from the moon landings to the latest iPhone. Visions of the future are provided by TV and film, from *Tomorrow's World* to *Avatar*. This is the dominant world-view in the developed world, espoused by intellectuals, scientists and opinion-formers. Many Christians, whatever their spiritual beliefs, would also subscribe to this viewpoint by default. This 'business-as-usual' world-view could be characterised as unthinking acceptance of the status quo. It limits political manoeuvre for issues such as climate change.

At the other end of the spectrum is the apocalyptic world-view. In the past nuclear war was a dominant concern. As this threat has receded, economic collapse, climate change and sometimes peak oil have taken its place. 'Doomsters' sometimes fixate on other possible causes of global disaster – such as an asteroid impact, or the eruption of the Yellowstone super-volcano, even coining their own disaster acronym TEOTWAWKI (the end of the world as we know it). Holders of this viewpoint are pessimistic about humankind's ability to deal with events, and see the comfortable lives we live today as temporary and unsustainable. Many Christians, particularly in the US, believe in apocalyptic end-times teaching drawing on parts of the Bible such as the books of Daniel and Revelation. However, the apocalyptic world-view is not limited to religious believers – there is a rich seam of it in popular culture. The *Hunger Games* books by Suzanne Collins imagine life in a dystopian future 100 years from now. *The Road* is a recent film version of Cormac McCarthy's bleak novel published in 2006, depicting a father and son as they journey through a post-apocalyptic landscape – and is only one of a slew of disaster movies in recent years. This theme is not limited to contemporary culture, a recent retrospective at the Tate Britain Gallery showcased the English painter John Martin, whose images of judgement and destruction found a huge audience in the eighteenth century. The idea of the apocalypse has taken hold in the popular secular imagination. Why this has happened is open to conjecture, possibly it's something to do with the financial crisis, or maybe the sheer number of problems both financial and environmental bearing down on humankind simultaneously.

In some ways these two ends of the spectrum are both myths. Unlimited economic growth is an overly optimistic view of humankind's progress, not being possible on a planet with finite resources. At the other end, apocalyptic concerns can be fatalistic ('we're doomed!'). A more balanced view would be to say that disastrous collapse happens only if we choose not to avoid it.

What follows are three future scenarios, based on looking back to today from the year 2030. As stated previously, predictions are difficult and quite possibly wrong; however, we offer these as three future routes that the world could follow. Although we are looking primarily at the impact of energy shortages, we include other factors. As stated elsewhere, this is not a book about climate change. However, we cannot ignore the prevailing scientific consensus that burning fossil fuels and the resulting carbon dioxide build-up in the atmosphere is leading to higher temperatures. We believe ignoring this will be increasingly impossible; therefore we include it in all the scenarios.

Scenario 1: 'Techno-fix'

The graphs show that oil production did peak and go into decline, but few people noticed. By 2015, after several years of high oil prices, it was *demand* for oil that peaked, as consumers found ways to do without it. A series of summits at the UN resulted in the adoption of a legally binding agreement to reduce demand for oil by 5 per cent per year. Once agreed, people found it easier than expected. Within two years the automotive industry had introduced a number of innovative vehicles which used far less fuel: Toyota's lightweight hybrid car ran on LPG and set new standards for frugality, and a breakthrough in battery technology by Renault extended the range of electric cars to several hundred miles. People still flew, but less often. The high fuel price had put half the world's airlines out of business, and flying was very expensive. Some aircrew even retrained as insulation fitters: the government's emergency insulation scheme introduced in 2017 was a great success. Millions of homes were insulated using huge numbers of previously unem-ployed workers to do compulsory energy audits and upgrading homes to the new efficiency standards. The use of feed-in tariffs meant that by 2020 most home-owners had fitted some kind of micro-generation technology, with thin-film solar panels being particularly popular. With the huge North Sea and Irish Sea wind farms now in place, renewable energy production had soared. Green electricity was whizzing around Europe on the new supergrid, and with smart meters in every home the supply of electricity could be managed far more efficiently. As renewable energy came on stream, most of the gas and coal plants were mothballed.

It wasn't all good news though. Food prices had rocketed and some items were in short supply. Material goods were more expen-sive and scarce, most were now made in the country rather than being imported. While carbon emissions were continually falling, the problems from historical emissions of CO_2 continued, although a mitigation fund helped developing countries, which had also suffered greatly from higher oil prices. One problem of the rapid deployment of the 'sustainable revolution' was that, once most houses had been insulated and fitted with micro-generation, work dried up and unemployment began growing. There was controversy over population control (most western countries introduced tax incentives for those having one child), and debate continued over GM food and onshore wind turbines. Since people swapped fossil fuel cars for electric cars and still used them for short commutes, ironically their very success put the electricity grid under strain. But these were all minor concerns. Overall the economy continued to grow, with hi-tech and food companies leading the way.

By 2030 CO_2 emissions are falling rapidly (along with oil production) and most electricity comes from a wide variety of renewable sources. Although only the wealthiest can afford to fly, a network of high-speed trains spans continents, and though people travel less, a joined-up public transport system gets them from A to B quickly and without pollution. Oil is now viewed by traders as simply one energy commodity among many. It is hard to believe we used to think it was so important.

Scenario 2: Disintegration

The Saudi Arabians kept very quiet about it, but in 2014 production from the world's largest oilfield – Ghawar in Saudi Arabia – went into steep decline. As oil demand started to outstrip supply, the price moved upwards once again – and kept on going. By 2015 it had reached US$250 per barrel, as supply tightened. The problem for many people was not the price of fuel, but simply not being able to get hold of it. Panic buying had led to petrol shortages and queues at the pumps, and the supply of fuel became intermittent. What was worse was the confusion. Governments did not seem to have any answers, or even an explanation for it, with ministers blaming the oil companies for lack of investment and oil-price speculators for profiteering. In off-the-record conversations with journalists, they blamed China and the exclusive oil supply contracts it had signed with Iran and other Middle Eastern countries. Nobody talked about geology or declining production. In America the President ordered substantial releases of fuel from the national reserve, and removed all restrictions on oil exploration. By 2016 world economies were rapidly contracting as businesses folded and unemployment soared. The UK government began a twin-track strategy, continuing to encourage renewable energy but also initiating an emergency programme to re-open the coal mines closed 30 years ago.

Inconsistent fuel supplies played havoc with the supermarkets' distribution logistics, so that while there was plenty of food sitting in warehouses and cold stores, often shop shelves were empty. When delivery lorries did arrive, Tesco staff found themselves having to operate a rough and ready rationing system to maintain order, with customers limited to just one basket of produce each. Farmers' markets were suddenly the busiest places, with stalls being swept clean of produce in a few minutes of frantic selling. A new middle-class fad came into being, moving to the country, buying land and aiming for self-sufficiency. The cold winter of 2017 was when things started to go badly wrong. With the pound dropping in value, the utility companies were unable to afford consistent imports of gas and energy was rationed. Many thousands of older people succumbed to hypothermia and other ailments in their own homes, as cold, lack of food and the collapsing healthcare system took their toll. Trees suddenly started disappearing from urban parks and gardens as desperate people chopped them up for fuel. Even water supplies became erratic, as companies struggled to obtain energy to treat water.

The year 2018 saw the first food riots in cities across the country, beginning a lengthy period of civil unrest. By the end of the year families living in the country were starting to find relatives from the cities arriving on their doorsteps – nephews, cousins, sometimes whole families needing a place to stay 'just for a few weeks, until things settle down'.

In 2020 London, Edinburgh and other cities saw the return of smog after 70 years.

Increased coal burning also meant soaring CO_2 emissions, and the climate was showing significant signs of change – weather patterns far outside the normal parameters, with erratic rainfall and extreme weather events becoming more common. Coastal flooding became more frequent as sea levels rose.

In 2030 many countries have no effective central government. International tensions over access to energy have resulted in several wars, but nobody has the capacity to fight a full-scale conflict any more. Fuel is rationed, but by price rather than any formal mechanism. The countryside is full of people eking out an existence of sorts on small plots of land abandoned by farmers, who don't have the fuel to farm them.

Scenario 3: Muddling through

The economic turmoil that had begun in 2008 continued for most of the next decade. Recessions were followed by short periods of sluggish growth, with the price of energy rising and falling with demand, and by 2015 the double-dip recession had become a triple-dip. Eventually the reason became clear: oil production had peaked. This was confirmed at an emergency meeting of heads of governments at the UN, when the Saudi representative announced that his country was experiencing production difficulties and would be unable to meet expected export volumes for the foreseeable future.

This revelation by the world's largest oil producer was a profound shock to the markets, but was swiftly followed by a similar statement from other OPEC producers. The oil price soared briefly to US$300/barrel before trading in oil futures was suspended. By then a number of countries had already instigated emergency conservation measures. Speed limits were reduced to 55mph and sales of petrol and diesel were rationed to avoid panic buying.

After lengthy negotiations an oil depletion protocol was adopted by most countries, a binding agreement to reduce oil demand so as to stretch supplies. Canada was one of the high-profile dissenters, preferring instead to ramp up oil production from its tar sands.

Globally economic growth stalled, inflation was high, and unemployment rose around the world. In Asia car sales and use continued to grow strongly, but in Europe and America sales fell, and the only cars that sold were smaller, more energy efficient models. A few electric cars were sold, but they remained expensive. Flying declined due to a steady increase in costs, and plans for a new London airport were quietly shelved. There was a renaissance in cycling, and it became common to see more bikes than cars. Despite governments cutting feed-in tariffs, renewable energy continued to grow steadily, particularly solar PV which saw a rapid increase in uptake as its costs fell. Higher energy prices meant buildings were gradually made more energy efficient. Due to the high oil price, the cost of food and chemicals rose, and around the world people went hungry as supplies of staple foods such as rice and maize fell short. Consumer goods became scarcer and more expensive, and as a result there was a revival of the skills required to repair things. Manufacturing gradually moved back to the West from China due to higher transportation costs and rising wages in China, although overall production still fell.

By 2020 the effects of climate change such as storms, droughts and floods were increasingly evident. After much deliberation and debate, the heads of governments reached a legally binding agreement to cut carbon emissions by 80 per cent by the year 2050. Even though climate scientists warned that this was too little, too late, the US President was unable to get Congress to ratify the agreement, although a watered-down lower target was later passed.

In 2030 oil production is significantly lower than in 2012. The world has made a wrenching adjustment to the new circumstances. Commercial aviation is a distant memory, and driving a luxury, but total collapse has been avoided. People are poorer, hungrier, many have no job, and they have to make do with less, but life still goes on.

All of these scenarios are flawed and simplistic. It is possible that elements from all of these, or from other visions (better or worse) may play a part as the future unfolds. The alert reader will have noticed common threads running through all of them. First, there is a lack of time before significant changes start to occur. Second, all three scenarios show humankind responding to the circumstances we face. But what if, instead of simply responding, we were proactive, actively planning for the future? This is the heart of an idea called Transition, an exciting movement conceived here in the UK, and the subject of the next chapter.

Notes

1   M. C. Ruppert, *Confronting Collapse*, Chelsea Green Publishing, 2009.
2   www.peakoildebunked.blogspot.com.

9

Transition – what's the big idea?

Maybe all this [Transition initiatives] sounds a bit goody-two-shoes to you – a bit ecofreaky – but what's wrong with that? We've been here before. When our food supplies were threatened in the last war the government urged us to dig for victory ... and we did. Never in our history have we had a more healthy diet. And the fact is that people are responding to Transition schemes. They're packing town and village halls around the country to support them. You don't believe there's any need even to think about this sort of thing? You reckon this latest oil crisis is just another scare and the danger of global warming is being exaggerated? Well maybe you're right. I hope you are. But if you're wrong, doesn't it make sense to think local rather than rely on politicians at national and world level to get us out of the mess they've helped create?

John Humphrys, *Sunday Mirror*, 25 November 2007

In the previous chapter we speculated what life might be like over the next couple of decades. A common thread in all three scenarios was humankind having to cope with the problems of resource depletion. In none of them did humanity voluntarily face up to peak oil. In this chapter we set out not just another scenario but another world-view: that proposed by the Transition movement.

History

The Transition concept started with Rob Hopkins. In September 2004 he was lecturing in permaculture[1] at a further education college in Kinsale, Ireland; he arranged for his students to watch the documentary film *The End of Suburbia*,[2] followed by a lecture on peak oil by a visiting speaker, Professor Colin Campbell of the Association for the Study of Peak Oil (ASPO). For Hopkins and his students it was a sudden and shocking immersion into the realities of energy depletion. He describes the effect as a 'double whammy', but what emerged was positive – a project in which Hopkins and his students envisaged how the town of Kinsale would manage without oil. After a lot of research and a community consultation exercise, they produced a document called the Kinsale Energy Descent Action Plan, detailing the steps the community would have to take to become less dependent on oil. The plan Hopkins and his students produced proved to be a significant step forward in formulating a response to future energy constraints.[3] When Hopkins moved to Totnes in Devon soon after, he continued to develop his ideas and these became the first Transition Initiative, Transition Town Totnes, launched in September 2006.[4] (The name refers to the *transition* from oil dependence to local resilience.) Other people concerned about peak oil and climate change were soon contacting him and several communities started to adopt the same idea. In 2008 Hopkins published *The Transition Handbook*, which explains the transition idea and sets out the steps communities can take to become more resilient. In the years since then the concept of Transition has gone 'viral', and worldwide there are now nearly one thousand initiatives underway.

What is it?

Perhaps we should start with what it is not. It is not just an environmental organisation. It is not political, in that it engages with all political parties and none. It is best described as a community-based attempt to tackle peak oil and climate change at a local level – the Transition movement's view is that these two problems are related and will deliver a series of economic and social shocks. The key idea behind the Transition movement is that of building resilience into communities, so that they can withstand these shocks. So, for example, growing more food locally would shield the community from climate-change-induced shortages or supply disruptions if oil runs short. In building local resilience, community involvement and environmental action is combined. This can be at a city, district, town or village level or even at a university (Edinburgh University has declared itself a Transition university).

The concept is best described in Rob Hopkins own words:

> Transition Initiatives are based on four key assumptions:
>
> 1. That life with dramatically lower energy consumption is inevitable, and that it's better to plan for it than to be taken by surprise.
> 2. That our settlements and communities presently lack the resilience to enable them to weather the severe energy shocks that will accompany peak oil.
> 3. That we have to act collectively, and we have to act now.
> 4. That by unleashing the collective genius of those around us to creatively and proactively design our energy descent, we can build ways of living that are more connected, more enriching and that recognize the biological limits of our planet.
>
> The future with less oil could, if enough thinking and design is applied sufficiently in advance, be preferable to the present. There is no reason why a lower-energy, more resilient future needs to have a lower quality of life than the present. Indeed the future with a revitalized local economy would have many advantages over the present, including a happier and less stressed population, an improved environment and increased stability.[5]

The aim of transition is for a community to devise and implement an energy descent plan which covers key areas such as food production, energy, transport and building. In each of these areas energy consumption must be reduced, or local sustainable energy production increased, so that the community becomes less and less dependent on uncertain imported energy, and increasingly dependent on its own resources and skills.

Many of the ideas and concerns of the Transition movement, such as renewable energy and local food production, have been on the environmental agenda for many years, but what makes Transition distinctly different is the way these ideas are linked within a collective community vision. Environmentalists have often painted a graphic picture of environmental meltdown as a warning to change damaging behaviours. The sort of positive vision of a low-energy yet abundant future that comes out of Transition seems to be more positive and compelling. The differences that Rob Hopkins sees between the conventional environmental outlook and the new Transition approach are summarised in Table 1 below.

Conventional environmentalism	The Transition Approach
Individual behaviour	Group behaviour
Single issue	Holistic
Tools: lobbying, campaigning and protesting	Tools: public participation, eco-psychology, arts, culture and creative education
Sustainable development	Resilience/relocalisation
Fear, guilt and shock as drivers for action	Hope, optimism and proactivity as drivers for action
Changing National and International policy by lobbying	Changing National and International policy by making them electable
The man in the street is the problem	The man in the street is the solution
Blanket campaigning	Targeted interventions
Single level engagement	Engagement on a variety of levels
Prescriptive – advocates answers and responses	Acts as a catalyst – no fixed answers
Carbon footprinting	Carbon footprinting plus resilience indicators
Belief economic growth is still possible, albeit greener growth	Designing for economic renaissance, albeit a local one

Table 1: Differences in approach between Transition and conventional environmental campaigning, taken from *The Transition Handbook*.

The differences in the two approaches are best illustrated for Neil by a recent BBC Radio 4 play *Getting to Zero*. In this entertaining comedy three real-life environmentalists, George Monbiot, Paul

Allen and Peter Harper (playing themselves), were set the task of reducing a fictional family's carbon emissions. They do this by taking away the family's car, altering their diet and removing many of the energy-using devices from the house, etc. However, leaving aside the compulsion factor and that the whole process came across as negative (if funny), the most controversial aspect was removing the family's freezer. Even in climate change terms this seemed a mistake, but from a Transition perspective, trying to build the household's resilience this definitely does not make sense. Of course it is good to have a very energy-efficient freezer and defrost it regularly. But growing food in the summer months in their garden and then freezing it for use throughout the year would make them less reliant on bought-in food.

While Transition initiatives often start with those who have already been campaigning on green issues, they seem to have the knack of drawing other people in. This may be because the first stage of the Transition process is raising awareness of the problems of peak oil and climate change, and seeking widespread community involvement.

How do you get involved?

If you live in a large town or city there may already be a Transition initiative somewhere in your area. If not, there are various resources available that would help a group of people set one up. Two of Rob Hopkins' books, *The Transition Handbook*, published in 2008, and *The Transition Companion*, published in 2011, are very useful reference points. There is also a Transition network website which carries the movement's news, as well as information about the location of existing Transition initiatives, and how to start one.[6]

What has Transition achieved?

For a movement that has spread around the globe, the central organisation is tiny, consisting of a handful of full-time staff assisted by volunteers. (Perhaps this is because Transition is really an idea rather than an organisation.) Apart from the website mentioned above, they have made two films. *Transition 1.0* provides an introduction to the whole idea and covers the early years of the movement, with examples from across the world of the things that have been achieved. The second film, *Transition 2.0*, was released in March 2012 and brings the story up to date. Some examples from the films and others known to us are given below.

Raising awareness

One of the significant achievements of the movement has been to provide people with a positive, viable alternative to the mainstream, consumer society. The first stage of any Transition initiative is raising awareness – firstly of the problems that humankind is facing, and then secondly the positive steps that people can take to mitigate these. Neil has been involved in several stalls for Transition Edinburgh where they have tried to raise awareness of peak oil. In 2008 they had a stall at the Forestry Commission's Woodland Fair. This was at the time when oil prices were near their all-time peak. They had a variety of responses, from denial that there was a problem, to wanting to join the Transition group. In 2011 Neil was involved with the stall at the Meadows Festival in Edinburgh. At this event there seemed to be less scepticism. The aims were to sign people up for the bulk purchase of solar panels, do a sustainability questionnaire, recruit new members and sign people up for energy surveys.

After a period of awareness-raising, local Transition initiatives launch their activities using what is known as an 'unleashing' event. This is described as 'a celebration of place, history and the possibilities of a low-carbon, post-oil future.'[7] At the unleashing of Transition Totnes the local mayor gave a speech and several people talked about peak oil. Andy went to the unleashing event at Transition Bungay in Suffolk, an evening which included a peak oil talk by author Shaun Chamberlin, a visioning exercise, music, food, discussion and networking. Lots of groups show relevant films such as *The End of Suburbia*.

Positive visioning

What sounds like some kind of New Age psychobabble is in fact a hugely useful tool for creative thinking about how the future could look. The process of Transition involves asking the question, 'What would we like our community to be in, say, 2025 or 2030, bearing in mind the energy constraints that we will face?' Having thought this through and come up with some ideas of what a good community might look and feel like, the next challenge is to set out the steps needed to get there. As Rob Hopkins writes:

> The tool of visioning offers a powerful new approach for environmental campaigners. We have become so accustomed to campaigning against things that we have lost sight of where it is that we want to go ... [We must] paint a compelling and engaging vision of a post-carbon world in such a way as to enthuse others to embark on a journey towards it.[8]

We are bombarded with positive visions every day in adverts, magazines and television programmes. In Transition the idea of contentment from things we could own or experience is turned on its head, and instead the vision is of how we could be content or even happier in a world with less energy and lower consumption.

Local currencies

This is one of the most high-profile ideas put forward by the movement and is shown in both of the Transition films. This concept was not invented by the movement; local 'currencies' are found all over the world, and here in the UK a scheme called LETS (Local Exchange Trading System) was a forerunner of what is happening today. The idea behind a local currency (technically speaking, a voucher for legal reasons) is to help build a vibrant local economy, keep money circulating within the area and stop it ending up in the bank accounts of large corporations. Rob Hopkins uses the image of money leaking out of a community like holes in a bucket, but the local currency won't fit through the holes. In the designated area pounds sterling can be exchanged for the local currency, usually at a rate of 1:1. Shops and businesses in this area can opt to accept payment with the local currency – and give it out as change. Totnes was the first town to do this when it launched the 'Totnes Pound' initially as an experiment in March 2007. Lewes, Brixton in London and other initiatives have followed suit. Surveys have shown that using local currencies to buy local food can re-circulate money in the community 2.5 times over, but buying food at a supermarket only 1.4 times over.[9] Future energy constraints will make our lives much more localised, and local currencies are one tool which could help communities become more self-reliant, less dependent on goods and services from far away, and therefore less dependent on oil.

It is fair to say the results have been mixed, with some people treating the notes simply as souvenirs for collection, but the schemes have attracted a high profile with national media attention.[10] Some economists have questioned whether they do what they are supposed to – stimulate the local economy, but the idea remains an interesting experiment and the results will become clear in time. As Hopkins wrote in response to a critic of this idea:

> firstly these [local currencies] are all experimental, and no-one claims to have yet created the ideal model ... secondly, you state that just issuing a local currency will make no significant difference ... you may be right, but you underestimate, I think, the potential of a well-designed local currency scheme as an awareness raising tool that can start to get people asking all kinds of questions about money and our relationship to it. It is, in effect, mindful money, and we rarely take into account the impacts of that.

In 2012 the largest currency yet, the Bristol pound, will launch, the first time this idea has been tried on a city-wide scale with a potential user base of over 1 million people.[11] Interestingly Greeks are setting up local currencies as a means of coping with their financial crisis.[12]

Landshare

After local currencies, landshare has attracted the most attention. Technically speaking this is not a Transition initiative, though it was inspired by an idea tried in Transition Totnes where people who had spare land (usually gardens) paired up with people requiring land to grow vegetables. The TV chef Hugh Fearnley-Whittingstall heard about the Totnes scheme, featured it on his TV programme *River Cottage* and, inspired by it, set up a national scheme called Landshare modelled on the Totnes idea.[13] A member of Neil's church has two people using part of her garden through this scheme. On the Landshare website each party signs up and posts their offer or request for land. Using postcodes, a Google map shows what is happening in a particular area and then landowners and potential growers can contact one another. In addition the site advertises gardening equipment, advice and even jobs.

Oral histories

One of the steps of Transition is to 'honour the elders' – the idea being that many older people have practical skills (see 'Re-skilling' below) and detailed knowledge about the local area. Many Transition groups have interviewed locals about the past.[14] In Totnes Rob Hopkins heard about several market gardens that had previously existed close to the centre of the town, providing fruit and vegetables. He also learnt that these had eventually been closed and paved over to make car parks! Without looking at the past through rose-tinted spectacles, this exercise can both show you that within living memory the economy was more localised and can give you some pointers as to how it could be again.

Re-skilling

Over the authors' lifetime people have gradually lost the ability to use a variety of important but mundane skills (e.g. how to garden, sew, knit, make jam and repair things). It is not that these skills have been totally forgotten, but that the people with these skills tend to be older, with many younger people either not having the opportunity or the interest to learn. As we cover later in the book, we think this matters (although there is a balance to be struck since many of these activities create employment). Re-skilling is a key part of Transition, and many initiatives hold training sessions in practical skills.[15]

Food

The security of our food supply is one of the major concerns for those aware of future energy constraints, and has been an early target for transition groups. Many groups such as Transition Carwen and PEDAL (Portobello Transition) have started planting orchards, more groups are planning to do the same. PEDAL has also started a farmers' market to promote local food. Other groups have set up food businesses such as bakeries, food co-ops and community-supported agriculture schemes. Transition groups around Edinburgh obtained money from the Scottish government's Climate Challenge Fund to promote local food production. North Howe Transition Town in Fife opened a community pub and a bakery.[16] Another example of community enterprise is the Slaithwaite Green Valley Grocer in West Yorkshire, which features in the second Transition film. This initiative came about when the local community had warning that their grocer was closing. They held a public meeting and established that there was enough support to rent the premises and set up a co-operative. After a successful share issue, they invited the local mayor to officially open the shop. Another co-operative business (a bakery) shares the premises, increasing both their trade. The baker raised capital by issuing shares in future bread production. Slaithwaite Green Valley Grocer aims to source as locally as possible and will buy garden produce brought into the shop.

Energy

Many Transition groups have made efforts in energy conservation and local energy production. Transition Edinburgh South used money from the Climate Challenge Fund to employ staff to work with householders on reducing energy consumption, and like other Transition groups have worked to organise bulk purchases of micro-generation equipment after the feed-in tariff was launched. Other groups such as Transition town Cheltenham are getting more ambitious, launching local energy co-ops.[17] The idea is to use community buildings such as schools or local government offices. These have PV panels fitted and get the benefits of lower bills, while those who have invested in the co-op receive a dividend from the feed-in-tariff revenue.

Tradable energy quotas (TEQs)

One proposal that is strongly associated with the Transition movement (but did not originate within it) is the idea of tradable energy

quotas, a radical long-term solution to rising energy bills and energy
depletion. This is a form of carbon rationing invented by economist
Dr David Fleming, but since his death taken forward by others.[18] In
principle the scheme is very simple: all adult members of the
population would have an entitlement to a certain amount of energy
use each week, given as TEQ units on an electronic card – (similar to
the Oyster card used to pre-pay for using the London transport
system). Other energy users such as government, industry etc.
would bid for their units at a weekly auction. When purchasing fuel,
electricity, or any type of transportation tickets, the corresponding
energy requirements are deducted from your card. Users who don't
use their full entitlement of units can sell the surplus, and if someone
needs more, they can buy them. However, the overall number of
units issued to everyone falls every year, with the percentage
decrease set by the climate change committee.

The key point about TEQs is that they provide an incentive for
everyone to reduce their energy consumption – and therefore the
whole country's energy use and emissions as a result. People would
quickly become aware of how much energy they use, and seek to
reduce it. Another advantage of such a scheme is that it is fair and
redistributive (poorer people might struggle with bills but tend not
to fly or use much energy, so should have excess units to sell). In
addition the TEQ system has an important philosophical basis in that
it assumes everyone has an equal right to pollute; if they want to use
more than their allowance, they must pay for the privilege. TEQs
also allow the user to decide their own lifestyle priorities, at least in
the short to medium term.

While the idea itself is simple, implementing it would be complex. Notwithstanding the difficulty of getting political approval,
there are a whole series of issues to be resolved. For example, do you
give the allowance to prisoners? What about people who have
learning difficulties, and at what age would you qualify for your own
quota?[19] One problem is that in some ways the system would give
you too much choice. (A fictional account of the introduction of
carbon rationing was written about in the *Carbon Diaries* series of
books by Sacci Lloyd, where one of the elderly characters spends the
proceeds from selling his excess points on drink and cigarettes.)
People who live in energy-inefficient houses should use their excess

units to improve them, but human nature being what it is, they may not. Another issue in the early years is that the rich might just buy extra units instead of conserving energy. However, as the quota of units gradually falls, even the wealthy would not be able to do this after a while.

Despite the difficulties and complexity, the concept of TEQs has much to recommend it. It has a fairness and equity which is compelling. It has advantages over another suggestion made by climate scientist James Hansen of a rising tax on fossil fuels with the proceeds returned as a dividend on a per capita basis. This latter idea is a tax (therefore a harder sell) and also doesn't put people as much in touch with their energy use. Under the TEQ scheme, to have excess points to sell you have to conserve energy or install carbon-saving technologies ... it's not a right, it has to be earned. In the coming era of depletion, energy will be rationed, it's just a case of whether it is done by high market prices – which is crude and unfair and hits the poorest hardest – or some more rational method such as TEQs.

Is there life beyond the Transition movement?

Transition is not the only way that communities are responding to the threats of climate change and reduced energy availability. There are communities which are focused on action on climate change, doing many of the same things as Transition but without buying into the whole concept. The village of Ashton Hayes in Cheshire is one example. It has set itself the task of becoming the UK's first carbon-neutral village, and over six years has reduced CO_2 emissions by 23 per cent through encouraging behavioural change.[20]

Another example is the city of Willits, California, where efforts are being made in economic localisation.[21] Judging from their website, the activity in Willits is along the lines of the Transition model, with localisation efforts in food, energy and transportation. A problem in finding non-transition groups is that they keep joining the Transition movement, for example Linlithgow had a very active 'climate challenge' group which has now been subsumed into Transition Linlithgow.

Criticism of Transition

The concept and practice of Transition has received its share of criticism, which can be divided into two different types. There are predictable brickbats from peak oil sceptics who claim that the Transition movement is 'mistaken, appalling and dangerous.'[22] At the other end of the scale, Transition receives criticism for not being radical enough. In a detailed but friendly critique, Australian radical Ted Trainer argues that Transition should not just be tinkering around the edges of society:

> Its implicit rationale is that it is sufficient to create more community gardens, recycling centres, skill banks, cycle paths, seed sharing, poultry co-ops, etc. It is not in general motivated by the clear and explicit goal of replacing the core institutions of consumer-capitalist society.

He goes on to suggest that the Transition steps are too focused on the procedure of setting up an initiative, and not enough about the actual nuts and bolts of what will make communities more resilient.

Another criticism of Transition is that it is predominantly a middle-class undertaking. This is recognised by the movement, and both the recent film *Transition 2.0* and the book *The Transition Companion* address this. Transition Moss Side (shown in the film) have gone out door to door and brought working-class ethnic minorities into their group.

Another criticism that could be levelled at the Transition movement is its focus on localisation. To overcome what are the global challenges of climate change and peak oil we also need both governments and big businesses to act. Eventually the Transition movement will have to engage with national politics. There does seem to be some recognition of this. In *The Transition Companion* there is mention of a 'Transition enabling act', a bill which would rapidly accelerate localisation and de-carbonisation of UK society. Discussions within the movement on what this would involve have started and the reader is invited to join in through the Transition website.[23]

Transition and Christians

Some Christians and churches are involved with Transition initiatives (some examples of this kind of interaction are found in Chapter 11). One interesting parallel between Christianity and Transition is that they both invoke a powerful vision of the future: with Transition, the future is a sustainable, resilient, vibrant community; for Christians, the future is the full appearance of the Kingdom of God.

A Transition scenario

Having made three possible future projections in the previous chapter, here is another, based on the Transition concept:

> The combination of a high oil price and the continuing financial crisis in the years up to 2015 led to an increasing debate on the reasons for the mess. While many did not make the connection between the financial, climate and resource crisis, a growing minority did and this was in part due to the awareness-raising of the many Transition initiatives. The movement gained in strength with an increasing number of local authorities formally embracing the Transition model, declaring themselves Transition cities, towns and regions. Many recognised the movement's localisation model as a means of keeping jobs in their area if nothing else. In countries like the UK an interest in traceable, local, seasonal food continued to grow; this was an entry-point into the movement for many. Local groups became ingenious at locating land that no one was using – unused building plots, roundabouts, even the sides of canals and railways were planted up with fruit trees and vegetable beds. Many councils adopted a policy of planting only productive trees in parks and other spaces, and allowed anyone to pick fruit or nuts from them in season.

> A frustration with high energy prices and the profits made by the big energy companies led to a plethora of community

energy schemes. In country areas these tended to be community-owned wind and hydro schemes; in urban areas large PV systems were installed on community-owned buildings. The profits were initially used to raise the energy efficiency in private and community-owned buildings, and after that dividends were shared among co-op members. The money for these schemes was raised by a mixture of local share issues and borrowing against the revenues of Transition-owned businesses such as bakeries, consumer goods, repair and cycle shops. One group in the UK opened a factory making solar hot-water systems.

Transition groups started setting up community-owned bike rental schemes modelled on those in Paris and London. These groups pressured local authorities that had signed up to Transition, to expand off-road cycle lanes and ran courses to encourage people to start cycling. Other groups started community car rental schemes using electric cars. As local government pulled back from funding local bus services some Transition groups took them over, running them as social enterprises. In the UK two Transition groups even started the most ambitious projects yet undertaken by the movement, reopening railway lines closed in the 1960s. Aiming to own the track 50:50 with Network Rail but run the trains themselves as a franchise, they persuaded a variety of local groups including local government to invest money in the schemes. The economic model was based on renewable energy projects to subsidise the running costs and provide the electricity for the trains. In 2020 political pressure by the Transition movement and others forced the UK government to introduce a carbon ration.

By 2030, although still only a minority of people were formally involved with Transition, the movement had influence far beyond its size. Transition had become the spirit of the age. The UK and other countries had taken on an increasingly localised outlook with most food and increasing amounts of energy locally supplied. Energy use was falling, people tended to walk and cycle, meaning they were healthier. Imported foods such as bananas and chocolate were expensive luxuries and many people were unhappy with this situation. While the carbon ration had helped poorer people make energy-efficiency improvements, fuel poverty was still a major problem. There were increasing numbers of people saying the Transition movement had got too powerful, but with dwindling oil supplies and increasing energy prices there didn't seem much alternative.

The future of Transition

No one in the movement would claim to know its future and freely admit it may fail. In our opinion, the Transition movement is the best attempt to tackle the problems of climate change and peak oil. Its strengths are an emphasis on local community action, and its ability and willingness to work with any political or community group.[24] Unlike conventional environmentalism it offers a positive vision of the future.

Notes

1   http://www.permaculture.org.uk/. Permaculture is a theory of ecological design which aims to develop sustainable human settlements and agricultural systems modelled from natural ecosystems.

2   A 2004 documentary film exploring the likely impact of peak oil on the suburban lifestyle.

3   http://transitionculture.org/wp-content/uploads/ KinsaleEnergyDescentActionPlan.pdf.

4   http://www.transitiontowntotnes.org/Central/About_us.

5   R. Hopkins, *The Transition Handbook*, Green Books, 2008.

6   http://www.transitionnetwork.org/3.

7   Hopkins, *The Transition Companion*, Green Books, 2011.

8   Hopkins, *The Transition Handbook*.

9   http://www.transitionnetwork.org/3.

10 http://www.bbc.co.uk/programmes/p0092m3f.

11 http://www.bristolpound.org/.

12 http://www.guardian.co.uk/world/2012/mar/16/greece-on-breadline-cashless-currency.

13 http://www.landshare.net/.

14   http://totnesedap.org.uk/book/part2/.

15   http://transitiontownworthing.ning.com/group/reskillinggroup. Also see
     Hopkins, *The Transition Companion* for more examples.

16   http://nhtt.org.uk/.

17   http://www.transitiontowncheltenham.org.uk/gcec.php. Also see the film
     Transition 2.0.

18   http://www.teqs.net/.

19   These problems are not insurmountable since the elderly and those with
     learning difficulties have to have someone to pay for their energy use now if
     they are not capable of doing it themselves.

20   http://www.goingcarbonneutral.co.uk/.

21   http://well95490.org/.

22   R. M. Mills, author of *The Myth of the Oil Crisis* Greenwood Press, 2008.
     Also try a web search for 'Transition Watch'. The site has not been updated
     for some years. As for its content we will let the reader draw his or her
     conclusions.

23   http://transitionculture.org/2010/12/20/needing-your-thoughts-for-a-
     transition-enabling-act/.

24   This is very apparent in the film *Transition 1.0*.

Does the Bible have anything to say here?

Towards a theology of peak oil

At that time the kingdom of heaven will be like ten virgins who took their lamps and went out to meet the bridegroom. Five of them were foolish and five were wise. The foolish ones took their lamps but did not take any oil with them. The wise ones, however, took oil in jars along with their lamps. The bridegroom was a long time in coming, and they all became drowsy and fell asleep.

Matthew 25:1–5, NIV

For Christians, the Bible represents the primary source of understanding, wisdom and truth. Reading, studying and grappling with the Bible is fundamental if we want to try to understand God and his purposes. As the apostle Paul wrote to his protégé Timothy, 'All Scripture is God-breathed and is useful for teaching, rebuking, correcting and training in righteousness' (2 Timothy 3:16). And yet at first glance we might struggle to think how wisdom and teaching from the Bible can be applied directly to the problems of oil depletion, energy security and climate change.

Clearly the world was very different place back in biblical times – oil, gas, coal and uranium were not significant sources of fuel or energy, so there is no direct teaching in the Bible about their use. However, what we can draw out from scripture are some principles and examples that we can apply to today. At this stage it is probably a good thing to state that neither of the authors are trained theologians, so what follows is simply our views as laymen of how the stories and principles found in the Bible could apply to this situation.

Central to the narrative of the Bible is the life, death and resurrection of Jesus Christ, whom Christians believe to be the Son of God. Jesus' life was without sin, utterly selfless, and yet fully human. His teaching provides some intriguing insights that we will explore in more detail later on. One of Jesus' parables, the story of the wise and foolish virgins, has provided us with the title of this book. But before we look at Jesus' teaching, we will first go back to the Old Testament, to the very start of the Bible.

That tricky word 'dominion'

As we mentioned briefly in Chapter 2, much of the controversy over Christian attitudes to the environment rest on certain key verses in Genesis chapters 1 and 2. Some Christians take the creation accounts absolutely literally, others metaphorically, but however you understand them, we believe these verses have some lessons on stewardship of resources from a climate change and peak oil perspective.

The key verses concerning dominion occur in Genesis chapter 1:27–28:

> So God created man in His own image; in the image of God He created him; male and female He created them. Then God blessed them, and God said to them, 'Be fruitful and multiply; fill the earth and subdue it; have dominion over the fish of the sea, over the birds of the air, and over every living thing that moves on the earth.' (New King James Version)

This is the part of the creation narrative where God invites humankind to share responsibility for his creation. You may have noted that the translation we have used here uses the word 'dominion', which, as we saw in Chapter 2, has been a problem. For some, it implies humankind being given a free hand to exploit nature, and this is the hook on which has been hung criticism of Christianity's attitude to the environment. Modern translations (such as the NIV) have replaced the word 'dominion' with 'rule over' or 'govern', which essentially have the same meaning, but perhaps without the negative connotations. What is clear is that humankind, as the only creature described as 'Godlike', has responsibility for the earth. As we see later in the Bible, in the life of Jesus, ruling in God's world should not be exploitative; what is meant is a gentle stewardship of the earth. Nowhere in scripture does it say that humans should use up the earth's resources and then escape to heaven when we die or Jesus returns. In fact the opposite is true – the Old Testament law contains specific instructions for the Israelites to care for their most important natural resource: the land. In the book of Exodus (23:10–11) and also in Leviticus 25, God decrees that the land should be rested from cultivation once in every seven years – a practice known as the land Sabbath. The idea of this practice is that soil fertility will be restored by periodically leaving the land fallow (a practice still carried out in some parts of the world). In addition, Psalm 24:1, 'The earth is the LORD's, and everything in it, the world, and all who live in it,' reminds us that even after what was said in the verses above from Genesis, the earth still belongs to God. A final point to note is that seven times in Genesis 1 the Bible says 'And God saw that it was good', and the final time in verse 31 is translated 'and it was very good'.

However, the verses on dominion are not the only ones in Genesis 1 and 2 relevant to peak oil and care for the environment. Genesis 2:15 states that 'The LORD God took the man and put him in the Garden of Eden to work it and take care of it' (NIV). The words 'work' and 'take care' both imply stewardship, being translated from Hebrew words meaning 'serve' and 'protect' respectively. Genesis 1:26 is also very interesting in this context. The NIV translates this verse as, 'Then God said, "Let us make mankind in our image, in our likeness, so that they may rule over the fish in the sea and the birds in the sky, over the livestock and all the wild animals, and over all the creatures that move along the ground".' The use of the plural 'that they may rule' is very radical for the time it is written. In other literature of the time a single human king would be designated ruler. The implication is humans are put as stewards on the earth and we all have shared responsibility for its care. No one could argue this is what happens at the moment.

So how can we apply the principle of humankind's responsibility for creation to our use of the world's resources such as oil? Geology and the other sciences have shown us that these resources are effectively a finite reservoir that we have exploited massively over the last few centuries. Since we will be leaving succeeding generations with a world largely depleted of these fossil energy resources (and also suffering the environmental and climatic consequences of their use), it is difficult to see how humankind's actions could be described as good stewardship. Energy does some wonderful things, providing comfort and convenience to our lives, yet once we understand the cost to creation of using energy and the limited future supply of fossil fuels, this must surely challenge us to reduce our use of them, stop thinking of ourselves as consumers, and start behaving like stewards. However we understand the first few chapters of Genesis, the fact that God called his creation good should give us pause for thought as humankind uses up the resources we have been given and in doing so makes a mess of the world.

The law and the prophets – the principle of justice

When God called his chosen people out of Egypt it was a decisive event in the formation of a nation. It was also a huge act of liberation, freeing thousands of slaves from an oppressive and unjust regime. When God meets Moses at the burning bush and tells him of his plans, the focus is on the oppression that the Israelites are suffering:

> I have indeed seen the misery of my people in Egypt. I have heard them crying out because of their slave drivers, and I am concerned about their suffering. So I have come down to rescue them from the hand of the Egyptians. (Exodus 3:7–8, NIV)

> Therefore, say to the Israelites: 'I am the LORD, and I will bring you out from under the yoke of the Egyptians. I will free you from being slaves to them, and I will redeem you with an outstretched arm and with mighty acts of judgement. I will take you as my own people, and I will be your God. Then you will know that I am the LORD your God, who brought you out from under the yoke of the Egyptians. (Exodus 6:5–7, NIV)

The writer Ronald Sider argues that the Exodus from Egypt is one example among many key points in the Bible, where God, in acting decisively to achieve his purposes, reveals his heart's concern for the poor and oppressed. Having rescued his people from slavery, during their years of wanderings in the wilderness they are given the laws they must follow as a nation – set out in detail in the books of Exodus, Leviticus, Deuteronomy and Numbers.[1] This law provides a wide-ranging set of rules for an equitable society, including stipulations for fair conduct between neighbours, husbands and wives, and for treatment of the poor and marginalised. When Moses spoke to the Israelites about the law, he confirmed that it spoke about the nature of God:

> For the LORD your God is God of gods and Lord of lords, the great God, mighty and awesome, who shows no partiality and accepts no bribes. He defends the cause of the fatherless and the widow, and loves the foreigner residing among you, giving them food and clothing. (Deuteronomy 10:17–18, NIV)

Both the law and the events recorded in the Old Testament speak of a God who is concerned about justice, providing a template for his people to live peacefully together. When they followed his law, they were blessed. When they ignored it, they were challenged and eventually came under God's judgement – which included Israel being conquered and the people being taken into exile. Among the prophets calling God's people to account was Amos. He lived in the eighth century BC, a time of economic success for the country. Yet behind this prosperity Amos saw greed, exploitation of the poor and

idolatry. Archaeologists have found that in the early years of the
nation of Israel there was little difference in the size of houses,
indicating a similar standard of living across the country, but by the
time of Amos, differences were pronounced, with some large,
well-built houses and others much smaller. Clearly the checks and
balances that the law contained to prevent people falling into
poverty, such as the year of jubilee, were being ignored. Amos
denounced the oppressors in clear terms:

> This is what the LORD says: 'For three sins of Israel, even for
> four, I will not relent. They sell the innocent for silver, and
> the needy for a pair of sandals. They trample on the heads of
> the poor as on the dust of the ground and deny justice to the
> oppressed. (Amos 2:6–7, NIV)

A couple of chapters further on he calls judgement on rich women
who were exploiting the poor: 'Hear this word, you cows of Bashan
on Mount Samaria, you women who oppress the poor and crush the
needy and say to your husbands, "Bring us some drinks!" ' (Amos
4:1, NIV).

Sadly the warnings of Amos were ignored, and within a few years
the northern kingdom had fallen to the Assyrians, and many
thousands carried off into captivity. Other prophets – Isaiah, Jer-
emiah and Micah – also warned about oppression and injustice.
Occasionally their words were heard and acted upon, but at other
times God chose to allow foreign nations such as the Babylonians to
be used as his instrument to purge the evil from his people.

So how does this overarching principle of justice for the poor,
which God values so strongly, apply to the concerns of this book?
Do oil, gas and the other energy sources play a part in oppression?
(Some would argue that energy-using devices such as the washing
machine have liberated many people from the drudgery of manual
labour.) When we look around the world today, it is clear that there
is inequality. In fact, the disparities between rich and poor must be
even more pronounced than in Amos' time. In our globalised
economy, hugely dependent on energy, some have benefited enor-
mously while others are losing out. Geologically, resources such as
oil, coal and gas are distributed unequally around the globe, histori-

cally giving countries like the UK, USA, Saudi Arabia, Kuwait and others an advantage – but that's not the whole story. Some countries have, for various reasons, more access to energy than others. Early industrialisation and exploitation of other countries through colonisation and slavery skewed trade terms – all have played their part in raising some countries up while others have struggled. For those countries like Britain or the United States, where our current economic and industrial strength, partly based on history, gives us access to energy today, the biblical teaching on justice must challenge us about how we use our position in the world. This may involve dealing with the past – setting right historical wrongs by making reparation to those that our country has exploited in reaching our current wealth. For the present – do we continue to use energy in seeking continued economic growth and even higher living standards for ourselves, or do we reach out and try to lift others up? And thinking of the future, in a world with energy in short supply, how will we help developing countries without access to oil cope?

The other area where the principle of justice impacts on our use of energy is the unwanted effects – pollution and damaging climate change. The overwhelming majority of climate scientists believe that rising levels of carbon dioxide and other gases, released by the burning of fossil fuels over the last couple of centuries, are part of the reason our climate is warming. (For some this is a controversial statement but we believe the evidence is clear and mounting.) The *benefits* of using energy are enjoyed mostly by the citizens of developed countries – cars, electricity, central heating, air conditioning and all the other things that an industrialised economy brings. However, the *costs* of using the energy are externalised: the carbon pollution caused by using coal, gas or oil does not impact directly on the user, or even on the country of the user. It is shared around the whole world. If scientists are correct and this is leading to climate change with the sort of impacts that are predicted, those who are likely to feel the first effects (and are arguably already experiencing them) are some of the poorest and most vulnerable people on the planet. Here is a clear example of injustice. People living precarious lives in the low-lying coastal areas of Bangladesh and eastern India, whose lifetime use of energy is minuscule, are likely to be the first to suffer as global warming causes sea levels to rise. Subsistence farmers across Africa, who may have never lived in a house with electricity and will never own a car, are already finding themselves suffering the effects of others' energy use in changing weather patterns, as crops wither and harvests fail. Two other groups will also suffer the effects of humanity's use of energy while contributing precisely nothing to the problem themselves: people yet to be born, and species that also share our world. Whether we accept it or not, our energy use has unintended consequences which we must face up to, both as individuals and nations. Taking justice seriously must mean examining our actions and changing how we live, reducing the negative impact of our lives on others.

Ecclesiastes – human wisdom and frailty

Before we leave the Old Testament, there is one other book with some useful lessons for the predicament we find ourselves in today. This is the complex and subtle book of Ecclesiastes. Most Christians of a certain age know the book for providing the lyrics for the song 'Turn, turn, turn' written by Pete Seeger and recorded by the Byrds and Peter, Paul and Mary (among many others). Others get no further than the words of Ecclesiastes 1:2: ' "Meaningless! Meaningless!" says the Teacher. "Utterly meaningless! Everything is meaningless." '

Traditionally the book has been seen as being written by King Solomon, though the author stops just short of declaring himself as such.[2] Recent biblical scholarship has led some to a different conclusion, that the writer was a man of wisdom who 'plays the part' of a Solomon-like figure in the early chapters, to make a point. The actual title he uses, *Qoheleth*, is untranslatable, but 'the Teacher' is probably the closest match we can achieve. While he ends the book by urging his readers to, 'fear God and keep his commandments', he takes a circuitous route to get there, including exploring everything 'under the sun' – as though he has to gain wisdom from nature and life, with God at a distance.[3]

Throughout the book the Teacher emphasises that materialism is not the route to happiness, and we should be satisfied with having our basic needs met.[4] In fact the acquisition of material possessions gives no lasting gratification: 'Yet when I surveyed all that my hands had done, and what I had toiled to achieve, everything was meaningless, a chasing after the wind; nothing was gained under the sun' (Ecclesiastes 2:11, NIV).

While the Teacher clearly values being wise, 'The wise person has his eyes in his head, but the fool walks in darkness' (Ecclesiastes 2:12, ESV), he also believes human wisdom has clear limits:

> I said to myself, 'Look, I have increased in wisdom more than anyone who has ruled over Jerusalem before me; I have experienced much of wisdom and knowledge.' Then I applied myself to the understanding of wisdom, and also of madness and folly, but I learned that this, too, is a chasing after the wind. For with much wisdom comes much sorrow; the more knowledge, the more grief. (Ecclesiastes 1:16–18, NIV)

The Jerusalem Bible translates verse 7:29 in a very interesting way: 'God made man simple; man's complex problems are of his own devising.' We would argue this is true of the predicament we have landed ourselves in, but also we need to be wise when it comes to solutions for peak oil, not to make things worse for ourselves.

Although the Teacher seems to have had few problems in his life and was wealthy there is an underlying hint within the book that this is as good as things are going to get and an uncertainty as to what comes next. This is best seen in 2:18, 3:22 and 6:12, for example: 'So I saw that there is nothing better for a person than to enjoy their work, because that is their lot. For who can bring them to see what will happen after them?' (3:22, NIV).

Does this book and its author writing some three thousand years ago have anything to teach us in an era of climate change, peak oil and financial crisis? The Teacher's musings on materialism echo eerily down the centuries, research has consistently shown that beyond a certain level of human need we are no happier with more.[5] Perhaps this is just as well, for the Teacher's instruction that we should 'be happy with work, food and drink' is one we will learn to recognise in the coming era when oil-derived goods become scarce and expensive. There is also a clear statement that work is good and people should derive satisfaction from it. There are two aspects to this. First, people should want to work, but also there should be work with dignity for them to do – something that society at a time of high unemployment and economic uncertainty would do well to recognise. The Teacher would certainly recognise a lack of work as a grave injustice. What peak oil will mean for work is something at the moment we can only guess at. The early years of a crisis could bring recessions (as oil shocks have in the past). Some areas of industry may disappear (air transport, aerospace) but many more could be created in manufacturing and maintaining renewable energy equipment. Farm work may become more labour intensive again and inevitable re-localisation will be good for jobs.

As Christians entering the time when oil production has peaked, it would be very easy to rely on our own wisdom. Neil at the time of writing had just attended a series of climate change talks. At one of these a variety of speakers put forward their solutions for maintaining our current energy use. They were clever, talented people and many of their energy efficiency or renewable energy solutions merited attention and investment, but Neil was left with the overwhelming impression that their human wisdom had missed the main point – that there is probably no totally satisfactory way to carry on living as we live now. To rely on such wisdom alone may not solve the problems we face, but actually make things worse.

We undoubtedly live at time of great uncertainty, something we think the Teacher shared. Our suspicion is that in the developed world we are living at our environmental limits and the next generation will be inevitably materially worse off. (This view is widely shared, as shown in recent opinion polls although for different reasons than ours.[6]) Ultimately Ecclesiastes teaches us that we need to trust in God rather than our own wisdom, which is a useful lesson in uncertain times.

Jesus' ministry and teaching

We cannot examine the teaching of Jesus without also reflecting on his actions, and in particular the central act in history: Jesus' death on the cross and subsequent resurrection. These events form the heart of the Gospel and for Christians they challenge, inspire and shape our response to all that life throws at us. Jesus set out the ultimate aim of his ministry in a discussion with his disciples: 'For even the Son of Man did not come to be served, but to serve, and to give his life as a ransom for many' (Mark 10:45, NIV).

The sacrifice of Jesus opened the possibility of a new relationship between God and humankind, and also a new relationship between humankind and the rest of creation. Because of Jesus, we can be free from our slavery to sin, from patterns of damaging behaviour, from our habit of selfishness. And we can live lives that are joyfully submissive to God, that grow in love for our fellow human beings, and that show care for the rest of creation.

However, from coverage of the Church in newspapers or on television you could well form the opinion that the Church is obsessed by sex: same-sex relationships and the gender of priests and bishops feature highly. In that context, it's interesting that in a search of the NIV New Testament the word 'sex' appeared 33 times, but the word 'money' 61 times.[7] As Richard Foster writes in his book *Celebration of Discipline*, 'Jesus spoke to the question of economics more than any other single social issue.' Sexual attitudes are clearly important, but maybe we've got some of our priorities wrong. Western society's obsession with greed and acquisition has got us into our current ecological and financial mess, yet we all find it hard to escape the all-pervading influence of materialism.

Among the many things that Jesus taught, one brief comment contains particular relevance to the subject we are discussing. Jesus is teaching a crowd when a man calls out to him:

> 'Teacher, tell my brother to divide the inheritance with me.' Jesus replied, 'Man, who appointed me a judge or an arbiter between you?' Then he said to them, 'Watch out! Be on your guard against all kinds of greed; life does not consist in an abundance of possessions.' (Luke 12:15, NIV)

Usually the older son inherited twice the younger son's portion, so either this was a disadvantaged younger son speaking, or possibly an older brother complaining that the younger son had got his hands on more than he was entitled to. Either way, he expected Jesus to help, since Rabbis were often called to intervene in such disputes. Jesus must have disappointed him. Instead of getting directly involved, he made the brief but telling comment recorded above and then told the parable of the rich fool, warning of the dangers of both acquiring possessions and making this your life goal (Luke 12:13–21). A modern paraphrase of Jesus' key words might read: 'Life is not about stuff' – surely a powerful counter-cultural message that the world needs to hear, and one that echoes the words from Ecclesiastes we have already examined.

Next, Luke records Jesus telling his listeners not to worry or concern themselves with material possessions, but to rely on God:

> Then Jesus said to his disciples: 'Therefore I tell you, do not worry about your life, what you will eat; or about your body, what you will wear. For life is more than food, and the body more than clothes. Consider the ravens: they do not sow or reap, they have no storeroom or barn; yet God feeds them. And how much more valuable you are than birds! Who of you by worrying can add a single hour to your life? Since you cannot do this very little thing, why do you worry about the rest?' (Luke 12:22–26, NIV)

This passage encourages us not to worry – a difficult thing in a culture that encourages complexity and provides a thousand ways for us to be busy and spend money. One way of reducing our stress and worry is to cultivate simplicity in our lives. For further study on this we can do no better than point you towards the books *Freedom of Simplicity* and *Celebration of Discipline* by Richard Foster.[8] We can only draw out a couple of salient points here. First, simplicity is not the same as asceticism. There is a long and complex role of asceticism in the history of Christianity, where people have seen spiritual value in denying themselves various pleasures for a time or as a lifetime vow. By contrast, Richard Foster writes that simplicity is a reliance on God as expressed in the beatitudes.[9] He also believes simplicity has both an inner working (the reliance on God first) and also an outer working, which is a series of practical steps; many of these coincide with the recommendations for personal action that we make in Chapter 11.

One aspect of peak oil that is sometimes overlooked is its effects on the supply of consumer goods, clothes and food, all oil dependent. We are simply going to have to make do with less. There are four aspects as we see it where Jesus' teaching is relevant to this. First, the verses we have examined emphasise that we should rely on God for the basics in life, but no more. Second, materialism may still be a problem. After all, in the New Testament era people did not have even a fraction of the consumer goods we have today and yet could still be materialistic (hence Jesus' comments). In other words, this particular teaching is eternal and we will need to continually challenge ourselves, even when we have less. Third, this must open up a very significant evangelistic opportunity to reach out to people who have not yet become Christians. Most of our contemporaries put their 'faith' not in God but in the acquisition of more money or consumer goods. When this opportunity for acquisition is curtailed we can only hope and pray this opens up space for Christians to proclaim the good news of God's Kingdom, where it is more blessed to give than to receive, and where life does not consist in the abundance of our possessions. Lastly, this teaching should remind us that many of our brothers and sisters do not have their basic needs met even now, and in a world where resources are depleted this will get worse. This should disturb us and call forth our compassion.[10]

Celebration – learning to rejoice as we move away from oil dependency

Amid all the doom and gloom concerning peak oil another lesson we can learn from a study of the Gospels is to celebrate. Our Saviour clearly enjoyed eating, drinking and the company of people, he and his disciples frequently provoking comment or criticism when they did so.[11] Jesus' first recorded miracle in the Gospel of John (one of the few John recorded) was Jesus turning water into wine when a wedding celebration had run dry.[12] Jesus also provided food during his own teaching sessions and, when he was a guest at other people's meals, used them as opportunities to teach both his hosts and others (Luke 14:1–24).[13]

Jesus told us that he has come to bring life to the full (John 10:10). A verse that has led to some confusion, as Mark Powley argues in his book *Consumer Detox*:

The connection with the consumer dream is obvious. You want to maximize your life? Jesus came to make it happen! Alarm bells should start ringing, though, when Jesus and the advertisers say the same thing. Actually, Jesus saying 'Maximize your life' would have been as likely as him ordering a ham and pineapple pizza for the Last Supper. But because we're so conditioned to maximize our lives, we naturally hear Jesus' words that way. We easily imagine a bigger bubble of possessions, a greater collection of experiences. We confuse 'life to the full' with a full life.[14]

We should celebrate both what oil has done (and let's face it, it's not all bad!) and, perhaps more importantly, frequently celebrate as we move away from dependency on it. The Transition movement suggests frequent celebrations within its groups. Why not try a celebration meal with food you've entirely grown yourself, or try sourcing a meal using produce grown within the boundaries of your city or town? Make your own cider or wine (or fruit juice if you are teetotal). The ride up to the oil peak was fun for many (albeit damaging fun), there's no reason to think the ride down the other side should not involve a party from time to time either.

The early Church – living as a community

So far we have looked at dominion, justice, human frailty, simplicity and celebration.

Another relevant theme is the example of community as shown in the early Church. Our expectation is that in the future there will be constraints on the supply of many goods and resources that we take for granted today. Many things will be more expensive. One way to cope with this is to share and co-operate in ways we do not at the moment, at a very local level (i.e. build community). There is a useful template of this kind of interaction described in the book of Acts:[15]

All the believers were one in heart and mind. No one claimed that any of their possessions was their own, but they shared everything they had. With great power the apostles continued to testify to the resurrection of the Lord Jesus. And God's grace was so powerfully at work in them all that there were no needy persons among them. For from time to time those who owned land or houses sold them, brought the money from the sales and put it at the apostles' feet, and it was distributed to anyone who had need. (Acts 4:32–35, NIV)

There are two aspects of this passage that we think are helpful: the part about sharing in verse 32, and about meeting people's needs in verses 34–35. In a future where consumer goods are both more costly and scarcer, it makes little sense for us to duplicate many of the things we own individually. A simple example: in an average suburban street in Britain today the gardens are small, yet typically each household will have their own lawnmower when one machine shared would probably be adequate, thus saving money and storage space. This kind of arrangement requires more than just interaction and flexibility between households – it requires a change in our mindset about ownership and individuality. Another example that comes readily to mind is a car. A few people are already experimenting with car-sharing and some belong to car clubs where you rent a car when you need it rather than owning it. A positive example we have heard about is a street in Edinburgh that, after the 2009/10 and 2010/11 winters, clubbed together and bought a snow-clearing machine.

It may be that as Christians we are already holding our possessions a little looser, and are prepared to lend or share things within our church family. The example of the early Church appears to go beyond this to a deeper level of community and living which some people are experimenting with today. The author and futurologist Tom Sine has been advocating that Christians should be trying out different ways of communal living and sharing because he believes that this can free up time and resources which we otherwise spend on buying and looking after our own properties.

The second aspect is financial help for those in need. When Neil was talking to a friend about this book, he happened to mention that one outcome of peak oil will be that energy prices will rise steeply. Neil's friend challenged him about what he would do. Neil replied with some ideas to lobby energy companies and government about. His friend repeated the question – 'What are *you* going to do about it?' The challenge for us as individuals is that we may have to help pay people's energy bills directly (both people in the Church and those in need outside the church community) as well as helping them to find ways to live less energy-using lives through changing their habits, expectations and infrastructure.

The end-times prophecies

The passages in the Bible which deal with the end times are difficult to understand and have produced a wide range of interpretations (and lots of misunderstandings) over the centuries. Passages emphasising different aspects of the future can appear contradictory and confusing. The author and former bishop Tom Wright puts it succinctly:

> All language about the future is … simply a set of signposts pointing into a fog. 'We see through a glass darkly', says St. Paul as he peers towards what lies ahead. All our language about future states of the world, and of ourselves, consists of complex pictures which may or may not correspond very well to the ultimate reality.[16]

Yet this difficulty should not prevent us from grappling with these issues – in fact it is critical that we do. Our understanding of God's plans for the future can affect our actions today. If we believe (as many Christians do) that the second coming of Christ is part of a scenario where all believers will be swept up into heaven to be with God, we may have little care for the world we will one day leave behind. If however we understand God's ultimate plan as the redemption, renewal and rebirth of all creation, (and that since Jesus is alive this process has already started) then practical action that helps care for this world today is meaningful as part of building for God's Kingdom. Tom Wright puts it clearly:

> To hope for a better future in this world – for the poor, the sick, the lonely and depressed, for the slaves, the refugees, the hungry and homeless, for the abused, the paranoid, the

downtrodden and despairing, and in fact for the whole wide, wonderful and wounded world – is not something else, something extra, something tacked on to 'the gospel' as an afterthought. And to work for that intermediate hope, the surprising hope that comes forward from God's ultimate future into God's urgent present, is not a distraction from the task of 'mission' and 'evangelism' in the present. It is a central, essential, vital and life-giving part of it.

Some churches and Christians, it seems particularly in America, are fixated with the second coming of Jesus and the events that might presage it. Conflicts, political events and groupings of countries are often assessed to see if they could fit with the various prophecies and pictures that the Bible provides. Is the re-emergence of the nation of Israel the 'budding of the fig tree' that Jesus describes as a sign of the end of the age? Could the European Union be the beast with ten horns and seven heads described in Revelation 13? Some of the speculation is informed not so much by biblical scholarship, but by the best-selling books and films which have woven the supposed events into fictional narratives. Part of the problem is that many of the passages concerned are multifaceted. A passage can contain verses which relate to the time when they were written or spoken, another part relating to the reader's lifetime, and another the distant future. The clearest example of this is the passage in Matthew 24 and an almost identical one in Mark 13. It appears Matthew 24:4–14 perhaps applies both to the disciples and to us today; verses 15–22 is a future prophecy about the destruction of Jerusalem (which happened in AD 70) and verses 23–31 are about Christ's second coming. The different sections merge into one another with no clear delineation, making their interpretation challenging.

A number of recent embarrassments have occurred with prominent Christians making confident predictions of the end of the world. However, this is not new; it started as early as the New Testament era and has continued ever since.[17] In the eighteenth century the prominent Plymouth Brethren leader J. N. Darby made end of the world predictions. In the 1970s it was Hal Lindsey (who is still going).[18] The best known in recent years is that of US radio broadcaster Harold Camping, who has made multiple failed predictions in this area.[19]

Theologians such as John Stott, Michael Green, John Drane and more recently N. T. Wright (the latter three recognised as prominent New Testament scholars) are very critical of this theological approach.[20] As Michael Green says,

> The purpose of prophecy is not to give us history written in the future tense, but, like film previews and hazard warning lights on the motorway, lift our hearts in expectation or in warning. The whole date fixing approach neglects this, and by its mixture of literalism and speculation militates against patient faith and social involvement.[21]

In the same book Michael Green sees no significance in the budding of the fig tree as far as the current status of Israel is concerned. He makes the point that Jesus made no pronouncements about the future of Israel in a political sense and that the Church takes the place of Israel (Acts 15:16). Such theology about the fig tree misses the point, as did many people in Jesus' time, seeing his mission as a nationalistic one, when it was to inaugurate the Kingdom.

What seems to be true (as an overarching comment) is that the time leading up to Jesus' second coming will be difficult and chaotic. Both Jesus and Paul use the same metaphor – that of a woman giving birth – to describe the process: In the Matthew 24 conversation with his disciples about the signs of his coming, Jesus talks of several events, and then says, 'All these are the beginning of birth-pains' (Matthew 24:8, NIV). Paul, in his letter to the Romans, writes that '… the whole creation has been groaning as in the pains of childbirth' (8:22). Though some births can be peaceful and smooth, this is not typical and surely not what is meant here. As Tom Wright says, 'This is no smooth evolutionary transition, in which creation simply moves up another gear into a higher mode of life. This is traumatic, involving convulsions and contractions and … the drastic and dramatic birth of new creation from the womb of the old.'

From what we have seen in earlier chapters of the impending difficulties of oil supply, there is clearly the potential (unless we choose otherwise) of significant trauma for the world as it currently operates. Could peak oil and climate change play a part in the 'convulsions and contractions' which may affect our world in the last days? That is a scenario that some are contemplating – in fact there is at least one book which has linked the looming energy crisis directly to biblical prophecy and a timetable of apocalyptic events leading up to Christ's return. A word of caution seems appropriate here. The Bible makes it very clear in several places that the hour of Jesus' return is known only to God the Father – the events are in his hands and not in those of humankind.[22] God is in control. It may well be that the concerns outlined in this book lead to a significant and wrenching transformation in our way of life – even the 'collapse' of industrial civilisation – but still not be part of God's ultimate plan to end history. To borrow a phrase, the end of the world as we know it is not necessarily the end of the world.

In this chapter we have attempted to tease out some biblical principles that relate to the problem of future energy constraints. These include our stewardship of the earth, God's concern for justice and how our current arrangements fail to provide it to many, the principle of living a full life without it being full of 'stuff', and the need to see our future role not as escaping the earth, but being part of God's redeeming plan. We started this chapter (and have taken the title of the book) by referring to one of Jesus' parables, the story of the wise and foolish virgins and their oil lamps. While useful in providing a title, this parable is not really about oil, but about believers being ready for Jesus' second coming into our world. But while it is not about depletion, it is a story about preparation, about being ready. In this book we have attempted to prepare you for the different future that peak oil is bringing. The next two chapters look at some practical steps you can take, and what churches can do to prepare themselves and their congregations for the changes ahead.

Notes

1 R. J. Sider, *Rich Christians in an Age of Hunger*, Thomas Nelson, 1978.

2 Ecclesiastes 1:1, 12, 16; 2:4–9; 7:26–29; 12:9.

3 Ecclesiastes 12:13.

4 Ecclesiastes 1:2–4; 2:3–11, 24: 3:13; 5:10–11.

5 R. A. Easterlin, 'Will Raising the Incomes of All Increase the Happiness of All?', *Journal of Economic Behavior and Organization*, 27 (1995), pp. 35–47. The research is a little dated but covers 30-year trends. Also see http://www.worldvaluessurvey.org/wvs/articles/folder_published/

article_base_106. There are some upward trends on some data sets but they are very modest and don't suggest that becoming wealthier makes us much happier.

6   http://www.guardian.co.uk/society/2011/dec/03/britons-children-lives-parents-poll.

7   Using Xiphos 3.1.4.

8   *Freedom of Simplicity* is currently out of print, though available second-hand.

9   Matthew 6:25–33.

10 James 2:15–16.

11 Matthew 9:11; 11:19; Luke 5:33; 15:2; 19:7.

12 John 2:1–11.

13 Matthew 14:16–22; 15:29–38.

14 M. Powley, *Consumer Detox*, Zondervan, 2011.

15 It is interesting to note that we don't have firm evidence that this pattern of living was exported to other early Church locations, and there is a question mark over whether it was sustainable. Later on aid has to be sent to the impoverished Christians in Jerusalem. Nevertheless it is a good model for the twenty-first century.

16 N. T. Wright, *Surprised by Hope*, SPCK, 2007.

17 2 Peter 3.

18 http://www.hallindsey.com/.

19 http://abcnews.go.com/blogs/business/2011/10/harold-camping-doomsday-prophet-wrong-again/.

20 See J. Stott, *Issues facing Christians Today*, Marshalls, 1984; J. Drane, J*esus and the Four Gospels*, Lion, 1984; and the essay by N. T. Wright in *The Green Bible*, HarperCollins, 2008.

21 M. Green, *Matthew for Today*, Hodder and Stoughton, 1988.

22 Matthew 24:36.

What can I do?

Throughout history, the really fundamental changes in societies have come about not from the dictates of governments and the results of battles, but through vast numbers of people changing their minds, sometimes only a little bit.

Willis Harman

It is quite possible that this book is the first time you have been confronted with the problem of energy depletion and its likely consequences, in which case you may want to research and read more to corroborate what you are reading here. Don't take our word for it – there are several books and websites which provide a range of perspectives on this subject, and which go into more detail than we can here on some aspects of the problem.

Starting to understand the problem of peak oil, and grasping the implications for the way we live, can be a profound shock. What is sometimes wryly called 'post-petroleum stress disorder' can emerge in a variety of ways: fear, denial, bewilderment or even elation. A common response in America is survivalism – buying a shack way up in the hill country and stocking up on cartridges and dried food rations ready for the day when society starts to fall apart. The instinct to protect ourselves and our loved ones from future uncertainties is a good one, but we need to channel it wisely into practical actions which will protect not just our own well-being, but also that of our neighbours, our community and maybe even our entire world. In the face of these huge global problems individual action can seem futile, yet we have to start somewhere. Mother Teresa of Calcutta was reportedly once asked, 'How can we ever hope to feed a million starving children?' Her answer: 'One at a time.'

Individual actions will of course have the most impact if carried out within the framework of a community or church-led effort with people working together; we will go on to examine this in the next chapter. Even better would be a national effort (such as tradable energy quotas[1]), to reduce our dependence on oil and other fossil fuels. Unfortunately that sort of radical country-wide campaign to cut our energy use looks unlikely at present, and what efforts there are in this direction are distinctly grass-roots and bottom-up.

Before we look at practical actions, it is really important that we get our thinking straight. Getting our head round peak oil and other energy constraints and how they are likely to impact us is the first step. We have literally to 'change our minds' – begin to think differently about the way we currently live our lives and the way we use energy. The word 'repent' may feel too strong a word here (we are not labelling energy use as sin) but the meaning of repent is 'to turn away'. We need to change direction, turn away from our old ways of thinking and from damaging patterns of living. Understanding the full gravity of our situation provides some of the incentive and the impetus to do that, but we need to have more than concern or even fear about the future as our motivation. We need to develop a positive vision for what life could be like with reduced energy use, and let that be our primary inspiration. The Transition movement advocates the development of this kind of positive vision for towns or communities following their process, and we think it is equally important for individuals and households to have their own positive vision of a low-energy future. As has been said elsewhere in this book, there could be many benefits from reduced consumption of energy and all that comes from it: more walking and cycling will make us fitter and healthier; less food being transported from the other side of the globe will make us appreciate food in its season; our streets will be quieter and safer with less cars; our communities more interdependent. The list of potential benefits could go on – and hopefully act as an encouragement for action.

The one big answer to the question 'What can I do?' is to reduce your dependence on energy from fossil fuels. This helps in several ways, In a changing world, you are less reliant on uncertain future supplies, and will be better prepared for when resources get tight. In addition, you are contributing less to carbon dioxide emissions and climate change. Third, you will be saving money. If everyone reduced their use of energy, the remaining fossil fuels would go a lot further and make the transition to more renewable energy easier.

The old wartime motto 'Keep calm and carry on' seems to be emblazoned on T-shirts and bags everywhere at the moment. A slightly less catchy slogan, but more appropriate to our times would be 'Keep calm and start doing things differently'. What we share here are some practical ideas which, if implemented, would make a significant difference at the personal or household level. These are broad suggestions, but each person who reads this book lives a unique lifestyle in their particular community, interacting with others in a specific way. We can only give some initial pointers and ideas. We hope we can inspire you to start the journey.

We have divided our suggestions into the main challenges of peak oil, namely energy, transport, food and chemicals, and for each area we have provided ideas for action at three different levels: easy, challenging and difficult. We also consider at the end of the chapter some possible communal ideas and skills. The ideas below are not mutually exclusive; you can start with the easy ideas and work upwards. In some areas you may want to take professional advice, and in fact this is required if you are planning to make use of the help available under the government's new 'Green Deal'.[2]

Energy

Easy ideas

Most readers of this book will have come across many of the easy measures, and hopefully are already doing some or all of them:

- Turn your central heating thermostat down one or two degrees – the difference in comfort is minimal but the energy savings can be substantial.
- Make sure all your appliances are energy efficient (especially white goods).

- Use energy-efficient lights, and switch them off when not required. Compact fluorescent bulbs are good, but LED light fittings (though a little more expensive to buy) use even less electricity.
- Lag pipes and your hot water tank.
- Defrost freezers regularly and open the doors as infrequently and for as short a time as possible.
- Switch off computers and wi-fi routers at the wall if not in use.
- Don't leave appliances on standby (count these- the sheer number could well amaze you). Plug any with USB connections into computers to charge, then when you switch off the computer you are not leaving these on standby.
- Whenever possible, hang clothes up to dry rather than using a tumble dryer.
- Ensure washing machines, tumble dryers and dishwashers are full when used. Freezers also work more efficiently when full.
- If your radiators are below windows, tuck the curtains behind the radiator to keep the heat in.
- When using a kettle, boil only the water you need.
- Cover pans when cooking food. This saves energy by bringing the water to the boil quicker.
- Draught-proof doors, windows and the loft hatch (easy to forget this last one; stick insulating boards on the (upper) loft side of it as well).
- Consider switching to a green energy tariff with your supplier. Remember that the electrons that you get are exactly the same from the same sources, but you will be encouraging more investment in renewables.
- Close curtains or shutters at sunset to retain heat.

After a while most of the ideas listed become habits and you won't notice you are doing them. However, if we had to choose one stand-out action to take in this area it would be to properly insulate your loft (Figure 1 shows the level of energy loss through the average roof).

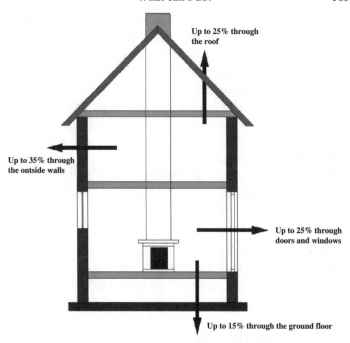

Up to 25% through the roof

Up to 35% through the outside walls

Up to 25% through doors and windows

Up to 15% through the ground floor

Figure 1: Potential sources of heat loss in the average house.

In the UK many lofts are not properly insulated. The reasons for this are unclear, but one reason may be that lofts become storage spaces for things people cannot quite bring themselves to get rid of. We would encourage you to clear your loft, and then make sure there is at least 270mm of insulation in it. The insulation layers should criss-cross and not quite reach the edge of the roof eaves to prevent build-up of damp in the roof space. If your cold water tank is in the loft don't put insulation underneath it – this helps to prevent it freezing – but insulate the top and sides of it.

There are several types of insulation suitable for lofts: the most common is glass-wool. Though cheap and effective, if installing it yourself, make sure you wear gloves and a face mask – the fibres are an irritant and can be inhaled.[3] There is a new type of insulation made from recycled plastic bottles. While this is slightly more expensive than the glass-wool material, it has lower embodied energy and has none of the itch and fibre-inhaling problems.[4]

Eco-insulation products include one made from treated sheep's wool, which is effective and natural but expensive, and 'Warmcel', which is made from treated recycled newspapers. If fitting insulation seems daunting, then get a professional installer to do it for you. Until recently energy companies in the UK had an obligation to insulate a certain number of their customers' houses, but this arrangement has now been replaced by the new Green Deal. Under this scheme, the insulation is installed and the money paid back through savings in your energy bills.[5] However you go about it, insulating your loft is easy, the energy savings are large and the financial payback is quick.

More challenging suggestions

Figure 1 suggests that a considerable amount of heat energy is lost through the walls of your house (35 per cent – more than the roof) and also through the floor (up to 15 per cent). These losses are not as easy or as cheap to deal with as the loft space. There are three options relating to walls – put insulation on the outside, in the middle (as Andy has done) or on the inside of the walls (as Neil has done). The complete set of options is beyond anything but a brief description in this book but here are a few details. Many homes have walls with two skins of masonry and a gap in the middle. This cavity can be filled with insulating material. Cavity-wall insulation is the cheapest of all the various options. It has been associated with damp problems in the past, but the technology has improved and if you do have cavity walls this is the route to go.[6] External insulation can be put on the outside and then rendered over. It can be very costly and will in most cases alter the external appearance of your house – something which may be prohibited in conservation areas. Insulating the inside of a wall is usually done with special insulation boards (dry lining).[7] The problem with this is that again it's expensive, also disruptive (major redecorating required) and will bring the walls of your house in, slightly reducing the size of the rooms. Both types are very effective in terms of cutting heat losses through walls, although external insulation is said to be more effective. However, for those of us without a cavity and who cannot fit external insulation there are cheaper, less effective options for insulating the inside. Neil has used insulating lining paper and has found it reasonably effective. The temperature in the rooms concerned has warmed up by a few degrees when compared with similar cold weather conditions before it was fitted, and the house cools down slower and warms up faster. In addition the warmth in the room no longer seems to come from the radiator but from all directions. There are two grades; if possible use the more expensive grade. This cuts heat loss through the wall by 36 per cent. Using insulating lining paper is in the more challenging section since it involves redecorating, but is less disruptive than the alternatives. The paper, about 2mm thick, is easily applied with a special glue. For aesthetic reasons it needs covering with another layer of conventional wallpaper.

Floors are another area of heat loss. There are various methods of insulating floors, such as sticking insulating boards or glass-wool insulation up between the floor joists (with netting to hold it up in the latter case). Neil has used another method – an insulating carpet underlay called 'Cloud 9' which is made from recycled foam. (This is so effective at insulating that its manufacturers state that on no account should it be laid on top of under-floor heating.) Why not next time you are replacing carpets ensure that this underlay is used? Indeed, why not keep weekly records of your energy usage using a spreadsheet (we plan to make one available through our website)? UK homes will soon start to get their electricity meters exchanged for smart meters. We hope that these will have the ability to download data to computers via wi-fi, bluetooth or through a USB. All these tools can help you keep a track of your energy use. You can correlate it with lifestyle changes, weather or conservation measures.

Difficult

The 'difficult' in many ways means the most expensive measures. As we stated in an earlier chapter, all the energy conservation in the world won't be enough since we still need to use some energy. However, before we turn to energy production we need to look at one last form of conservation, double glazing. Windows are one of the most significant areas of heat loss in any building. Double glazing is one of the most popular energy conservation measures and is fitted for a variety of reasons such as noise reduction, aesthetics or simply because the old windows are worn out. Only recently due to the massive rise in gas prices is this technology looking like it may pay back financially in its lifetime. Having windows ripped out and replaced *is* disruptive, but after loft insulation this has to be the easiest way to save energy. Ensure your double glazing uses 'low E' glass that traps infra-red heat inside the building. For those in conservation areas check with your local planning office, but you can fit secondary glazing on the inside even in these areas.

The measures we have outlined above will reduce your energy/ electricity *consumption*. We now turn to energy *production* using micro-generation. Once you start producing electricity yourself, you can at times produce all that your household needs, and even export the excess.

If you are lucky to live in windy open country then we would encourage you to contemplate a wind turbine. If you are fortunate enough to have flowing water on your land then a hydro system is worth considering. But for most of us, our options are limited to solar panels. In our experience, both solar hot water and photo-voltaic panels (PV) are useful technologies that work well. The costs of PV have reduced considerably in the last couple of years, and are fast approaching the levels where no subsidy is required (about £8K for a 4kW system), but the feed-in tariff scheme means that you can be rewarded with a payment for each unit of electricity generated, and a further small payment for any units exported. (The renewable heat incentive to be introduced in 2013 will similarly support sustainable heat energy.) Taken together with the savings on electric-ity, the installation will pay for itself after about 10 years, and with the feed-in and export tariffs guaranteed for 20 years (and rising with inflation) it can be a very sound investment, potentially paying back the initial cost several times over. Of all the technologies this is the one we strongly recommend since it is 'fit and forget' – once installed there is usually no maintenance beyond keeping the panels clean. The bigger the system the better in terms of financial payback. The most important thing to consider is system shading; the effec-tiveness of the panels is reduced if trees or other obstructions get in the way, though this can be mitigated by using more than one inverter.

In terms of heat energy, the major gains are to be made by insulating your house to a higher standard as described above. The concerns over future wood supply mean that we cannot wholly recommend you switch to biomass central heating. However, we strongly recommend wood-burning stoves as a supplementary heat source. Scrap wood to fuel a small stove can be scavenged for free even in cities.

Before we leave energy it is worth stating that this whole area is moving fast and new insulation technologies are constantly under development. Historic Scotland are running scientific trials on a number of new and existing technologies (for example using wooden shutters in conjunction with single glass windows gives the same levels of heat loss as double glazing). The results are being published on their website.[8] Finally, once you have put additional insulation in, you should be able to keep the heating off for longer.

Transport

Easy ideas

Again the easy measures are well known and we hope you are doing this already.

- Reduce your car use: Is your journey necessary? Many car trips, particularly urban journeys, are short, and could be done by walking, cycling or taking public transport.
- Is your car fuel-efficient? Driving more gently, avoiding rapid acceleration and sharp braking will increase how many miles per gallon you get from it – as will keeping it well maintained and inflating the tyres to the correct pressure.
- Air conditioning uses more fuel – try to reduce your use of it.

More challenging suggestions

Try taking up cycling, not just for leisure purposes but as a regular means of transport. If you are a reader in Germany, Holland or Denmark you will likely live in cities where cycling is very common or even the predominant mode of transport. This applies to some cities in the UK such as York and Cambridge, and Portland in the US. We strongly recommend that you don't just buy a bike, jump on it and set off into traffic. In many towns and cities there are groups set up that will take you out and show you how to ride safely in an urban environment. Groups such as the London Cycling Campaign or Spokes in Edinburgh are a good place to start. Cycling is a low-cost activity; bikes can be easily bought second-hand. Surveys have shown that once the number of journeys undertaken by bike reaches about 3 per cent of all journeys, the number of accidents falls dramatically.[9] Always wear a helmet.

Use public transport more. Neil encourages his children to use buses so that they are not ferried around by car all the time. They are given bus money, but often walk one way and save some of the money.

Difficult

Give up flying, or at least severely reduce the amount you do. This is not difficult in most cases but just seems so. Obviously this *is* difficult for intercontinental journeys, but are these necessary? Why not holiday closer to where you live? Travel by train uses much less energy than either driving or flying. On shorter journeys, taking the train can be as quick as flying.[10] Consider that trains take you from city centre to city centre; this saves time since airports are generally on the edge of cities. In addition you don't have to arrive one or two hours before the flight, or take time to go through the airport security. So, for example, for journeys such as London to Edinburgh or London to Paris or Brussels the train can often work out quicker than the plane. Consider cost. First, cheap flights are not generally as cheap as the headline figure might suggest. Budget airlines have a reputation for tacking on a variety of costs for baggage, using a credit card etc. You also have to consider either car parking charges or public transport to and from the airport, both of which are expensive and are rarely taken into account.[11] Buying rail tickets in advance can get you some bargain fares, sometimes newspapers do special rail ticket offers as well. Train travel to southern Europe from the UK is more time consuming, but even here there are alternatives. Eurostar run direct trains to the Alps in winter and Avignon in summer, and soon trains will run direct from London to Frankfurt, Cologne and Amsterdam. There is also a new TVG line from Paris to Barcelona (six hours) and another under the Alps between Zurich and Milan on its way. If you are not rushed, another alternative is to take the sleeper. For general travel advice on train travel anywhere in the world, an excellent website is 'The man in seat 61'.[12] Both of our families travel a lot by train and in general we find trains in the UK modern, comfortable and reliable.

Perhaps the most challenging area is our relationship with the car. The measures outlined above are good, but don't address the big central issue – could we manage without our car altogether? For many families with two working parents, the idea of managing without *two* cars would be a challenge. But considering the constraints that we anticipate coming in the next few years – high fuel costs and even actual shortages of fuel – we need to start planning for reduced car use (there are some signs this is happening[13]). Part of the problem is that we have become very used to the convenience that the car provides, and we have developed patterns of living that are dependent on it. So reducing our car usage is not just about deciding it is a good thing, it requires us to start rethinking the connections that make us dependent. For all sorts of good reasons we may live some distance from where we work, where we worship, or where we shop. Radically reducing our car use, or giving it up altogether, may mean some difficult decisions about these journeys. It may be much easier to avoid the issue for now, but this will not prepare us for the future. What steps could you take to reduce your dependence? Could you use a car club, or car share with one or two other people? Could you buy a more efficient smaller model or even an electric one? Like PV, the costs of electric cars will only fall when they start selling in quantity. Challenging the ubiquity of car use may require some major changes to the pattern of our lives. However, to put this in a global context, less than 10 per cent of households in the world own a car.

Overall we need to realise that constrained oil supplies will inevitably limit the amount of travel we will be able to do in the future compared with today. There is no realistic alternative to oil for aviation fuel, meaning that flying will be curtailed. Even switching to the most fuel-efficient hybrid or electric cars will only put off fuel shortages for a while if we continue to depend on the car as much as we do today. Trains and other forms of public transport could be run on sustainably produced electricity, though this is still some way off in the future. Cycling will become much more important, as will finding ways to live which reduce our need for travel.

Food

Easy ideas

Again we would expect most readers to know and do the following:

- Buy less packaged 'convenience' foods.
- Use more fresh local seasonal food – this reduces the energy used in food transport and storage.
- Don't waste food. If you have space, create a compost heap, food which has spoiled (apart from meat) can go on the heap and the resulting compost used to feed your garden.
- Organic food production uses less energy than conventional farming so buying organic, preferably direct from the farmer or grower, supports a sustainable local food economy.
- Our stand-out action is to learn to do some preserving, why not start with something easy, for example jam-making. Few people we know do this. It is surprisingly easy and we give a sample recipe in the documentation on our website.

More challenging suggestions

Start to grow your own food. Many fruit and vegetables are easy to grow (subject to the vagaries of the weather). Very few of us have the land area to enable us to be self-sufficient, but almost everyone can grow something (even on a window box).[14] Neil has found lettuce and spinach very easy to grow. If you want to try growing fruit, Neil recommends gooseberries. They take very little care, crop heavily and suffer from very few pests and diseases.[15] If you have large apple or plum trees, share your fruit with those in need or turn your fruit into jam, soft drinks, or even alcohol such as cider.[16] The advantages of growing your own food are that you learn to appreciate the seasons, are more in touch with nature and are saving on food miles. Growing your own also opens up a whole range of culinary possibilities including tarts, crumbles, and fools. Try baking your own bread. Second-hand bread-makers are easy and cheap to purchase at car boot sales, or use your oven.

Difficult

As discussed in the food chapter, the supermarkets provide convenience and low-cost food. However, their arrival in a town often means the end of a local food economy as greengrocers, butchers and other small shops shut down. By cutting down on supermarket shopping and instead using farmers' markets, local shops and growing as much as you can yourself, you can promote a more resilient, less oil-dependent food culture. At this point the freezer is your friend, but make sure it's energy efficient. Cutting supermarket use is difficult because it is less convenient and requires more time and planning. There may not be many small shops left in your locality, but in many towns or cities it can still be done. Supermarkets are usually but not always cheaper. Neil has found the farmers' market in Edinburgh to be cheaper for eggs and vegetables, but the meat is much more expensive (although of far higher quality). Meat production, particularly of intensive poultry and pork, requires large amounts of energy. Reduce your consumption of these meats, and if possible eat more beef or lamb which is largely raised on grass. One way of reducing meat use is to remove it from being the main part of the meal (meat and two veg) to being less dominant (for example in risotto or stir fry).

Chemicals

As we wrote in an earlier chapter, one of the biggest problems is our dependence on oil to make 'stuff', principally plastics but also chemicals and pharmaceuticals. The replacement of these products with alternatives derived from natural materials relies on scientific research which has (worryingly) barely started, so actions in this area are more limited. However, as we believe we will all have to do with less than now, there are habits to be formed.

Easy ideas

- Don't burn plastic.
- Preferably send it for recycling.
- Make sure any electronic goods you throw out are recycled (we need those rare earth metals which are in almost all electronics).
- Try to buy second-hand goods (charity shops or the internet are good sources).
- Make stuff last longer (don't upgrade).

More challenging suggestions

See if you can get things repaired. This is counter-cultural since we live in a throw-away culture. When the authors were young this was common and a whole network of businesses existed to facilitate repair of just about anything. Now it is much more difficult. Nevertheless it's still possible to get shoes and clothes repaired. Neil had a zip fail on his cagoule. This has years of life left in it so he paid a local clothes repair shop to replace the zip – it was far cheaper than getting a new coat. Andy has rescued furniture that was being thrown out and used it to make kitchen tables. While it's far more difficult to get stuff repaired, replacing consumer goods or parts of consumer goods has been made far easier by the internet. So when the Hollow family needed a replacement foot pedal for an old Singer sewing machine, we bought one off the internet. When a second-hand laptop keyboard had some letters fail Neil bought a new keyboard (having first ascertained that replacing the keyboard was really easy to do yourself). This was far cheaper than replacing the laptop. There are lots of websites, such as Freecycle or Gumtree, where you can pick up things for free.

Difficult

Buy less. People who work in charity shops say it's amazing how many people donate clothes which still have shop labels on! Have a try at making some things yourself.

Re-skilling and community

Another area where we can make a difference with personal action is to gain and develop useful, practical skills. As we discussed in Chapter 9, although we may have gained expertise in other areas, many people in our generation are de-skilled in the practical talents which will become more important in the future. Being able to make or repair things, or to build something using local or recycled materials, or to grow and process your own food may all be more important skills in the future than some of the talents we value highly today. Gaining these kinds of practical skills boosts our personal resilience, and if a range of these skills are available within our neighbourhood, working together builds up the whole community's resilience. If you have a particular skill, can you share it with others? We can learn some skills from books or the internet but generally speaking we learn best by being shown how and having a go. Neil extended a brick shed doing the work himself, but would have loved someone to show him how to do bricklaying. With friends he has tried his hand at dry-stone walling. After two years of unsuccessful bee-keeping, Andy is now being shown what to do by an experienced and helpful mentor. This sort of interaction needs to be encouraged and valued as benefiting individuals and the community.

Developing a vision

After all you have read in this book you may be despondent, or you may be fired up and looking for the next step. In either case, one way forward in your personal life may be to consider the Christian practice of meditation. There isn't the space to go into the full theology and practice here and again we recommend Richard Foster's book *Celebration of Discipline*.

As Richard Foster writes, meditation has been confused by Christians with eastern practices of meditation such as Transcendental Meditation (TM). The Christian discipline is not about emptying your mind, but filling it with God. Practices such as TM are also about detachment from the world, which we hope, as you have gathered from the book in general and this chapter in particular, is not what we are trying to encourage. Meditation is also entirely scriptural; see for example Genesis 24:63, Joshua 1:8, Psalm 1:2, Psalm 63:6 and Revelation 1:10.

What we would encourage you to do is catch a potential vision of an oil-free future and your place in it using some of the spiritual exercises Richard Foster outlines. Particularly relevant here are the use of scripture, prayerful meditation on the natural world and imagination (in this case about the future shape of your community and society). The aim is not so much prophecy about the future – the vision you imagine is not necessarily what will happen – but it is one you can relate to and work towards in your own life and alongside others.

One possible example of this in the Bible is what David wrote in Psalm 18 (a parallel version of the psalm appears in 2 Samuel 22:1–51). None of the dramatic events that David describes are recorded in either 1 or 2 Samuel when David was on the run from Saul, yet God saved David again and again from Saul's hand. In these passages David uses his God-given imagination celebrating his physical deliverance from Saul via earthquakes and hail. We are not expecting you to have such a vision as David had, but this passage shows using your imagination in a Godly way can be very powerful.

There are no set methods to do this; none of the passages in the Bible describe how to meditate. One possible way is to be alone and somewhere quiet. Light a candle and put on some music very quietly. We would suggest some quiet unobtrusive Christian music (Neil uses plainchant). Metallica probably fails on both counts. If you are using a Bible passage read it several times slowly and look for any words and phrases that stand out. Ask yourself what they mean and where God is taking you. You could start by using some of the passages we used above. This general idea can also be used in a group setting. Neil used a similar exercise in his home group after watching the film *Transition 1.0*. We split into groups of three, came up with different aspects of an oil-free vision of our community in 2030 and then prayed about it. We are not claiming that meditation in itself will usher in an oil-free nirvana, but it could play its part in encouraging and nurturing you for what at times seems an over-whelming task.

We have discussed in this chapter how our personal vision, lifestyle and choices can contribute to our preparedness for the changes ahead, but also how this is best done within the framework of a community or national effort to reduce our dependence and build resilience. But how could this look within the context of a community that many of us are part of – the Church? The next chapter looks at how individual church fellowships and the Christian community as a whole could respond.

Notes

1   See Chapter 9 for more details.

2   This is a (UK) government scheme where work to improve the energy efficiency of a house can be done without upfront payment – the cost is paid off from the savings in energy use.

3   http://www.thinkinsulation.co.uk/diy-installation.htm.

4   The glass–wool insulation is made partly of recycled glass bottles but partly from new glass, so will involve a considerable amount of energy to manufacture it.

5   For details and advice for all the 'Easy ideas' on energy, contact the Energy Saving Trust.

6   Check guarantee details carefully and use a reputable firm (this will be part of the green new deal).

7   We recommend *Eco-Refurbishment: A Guide to Saving and Producing Energy in the Home* by Peter F. Smith (Elsevier, 2004) throughout this section. It covers all the options in some detail.

8   http://www.historic-scotland.gov.uk/index/learning/publications/ publicationsresults.htm?pubcategory=Conservation,+repair+and+ maintenance&catbrowse=true.

9   This is because statistically there is always the likelihood of a bike visible to any car driver.

10   Train journeys of less than four hours are thought to be quicker than flying. http://www.guardian.co.uk/uk/2010/oct/19/high-speed-rail-europe-db?INTCMP=ILCNETTXT3487.

11   Neil took the sleeper from Paris to Barcelona for a scientific conference. Although this was more expensive notionally than flying, the return flight time would have meant another night in the hotel after the conference ended meaning the costs were about the same.

12   www.seat61.com.

13   http://www.autoexpress.co.uk/news/autoexpressnews/273682/ fuel_sales_plummet.html.

14 *The Complete Urban Farmer: Growing Your Own Fruit and Vegetables in Town* by
David Wickers (Fontana, 1977) is an excellent book which shows how to
grow fruit and vegetables in all sorts of weird and wonderful places. It is out
of print but available second-hand.

15 Only the Gooseberry Sawfly, but there are way to minimise attack and it
doesn't eat the fruit anyway. Wood-pigeons are another pest – possibly they
like dessert varieties, which Neil's aren't …?

16 Google 'Abundance'; there is no one website for the UK, but groups exist
in many major cities – London, Edinburgh, Manchester, York etc. They
harvest food people don't want and share it.

What can my church do?

There is nothing that unites a group of people more than work-ing together on a shared and urgent task.

Revd George Macleod, founder of the Iona community

Having looked at the actions we can take individually to prepare for a lean energy future, in this chapter we look at what our church communities could do. Our experience is that the issues explored in this book are not on the radar of most churches. Even churches that have some interest in environmental issues have often not connected with peak oil and its implications. There are perhaps two main reasons for this. First, they may simply be unaware of them – as are many if not most of the wider population. Second, they may not view issues of resource constraints as 'spiritual' issues which churches should get involved in. As we have tried to make clear throughout this book, the shortfall in future energy supplies will cause a considerable challenge to our lives in many areas, and churches will not be exempt from the effects. We believe that energy constraints will provide the context for our lifestyle in the years ahead. How we 'do' church will inevitably be affected. We will still be worshipping the same unchanging God, but the ways we have become used to doing this will almost certainly have to change. The ministry of Christians and the Church, both in our own country and overseas, is likely to change too, as different needs arise, and different constraints affect us.

The wider challenge for the Church is not just to adapt to the changing circumstances that peak oil will force upon us, but also to recognise that the Church has been part of the problem. Most Christians and churches have been full of participants in the dominant culture of consumerism, globalisation and economic growth, not questioning it in any meaningful way. Peak oil will fundamentally undermine this paradigm and therefore challenge not just our society, but our faith. We need prophetic voices pointing out to us how our attitude to, and our behaviour towards, God's world and its resources have been infected by the dominant world-view, and we need teaching which guides us into different ways of thinking and living.

Church leaders

Many issues in the past have seen Christian leaders speak out and engage in practical action: slavery, racism, injustice and poverty to name a few. Yet peak oil and its consequences will present a quandary for church leaders – a wide-reaching shift in circumstances without an obvious moral angle (though as we argued earlier there are moral issues inherent in our current patterns of energy use). This is not an issue where campaigning will change the underlying geological circumstances, yet Christians need leadership which addresses what will become a serious political, economic and social issue affecting everyone. There are three key areas where leadership can make a difference: first, communicating what is happening and the reasons behind it; second, promoting behavioural change which helps mitigate the problem; and third, helping people adapt to the altered circumstances.

The problem of future energy supplies is a complex one which defies easy explanations and simple solutions. However, the heart of the problem is humankind's consumption coming up against the God-given limits of our planet's resources. Current levels of energy use cannot be sustained and as a result we face a different future. While church leaders cannot be expected to have a complete understanding of peak oil, if they can grasp this central issue and communicate it, they can then point people in the direction of more detailed sources of information. Understanding the problem is the first step and leads people on to asking, 'What can we do?'

The kind of practical personal actions that we outlined in the last chapter are encouraged, reinforced and strengthened when people work together, and when the Church provides a lead, both in teaching and example. While some measures benefit the individual or the household, many help the wider community and all benefit the environment. In spiritual terms, reducing our dependence on oil is good stewardship – it conserves a valuable resource for important future uses, saves money and reduces our negative impact on creation. Just as many churches promote fair-trade products or back various campaigns, they could put their weight behind efforts to reduce our energy use and prepare for the lean-energy future. One important way for the Church to do this is to lead by example – reducing energy use by using some or all of the measures discussed in the last chapter (we look at some congregations that have done this at the end of this chapter). There is also scope for congregations promoting other energy-saving measures: for example promoting cycling or car-sharing for the journey to church, energy-saving measures becoming part of a church ministry to the wider community. The church could become a source of information and help, both for churchgoers and others. With rising fuel prices, many households and individuals are falling into fuel poverty and struggle to find money to keep warm.[1] A church could help people access grants or assistance with fitting insulation, or even by having work teams which go out and fit insulation for people unable to do it themselves – a very practical demonstration of God's care and concern. This is just one example of ways the Church could help people practically, and with God-given creativity and inspiration, there must be many more.

One response could be for a church to comprehensively examine each aspect of its life and ministry in a kind of 'peak oil audit', asking itself two key questions, 'How will this be affected by a reduced-energy future', and 'How can we change this to make it more resilient in the future?' Some areas may require only minor changes; others may need a fundamental rethink. A church does not need to do this kind of work alone. It can and should connect with the Transition movement where initiatives have started; some churches have already done so. And where there is currently no Transition work going on, why not the church as the initiator? In fact, we don't have to look back very far in history to see examples of the Church taking this kind of action: the pioneering work of George Macleod in Govan parish during the depression of the 1930s shows some remarkable similarities with actions that the Transition movement encourages today.

Practical implications

Looking at the potential impacts of energy constraints on churches, one of the first things that comes to mind is the practicalities of getting to church, whether that is for a Sunday service, or a midweek meeting in someone's home. A decade or two ago, churchgoers would mostly go to the nearest church of their chosen denomination. For those in traditional denominations with a church in virtually every city, town or village, there was no need to travel any distance at all; for other fellowships you may have had to go further. Fast-forward to today, and the situation is quite different. There has been a steady drop-off in attendance at traditional churches (with notable exceptions). Many such churches have closed, while an increasing range of new ones have emerged, which often meet in schools or other community buildings instead of having their own building. We have also had the emergence of a few very large 'mega-churches' around the UK. Churchgoers have a variety of reasons for attending a particular church – a style of worship and service that meets their needs; good teaching; a vibrant children's or youth ministry; or simply good fellowship. The end result is that many churchgoers travel some distance to attend a particular church. And for many this will be by car – as public transport often runs a reduced or no service at all on Sundays.

Clearly a reduced energy future will cause problems for this pattern of church attendance. For the individual or family with increasing fuel costs, or even at times finding it difficult to obtain fuel, the option of driving any significant distance to church may become difficult or even impossible. For a church whose congregation is 'gathered' from a large area, there is a fundamental challenge: how can we 'do' church if people are unable to get there? This model of church attendance we have described, like long-distance commuting for work or the supermarkets' delivery logistics, is a product of the age of cheap fossil fuels – and now that this age is coming to an end, inevitably this model will also be challenged.

There are some partial solutions to this problem. Cycling rather than driving – though most people are not used to cycling more than a few miles and even this would be difficult for small children, the elderly or infirm and possibly for everyone in poor weather. Car-sharing could help to some extent. The use of information technology such as live-streaming of services could provide one means of connection, though this is not really a substitute for actually meeting together. There is no escaping the fact that the new energy circumstances will be particularly challenging for larger churches with 'commuting congregations' and these churches should start thinking about organising themselves differently. Many churches already have smaller structures such as cell groups, house groups or cluster groups. These could become more locally focused involving inherently less travel, and these may have to become more important than the large Sunday meeting. Some radical creative thinking around church structures and patterns of meeting will be necessary. At the end of the day, however, the decision to drive some distance to attend church is a discretionary one. In an energy-constrained future people may return to attending their local church, and connecting with other Christians in their immediate locality, potentially a positive thing. The future could well be more, smaller churches rather than the recent trend of fewer and larger ones.

Overseas mission

It is interesting to see how the pattern of Christian work overseas has changed over time. The picture of a pith-helmeted missionary, with the Bible in one hand, a machete in the other and a phial of quinine in his pocket may be a caricature, but there are still people alive today who were pioneers, the first to bring the gospel to people and communities in the developing world. Today, the overwhelming majority of missionaries are cross-cultural workers from within their own country or continent – often unpaid pastors, evangelists and church planters who leave their home area and take the gospel into a different community, part of their country, or region. While never having worn a pith helmet, Andy has had two periods of time working for missionary organisations in Africa, first in Nigeria in the early 1990s, and then more recently in Malawi with a different organisation. Even the relatively short time span covering these two periods abroad showed changes in how missions work. Andy met missionaries in Nigeria who had first gone to the mission field in the 1950s. Before the age of widespread air transport, they had travelled out to Nigeria by boat, a six-week journey. A tour of duty was three or four years, with no visits home in the meantime. By the time Andy and his wife and went out in 1990 the journey was only six hours by plane, though we were still required to stay 'in the field' for two years without a home visit.[2] Their more recent experience in Malawi was quite different – while some traditional established missions still expected long commitments, many smaller or younger organisations were happy for people to come out for a year, a few months, and increasingly for a few weeks. Many people's experience of Africa or other developing countries is through short-term team visits, which often focus on a specific practical task such as building a church, roofing a school classroom, or running a youth leaders' conference. The opportunity to leave your own culture and partici- pate in a completely different one is an important experience in itself. These visits often provide a valuable taster experience, which for some can lead on to a longer-term commitment to overseas work, and consequently missionary organisations value them as part of their recruitment process. There is no doubt such short-term teams can achieve a lot. While people in the developing world do have building skills, a team coming in can bring energy, impetus and often funds. However, this type of short-term mission work has also attracted some criticism. The time period inevitably allows only a very shallow introduction to the host culture, and visitors can end up with a 'tourist' type experience with only fleeting interactions with local people. Then there is the question of cost and whether it would be better just giving the money to employ people locally to do the work. A two- or three-week trip to a developing country is becoming increasingly expensive. As well as the flights there may be vaccinations and malaria tablets to be paid for. Finally, apart from the financial cost, the carbon footprint for this kind of visit is enormous.

Setting aside the controversial question of whether short-term mission is a good thing or not, the question for the future is, will it even be possible? With oil supplies tightening, flying is likely to become even more expensive, and may even be restricted through lack of fuel availability. How high would air fares have to go before a church or mission decides the cost is too high? Unfortunately, for all the good things that short-term mission teams have achieved, our conclusion is that they will become more expensive and difficult to justify in the years ahead. Restrictions on flying will also affect medium- and long-term overseas Christian workers, and missions will have to review their activities in the light of these challenging new circumstances.

Peak oil will also provide a considerable challenge to the work of Christian relief and development organisations such as Tearfund, CAFOD and Christian Aid. As well as the logistical problems that high fuel costs will cause, they may be faced with a new set of needs around the world as the crisis unfolds. Missions and relief organisations should be factoring in the effects of what we have described into their planning scenarios, and be making preparations for a different future.

The issue of peak oil is one that the Church cannot ignore for ever. While keeping our eyes on the ultimate future, we must still address the needs of today and tomorrow. Hopefully this chapter has provided some pointers and ideas that churches can examine and act on. Some churches are already taking action, and here we share examples of these, churches that are addressing some or all of the four categories of challenge we have mentioned previously: energy, transport, food and material goods.

Bankfoot Church, Perthshire

Key features: renewable energy, recycled materials, local materials, food, use of building.
Bankfoot Church of Scotland met in a traditional stone church until in 2004 it was burnt to the ground in an arson attack (the ruined church can be seen from the A9 road). Rather than rebuild the existing church, the congregation decided to start again on a new site with a completely 'eco-friendly' design. Construction started in

2007 and finished just over a year later. The Church of Scotland largely paid for the new building but kept the insurance money for the old. What the congregation have created is a wonderful high-quality building that, if seen from above, forms the shape of a cross. The church has two very strong ethoses, eco-friendliness and community involvement, and these are reflected not only in its design, but in its everyday use.

The church has a very well-insulated roof. The windows are double glazed using low-E glass which traps infrared radiation inside the building. Heating is via a ground-source heat pump with its 'slinky' buried in a field the church owns adjacent to the building. (To save money, members of the congregation buried the slinky themselves, hiring a digger and driver; this work took five weeks as they buried 3.5km of pipes.) As we stated in Chapter 5, since heat pumps use a lot of electricity the church installed two 6.5kW wind turbines in the same field. The heat pump stays on 24/7 during the months of the year when heating is required; during the summer months the heat pump heats the water, with any excess electricity from the wind turbines being sent to the grid. Other eco features include rainwater being used to flush the toilets and the roof tiles being made from a mixture of quarry dust and resin which is 84 per cent recycled. The wooden frames that hold the building up are made entirely from wood from well-managed forests. All the splash-backs behind wash hand basins are made from recycled yoghurt cartons. The panels on the wall of the soft play area are made of recycled Wellington boots and mobile phone cases. The decorative insets in the youth café are from recycled CDs.

This extensive use of the heating system reflects the building's use, which is every day. The church itself takes up a comparatively small part of the building. Other users of the building include a community dentist and podiatrist, an older people's day care drop-in centre run by the council, an indoor sports area, a soft play area and a youth area. The church also has a nursery and a café. The day care and youth areas have their own kitchens and toilets; despite this they are either run by church members, or members are encouraged to interact with them. The chapel itself is very simple, as one would expect of a Presbyterian church. It does however make use of a number of locally made carvings and items of furniture. These include a beautiful Celtic cross above the altar, a communion table in two halves, a lectern and some wall carvings with scriptural quotations on. These were all made from an oak tree that had been blown over and stored in a barn for many years by a local farmer. He donated them to the church.

Finally, the church is working on projects to grow its own food. In conjunction with a local school the church is starting to plant an orchard around the building. They are also experimenting with raised beds to grow vegetables, although this being a country area the local rabbit population is voracious.

Problems encountered and lessons learnt

Obviously this example is at the extreme end of what most churches can hope to achieve. As Bankfoot's former minister Ian McFydan said, if he had a pound for every minister who had asked him for the name of his arsonist he would be a millionaire! However, we believe there are lessons to be learnt from Bankfoot. The reason why we were keen to include this church was because of the way they use the building. Not only do they utilise it to the maximum extent but they are trying to minimise car journeys to wider afield (such as Perth) by having a dentist use the building. If you are going to rebuild a church and then heat it 24/7 during the heating season then use the building as much as you can.

The church has had problems with the heating system. Someone put a nail through a pipe in the under–floor heating. Fortunately a church member knew someone in the fire brigade who turned up with an infrared detector and traced it. More seriously the winters of 2009/10 and 2010/11 were very cold. Particularly during the latter winter, the building was not warm enough and additional heating was used using bottled gas. They have found the temperature in different parts of the building varies even at the same thermostat settings (this was evident when Neil visited). Finally, they have had persistent problems with one of their wind turbines. Although sited immediately adjacent to one another one often doesn't turn (again Neil saw this) and its output is about 30 per cent lower. The heating problems using heat pumps bear out some of the reservations we expressed about this technology in Chapter four. Neil's feeling having visited was that assuming the floors, roof and walls are properly insulated, the heat loss is most likely through the large amount of glass present in the building, or the distance from the pump's heat exchanger to parts of the building. If you are going to use a low-temperature heating system then make sure your building is very, very well insulated. Monitor your renewable energy system's output closely. Most of us probably attend ancient buildings. Without burning them down, how can we drag them into the twenty-first century as far as energy use is concerned? The remaining examples look at the other end of the scale from Bankfoot.

St Nicholas' Church, Rochester

Key features: renewable energy, micro-generation, secondary glazing.
This medieval church building, which is immediately adjacent to the cathedral, houses the diocesan office. The building's age raises a whole set of issues both as to what you can physically and what you are allowed to do to make the building more energy efficient. In 2007 this church mounted 5kWp solar PV system on its roof and installed a 50kWp output biomass boiler system. They also installed secondary glazing.

Problems encountered and lessons learnt

Secondary glazing helped improve the levels of comfort in the offices. The biomass system has worked well but they have little space to store pellets. This means that these cost the church more than they would otherwise if they could order and store larger quantities. While this church is used as an office it is an historic listed building and does show what can be done to cut energy use.

St Paul's and St George's Church, Edinburgh

Key features: energy, roof insulation, raising awareness, transport, lend swap and share.
St Paul's and St George's is a thriving city-centre church originally built in the early 1700s but extended since. In 2008 it reopened after

a major renovation project. Balconies were put back into the main building and the hall space was greatly expanded. As part of the project the church had an under-floor heating system fitted in the main church building. Post re-opening the loft space was insulated with glass-wool insulation. The church also applied for, but failed to get, a grant for secondary glazing from the Scottish Climate Fund. Like Bankfoot the church is used by a variety of church-organised groups (parents and toddlers, Alpha, marriage preparation and marriage courses) and is also used by charities, government, Christian groups and businesses for conferences. Most of the groups mentioned above using the church consist mainly of non-churchgoers. This is also an opportunity and both the fair-trade and eco stalls have been present at the parents and toddlers group.

While the refurbishment was underway the church signed up to the eco-congregation initiative, and after moving back in the group looked at a number of eco issues. One of these was transport and one member of the group came up with a simple transport survey (shown in the appendix on our website). Shortly before this, additional cycle racks were installed (donated by half a dozen members of the congregation). The eco-congregation group twice paid for a bike doctor to come and do routine cycle maintenance during a morning service. The church has also shown the film *Transition 1.0* after an evening service during a sermon series on community, and this has also been shown in four home groups.

Currently the church is investigating the use of its website forums for allowing members to swap foodstuffs such as fruit, lend items and share skills. Seven categories have been created: food, IT goods, skills, tools, household items, children's goods and miscellaneous. The idea is to expand something that has been going on informally for many years, mainly with children's clothes and food. The church tried a free but commercial site, but found it had a number of major shortcomings.

Problems encountered and lessons learnt

Be very cautious when undertaking a major refurbishment. Building regulations seem designed to make sure your church uses more energy. St Paul's and St George's were forced to put in a smoke-extraction system, the control system of which uses a lot of energy. In addition the church had vents put in the roof of the church. Fans installed in the roof's apex above these were linked to part of the heating system. This combination of vents and fans pulled all the warm air out of the building! Even when they weren't on the heat was still literally flying out, since essentially the church's roof was open to the sky! Having established that these vents weren't part of the smoke-extraction system, insulation was laid over them. It was cheaper (and safer) to have someone install the insulation than for the church to do it themselves (in fact six cycle racks cost about twice as much to buy as the insulation). Putting in roof insulation is a very basic energy-saving measure but Neil has visited a few churches that have roof grills allowing you to see into the roof loft space and no insulation apparently present. In 2011 the church cut its gas use by about 30 per cent compared with 2010 consumption. This is despite the church building being used more and more. While some of the fall can be put down to milder weather, most is due to the church having confidence in the time the building takes to warm up, in part due to the insulation. As with Bankfoot, having invested money and energy in refurbishment, it makes sense to use the building as much as possible. Finally, the church is perhaps better at coming up with ideas than following them through: neither the transport survey nor the Transition film were followed up.

Emmanuel Church, Bungay

Key features: renewable electricity, climate change conference, environmental events, link with Transition.

Emmanuel church is situated in the heart of this small market town on the Suffolk/Norfolk border. In 2007 it organised and hosted a conference on climate change, with an impressive roster of speakers. A small group of people from the community met afterwards and as a result a group was formed – Sustainable Bungay, which subsequently became part of the Transition movement. Independent from the church, and in fact with few links between the two remaining, this small organisation has gone on to run a vibrant set of continuing activities in the town.

The church's highest-profile action has been to install an 11.44kWp PV system on their building in the heart of the town. Not only does this supply electricity for church activities, it is a major source of income for the church, although for various reasons they had to argue their case to qualify for the highest feed-in tariff rate. (Their situation helped to get the law clarified and set a precedent for such an installation.) The church has put effort into a campaign called 'Going Green', ring-fencing some of the FIT income so that it can be used for other environmental measures that they have planned – installing a ground-source heat pump and under-floor heating, increasing the insulation, fitting secondary glazing, installing solar hot water panels and rainwater harvesting for flushing toilets. The church sees itself as a showcase for green technologies and in July 2011 hosted an event, 'All under one roof', which promoted local firms and organisations involved in renewable power, recycling and more.

Like the other examples, Emmanuel wants its building to be used more; they try to use (and heat) appropriately sized rooms for the groups that hire them, including Sustainable Bungay. Recently the church were nominated as the Best Community Energy project in Suffolk, and came second at the awards.

Notes

1 The official measure of fuel poverty is when a household needs to spend more than 10 per cent of its income on heating and other fuel needs.
2 This policy was based not on the cost of travel to the mission, but also on the emotional toll that home visits can take. Once adjusted to and engaged with a different culture, 'popping home' can cause reverse culture shock. The experience of Andy and his wife was that, though difficult at times, staying abroad for two years was a good thing.

Where do we go from here?

You're blessed when you're at the end of your rope. With less of you there is more of God and his rule. You're blessed when you feel you've lost what is most dear to you. Only then can you be embraced by the One most dear to you. You're blessed when you're content with just who you are —no more, no less. That's the moment you find yourselves proud owners of everything that can't be bought. You're blessed when you've worked up a good appetite for God. He's food and drink in the best meal you'll ever eat. You're blessed when you care. At the moment of being 'carefull,' you find yourselves cared for. You're blessed when you get your inside world – your mind and heart—put right. Then you can see God in the outside world. You're blessed when you can show people how to cooperate instead of compete or fight. That's when you discover who you really are, and your place in God's family.

Matthew 5:3–9, The Message Bible

Over the last couple of hundred years, humanity has become gradually more dependent on non-renewable finite sources of energy. This was not a conscious decision, no political party stood on a platform of encouraging fossil fuel use, although plenty defend it now. As Wendell Berry wrote, this switch gave us power and an ability to shape our natural world, but at a high cost:

> What gave them power, and made them able finally to dominate and reshape our society, was the growth of

technology for the production and use of fossil fuel energy. This energy could be made available to empower such unprecedented social change because it was 'cheap.' But we were able to consider it 'cheap' only by a kind of moral simplicity: the assumption that we had a 'right' to as much of it as we could use. This was a 'right' made solely by might. Because fossil fuels, however abundant they once were, were nevertheless limited in quantity and not renewable, they obviously did not 'belong' to one generation more than another. We ignored the claims of posterity simply because we could, the living being stronger than the unborn, and so worked the 'miracle' of industrial progress by the theft of energy from (among others) our children. That is the real foundation of our progress and our affluence.[1]

This leaves us in an unenviable position of being addicted to a finite resource. The authors believe peak oil and peaks in other staples of our energy diet will force profound lifestyle change upon us. As Robert Hirsch's report (mentioned in Chapter 1) states:

The problems associated with world oil production peaking will not be temporary, and past 'energy crisis' experience will provide relatively little guidance. The challenge of oil peaking deserves immediate, serious attention, if risks are to be fully understood and mitigation begun on a timely basis.

This will not be easy, as Hirsch goes onto say: 'In summary, the problem of the peaking of world conventional oil production is unlike any yet faced by modern industrial society.'

The biggest challenges to be faced are our industrialised food system and the fact that we have no ready substitute for oil as a transportation fuel. As we have covered elsewhere we believe flying will be severely curtailed. Electrification of road transport, though technically possible, will mean generating a lot more energy, not just to power the cars but to build them too. Maintaining the current food system where food is shifted hundreds, thousands, or even tens of thousands of miles will not be possible in an era of depleted oil reserves.

It is difficult to be optimistic when politicians fail to rise to the most basic challenges. A recent example was a sensible proposal to get home owners in England to carry out basic energy-efficiency measures if they want to build an extension. This idea was put forward in a consultation document, but after pressure from climate sceptics in the national press it has been scrapped, even though one conservative council has been running such a scheme for years with no controversy.[2] Gaby Hinsliff wrote in the *Guardian* about this matter, and about the hosepipe ban brought into force over large parts of England in Spring 2012.

> Politicians of all parties fall over themselves now to swear there's no money left in the kitty, yet remain oddly coy about suggesting that within a generation there may not be enough water left either – or enough affordable oil, or cheap food – to maintain the cheerily wasteful lives that many of us take for granted.[3]

Rationing energy and building a new type of genuinely fair and sustainable economics are not even on the political radar. At the same time, global carbon emissions are rising inexorably.

However, there some signs which we should find encouraging. Renewable energy deployment is accelerating as the costs fall. This is particularly true of solar PV, the cost of which has plunged in the time we have been writing the book (requiring multiple additions and rewrites). At the moment this technology is poised to be a significant energy source of the future. Another technology that has come on to the market in the time we have been writing is electric vehicles. These hold great promise, although we have concerns about their unfettered use. More and more people are becoming aware of peak oil (as we wrote earlier in the book, this is just starting to be seen in popular culture). The high-profile 'occupy' movement has tried to raise questions about the current dysfunctional economic system, and in doing so has expressed underlying concerns many of us have about conspicuous greed and fair taxation. Perhaps the biggest encouragement for us personally is the Transition movement and the astonishing way it has both grown and taken root in so many communities.

No technology can substitute for oil and that is where vision and sacrifice come in. If this book was written about climate change we would not hesitate to use the word 'sacrifice'. We would try and link it to positive messages about the changes required and tell you that there are good reasons for lifestyle change. We hesitate to use the word in this context. We are going to be forced to live with a lot less energy and material goods than we have been used to, whether we like it or not. Sacrifice therefore does not seem an appropriate word under these circumstances. However, as we have covered in the book there will clearly be sacrifices required over and beyond this general squeezing of our energy-profligate lifestyles, particularly related to that of fuel poverty and food.

One of the questions we have tried to ask in this book is 'Is there a specific Christian response to peak oil?' In many ways we would say no. Obviously the change that is coming will affect how we 'do church'. For example people may no longer be prepared to travel so far to services, buildings will have to become much more energy efficient and we will need to use local food for church events rather than just popping down to the supermarket. Overseas mission and development will be drastically affected. In a church context these are issues specific to us and not wider society. However, as we have tried to express in the book, for humanity to survive and prosper on the second, downward part of the oil age we will need to co-operate as a community in ways we have not done for years. We need to join in enthusiastically with what our community is doing and not necessarily reinvent the wheel.

While there may be no specific Christian response to peak oil, there are both specific challenges to our faith and also significant opportunities. The first challenge is that for many Christians (particularly but not exclusively Evangelicals) our faith has become a consumerist pick-and-mix self-help system. Neil's minister said in a sermon recently that when he browses Christian TV stations on the satellite channels, at any one point in time 18 out of 20 are broadcasting health-and-wealth theology. This heresy will be severely challenged by the events of the years ahead. There is no record of Jesus owning anything and there is nothing in the Bible to suggest that this is what our faith is about. Jesus came to bring salvation, not material contentment.[4] More than a cursory glance at the New Testament shows that for many of his followers becoming a Christian was the start of their problems (for example 2 Corinthians 6:1–10). Jesus himself said he had come not to bring peace but the sword,[5] something that has been misinterpreted, but clearly implies that life is not going to be a bed of roses. Peak oil presents us with an opportunity to clear out the materialistic detritus and focus on what our faith really means. Following Christ is more than just about a narrow personal salvation, but is also about bringing into being the Kingdom of God, ('your kingdom come, your will be done, on earth as it is in heaven'). This can be seen practically in acts of service to individuals and the community.

This brings us to another challenge we will face: working with people whose lifestyles we don't agree with towards common oil-free community goals. Many of us won't find this easy, partly because the environmental movement and the Church have had little contact for many years (if ever). However, we believe such differences do not make churches and Christians co-operating with, for example, the Transition movement impossible, and indeed both sides would probably benefit from the encounter. There is an opportunity here for evangelism with a part of the community with whom most churches have little contact. As The Message Bible paraphrases Matthew 5:9–13:

> Let me tell you why you are here. You're here to be salt-seasoning that brings out the God-flavours of this earth. If you lose your saltiness, how will people taste godliness? You've lost your usefulness and will end up in the garbage. Here's another way to put it: You're here to be light, bringing out the God-colours in the world. God is not a secret to be kept. We're going public with this, as public as a city on a hill. If I make you light bearers, you don't think I'm going to hide you under a bucket, do you? I'm putting you on a light stand. Now that I've put you there on a hilltop, on a light stand – shine! Keep open house; be generous with your lives. By opening up to others, you'll prompt people to open up with God, this generous Father in heaven.

As we expressed earlier in the book we believe there is a huge opportunity to reach out to people who have built their lives based on materialism. As this collapses around them, this presents Christianity with an open goal (perhaps the greatest such opportunity for hundreds of years).

Finally this brings us to a vision of the future that politicians and conventional environmental groups are not currently offering. We have given you some ideas, resources and encouragement to get started, we can do no more than that. We think many of the things we have suggested you do, you will have to do. There may be things we have left out, ideas that no one else has thought of. Our backgrounds and communities are similar in many ways, but each one of us is created unique. Each one of us can bring our individual creativity as we together find a path through the difficulties ahead. The urgent task is this: develop a vision for what your own lifestyle, your church and your community could look like in ten or twenty years' time. Then, with God's help, find ways to make it happen.

Notes

1   Wendell Berry, 'Energy and Agriculture', from the *The Gift of Good Land*, Counterpoint, 1981.
2   http://www.businessgreen.com/bg/news/2168480/tory-council-happily-running-conservatory-tax-past.
3   *Guardian*, 10 April 2012.
4   Acts 4:12.
5   Matthew 10:34.

Some questions to ponder

Chapter 1: What's the problem?

Q1. The authors suggest that the earth's resources are not limitless. Is this something that you have considered before? How does this make you feel?

Q2. In the UK at the start of the credit crunch many articles were written and much discussion was had about whether this was the permanent end of the good times in the West and whether things could ever be the same again. As things (for many people) turned out to be not as bad as expected, this kind of discussion has faded. In the light of Matthew 6:19–20, what does this tell us about what happened, and do you think people were right to be worried at that point?

Chapter 2: What about Christians?

Q1. Have you come across any books/films/plays or any other cultural aspects concerning peak oil?

Q2. The authors outline five reasons why Christians have not taken any interest in the environment. Which do think is the most important for others and for you?

Q3. What do you understand by dominion? How does it differ from stewardship? (Also see Chapter 10.)

Q4. Read Genesis 37—43. How was Joseph prepared by God for his mission?

Q5. A little-noticed part of the story comes about in Genesis 47:13–20. Are there any moral lessons for us in preparing ourselves for lean years? Must the poor suffer due to rising energy prices or food shortages, are there any ways round this?

Chapter 3: Can't we make do with coal, gas and uranium?

Q1. Have you ever considered any of the moral issues we raise here? How can we do something about these issues?

Chapters 4 and 5: What about renewable energy?

Q1. Have you ever considered any of the moral issues we raise here?

Q2. Has your church measured its energy use or carbon emissions? If not, why not?

Q3. Has your church considered installing any renewable energy systems?

Chapter 6: Food and other stuff

Q1. The authors have covered many of the problems with the global food system. A recent report by a UK parliamentary committee echoes many of the concerns we have written about but can you think of any others?

Q2. What does the Bible have to say about food? Can you relate our problems today to any passages in scripture?

Q3. What can we learn from Jesus' attitude to food?

Chapter 7: Economics

Q1. Is capitalism 'Christian'?

Q2. What do you think are the essential ethical foundations of a just society? Clue – please look beyond everyone being a Christian.

Q3. What are the ethical foundations of an economic system?

Chapter 8: What are the consequences if we just carry on?

Q1. Which of the three scenarios do you think is most likely?

Q2. What emotion does thinking about the future bring out?

Q3. How can we look at the future in a positive light?

Chapter 9: Transition – what's the big idea?

Q1. Can you think of examples where the church has adopted ideas from organisations or campaigns which are not faith-based?

Q2. Who could you go to for information and lessons from the past?

Q3. What signs of resilience are present in your local community?

Chapter 10: Does the Bible have anything to say here?

Q1. Can you think of other verses/passages which are relevant to the problem of resource depletion?

Q2. Do you think the authors are right about celebration?

Q3. Does the biblical principle of forgiving debt through the Jubilee have any relevance today?

Chapter 11: What can I do?

Q1. What actions will you find easy to take?

Q2. Are there ways in which reducing your use of energy will improve your life?

Q3. How can we support and encourage one another in reducing our energy use?

Chapter 12: What can my church do?

Q1. How far do you travel to church, and what would you do if you couldn't drive there?

Q2. Is there a minimum size for a church?

Q3. How can your church start to tackle some of the changes that it will need to make?

Chapter 13: Conclusion – where do we go from here?

Q1. Do you have a positive vision for the future?

Glossary

Units of power

kW Kilowatt, this is a basic measure of power, named in honour of the Scot James Watt. It is equal to 1000 watts. Often known colloquially as the 'unit' when referring to electricity.

MW Megawatt = 1000 kilowatts
GW Gigawatt = 1000 megawatts
TW Terrawatt = 1000 gigawatts

When a small p is added to one of these units (e.g. GWp) this means the peak or greatest power output from the aforementioned capacity. So for example Neil's second PV array has a peak power out of 1kWp.

Units of energy

This is the rate at which power is produced or consumed. So 1kWh is 1kW of power used or generated over 1 hour. To put this in perspective, in 2006 global electricity production was 19,015TWh or 19,015,000,000,000kWh![1] Electricity that could be generated from renewable resources per year is estimated at 975,010TWh or 975,010,000,000,000kWh.[2] Remember, however, apart from the practicalities of harvesting this power, if we electrify all road and rail transport and space heating, demand would rise dramatically.

Grid parity

This term is referred to currently when discussing micro-generation, mainly PV. The expression means matching the price of electricity on the grid for electricity produced by PV. There are two types of grid parity: the first is the wholesale price of electricity; the second is matching the price of electricity coming up the garden path. The wholesale price of electricity makes up only around 40 per cent of the average bill; the remainder is made up transmission charges, environmental charges and profit etc. Thanks to the FIT we are close to the latter in many countries, but still some way off the former.

FIT (feed-in tariff)

A means of encouraging renewable energy generation dreamt up by a German, the late Dr Herman Scheer. Renewable energy generation systems are paid guaranteed rates per unit of energy produced. The rate is fixed for each technology and varies for each depending on how near to being able to compete with existing technologies they are (being lower for those that are). The rates paid undergo 'digression', that is, they fall year on year from the start of the scheme. So for example in the UK the FIT was set at 43.3p per unit generated for PV at its start in 2010; this was planned to fall at 7 per cent a year for 25 years after which the user would get nothing. The scheme in the UK is index linked (so the inflation rate is added on each year), meaning the cut is less than 7 per cent (and also tax free). New entrants the next year get the starting rate minus the cut, so for 2011 this should have been 40.27p (excluding inflation). The money is not government money but is paid by all other electricity customers out of their bills.

Right-wing think tanks are wrong to think FITS are a permanent subsidy to uneconomic technologies. The whole idea is to encourage production economies of scale and bring down prices. They do this by two basic competitive pressures. First, the user of technology has to pay its up-front cost, so encouraging the user to find the best deal. Second, year on year the rates paid for generation fall so unless the user can get an economic price they will not go ahead. This also puts a downward pressure on prices.

The main problems with FITs are caused by their sheer success. Governments get nervous about the perceived pressure on bills. Tariffs have been cut and altered in a wide variety of countries.

Another problem is that as installation prices fall, purchasers tend to make a windfall. This is particularly true just before a degression. However, feed in tariffs have been phenomenally successful in encouraging technologies like PV. Spain went from almost nothing to 3.5GWp in two years and Germany after 19 years has over 27GWp of installed PV capacity.

Tradable energy quota's (carbon ration)

This is a means of rationing energy by means of issuing points to individuals, charities and business. Every time the user purchases fuel, energy or transport a certain number of points are removed from their carbon account. The number of points reduces year on year.

Inverter

This converts direct current (DC) electricity (produced by most micro-generation systems) to 240 or 415V three-phase 50hz alternating current used by the grid. In actual fact the grid voltage varies at times of high demand both the frequency and voltage drop. The inverter monitors these and tries to match them.

Notes

1   'Plugging into the Sun', *National Geographic*, September 2009 .
2   *Ibid.*

Index